Healing Ghosts, Haunted Places, and Non-Human Beings

Training Manual to be a Supernatural, Multidimensional Medium and Healer

Tina M. Zion

Healing Ghosts, Haunted Places, and Non-Human Beings

Published by WriteLife Publishing
(an Imprint of Boutique of Quality Books Publishing Company)
www.writelife.com

978-1-60808-303-9 (p)
978-1-60808-304-6 (e)

Library of Congress Control Number: 2025942457

Book and cover design by Robin Krauss, www.bookformatters.com
Cover artwork by Corey Ford, www.coreyfordgallery.com
Toroidal Field illustration by Jacqueline Rogers, www.jacquelinerogers.com

Editor: Andrea Vande Vorde

Praise for Tina Zion and *Healing Ghosts, Haunted Places, and Non-Human Beings*

"This is the book I've been waiting for . . . a common sense approach to a not-so-common topic. Those of us who KNOW there is more to life than the physical realm are looking for ways to deal with the supernatural in a grounded, no-nonsense manner and Tina Zion has delivered helpful tools and information. I recommend *Healing Ghosts, Haunted Places, and Non-Human Beings* without hesitation."

— Lisa Bonnice
Author, Podcaster lisabonnice.com

"Tina's *Healing Ghosts* is not just a manual—it's a bridge. Whether you've spent years walking between worlds or are only beginning to sense what lies beyond the veil, her guidance meets you with clarity, reverence, and unwavering truth. She writes with the rare kind of integrity that neither dramatizes nor diminishes the unseen. Instead, she offers language, structure, and deep compassion for the work of healing — not only for the living, but for the struggling dead and the places they still inhabit. This book is an offering to all who feel the pull to serve what others overlook. It's a remembering, and an invitation."

— Phoenix Aerie
phoenixnestmagazine.com

"From a compelling biographical beginning, through its comprehensive dive into various spiritual phenomenon, Tina Zion's latest book will add greatly to the material available for students of metaphysics regardless of their current level of understanding. This workbook style publication will be an asset to students of all levels moving through our spiritual healing and prophecy educational programs. I highly recommend Tina's breakthrough work."

— Rev. Mark Thomas
Pastor, Fellowships of the Spirit

"Reading Tina's personal story brought me to tears. She is such a special soul in this world and knowing her story now makes it even clearer why she is the person to teach us about ghosts, haunted places and non-human beings. I wouldn't know any other person with her experience and love for all human and non-human beings. Be ready for a journey full of color that expands your horizon and opens your heart to the unseen world. I cannot thank Tina enough for everything she taught me out of pure love."

— Sonja Frey
Medical Intuitive & Lawyer www.sonjafrey.com

"A helpful treatise for the spiritual aspirant wishing to move through their guilt, fears, and frustrations of what lies beyond the veil. Unparalleled reference given the experience both personally and professionally by its world-renowned author Tina Zion."

— Rev Thomas Bundy, MD, FACMS

"Tina's new book is the pinnacle of knowledge, understanding, tools and methodology in the field of healing in the spirit realm. Her work is unequivocally ground-breaking, in completely preparing and equipping those of us that are called to serve . . . in releasing and assisting the suffering, the lost, and confused spirits beings. . . ."

— Vera The Attunitive
Australia www.theattunitive.me

"The tools and teachings provided in this book showed me how to remove all fears and step into my power. It feels as though you are being taken by the hand and guided safely whilst being shown exactly how confident you should be. Being taught how to do this is something of significant value to an individual and healer like me. . . . Truly an amazing source of valuable information as well as tantalizing read."

Carina H.
New Zealand www.alternativeapproach.co.nz

"Tina Zion's book is much needed and dispels the myths and fears about the afterlife and other worldly communications. This book is an educational manual filled with essential information for those who have experience with these non-ordinary realms and may be reluctant to share those narratives. She artfully takes us through her amazing journey of surviving numerous near death experiences and offers readers a handbook so they can navigate their own experiences with trust, clear vision and clarity. . . . I highly recommend this book!"

— Janet Roseman, Ph.D.
Assistant Professor, Integrative Medicine. Author of *The Eternal Bond: Daughters Honor their Mothers on the Otherside.*

"Finally, an authentic and practical book that addresses what has been thought to be illusive when it's been more elusive due to lack of understanding. . . . I have experienced the accuracy of the content in this book as Tina's guidance is comprehensive and practical and covers topics many are not aware of; don't want to acknowledge; and/or are afraid to discuss. . . . I am not aware of any other book, courses, or recorded media that includes so much content while other books have been lacking clarity on many levels. . . ."

— Maryann Kelly, B.S., R.T.R.
Intuitive Services Insight

"Goodness, Tina, you have shared an incredible story and manual. Thank you for giving me an opportunity to express how I feel after reading it. You won't find another book like this one. Tina Zion's, *Healing Ghosts, Haunted Places and Non-Human Beings* is more incredible than its title. It is a masterpiece."

— PMH Atwater, L.H.D.
Author of *Future Memory, The Forever Angels: Near-Death Experiences in Childhood and Their Lasting Impact, Aliens and the Near-Death Experience*

"Tina Zion's *Healing Ghosts, Haunted Places, and Non-Human Beings* is a practical and empowering guide that demystifies the nonphysical world with depth and clarity. Drawing from her personal experiences and decades of professional practice and teaching, Tina offers a grounded and compassionate blueprint for anyone called to be a healing medium. What makes this book unique is how clearly it guides the reader through healing work with both the deceased and non-human beings, territory that's rarely addressed with this level of insight and structure. Rather than ignoring fear, she embraces the topic, educates, and supports the reader in moving forward with greater understanding and confidence. It's a timely and important manual for those ready to step into multidimensional service with integrity and skill."

— Andrea Kennedy
MainstreamReiki.com

"Tina Zion takes our hand and walks us through the reality that exists around us. While reading this book I hear Tina's voice explaining and guiding me through a world that I wasn't brought up in, but now understand and give thanks for. Tina shows us while we are helping those troubled deceased, we are also helping the physical world find the peace we are all searching for. Thank you Tina, through your teaching and writings, you have helped many, many souls."

— Allen Wentland
Peace@The Lake

"In *Healing Ghosts, Haunted Places, and Non-Human Beings,* Tina Zion delivers a rare and potent blend of grounded wisdom, supernatural insight, and practical training. . . . She normalizes what many fear, and through story, step-by-step guidance, and radiant authenticity, she provides a luminous roadmap for stepping fully into multidimensional service. This book doesn't just inform; it initiates."

— Cyndi Silva
Founder of Metaphysical Wisdom

"Tina Zion offers a groundbreaking approach to mediumship and provides powerful tools for healing both - the living and the troubled deceased . . . she shares transformational stories and practical wisdom about death, dying and most important, selfcare for the healer. Her book gently dissolves fear around the spirit realm and guides readers to connect with the unseen in empowering and meaningful ways. . . . "

— Barbara Liniger
www.barbaraliniger.com

"Tina leads us in learning to enhance our own mediumship skills in a comfortable way as we work with the deceased who are confused and negative, . . . without fear of what we might encounter, . . . she has truly held nothing back. . . . Tina has finally made me realize on a deep level that those in Spirit are right here with us, and we can communicate with them easily as we heal on all realms. What a gift to have that knowledge!"

— Betty Ann Dean, R.N., B.S.N.
vibrantbodyworks.com

"Tina, you are such a beautiful soul and a master at turning the abstract and mystical into a practical and digestible process. You make it all seem so normal and real . . . I love it! This book is truly one of a kind; informative, instructive, and remarkably clear. It's a rare combination of spiritual insight and practicality. What a gift to society!"

— *G.G.* Psychotherapist

"I think of Tina's book as a personalized textbook. She added so many examples of her own personal information and experiences that enhance credibility and trust in what she is teaching in the book. It is a step-by-step instructional guide to work with spirit in any form it makes itself known to the medium. The book instructs how to collaborate with spiritual beings out of your heart center, not out of fear. Tina makes clear that a medium's work is to help them let go and move on in their true lives as spirit beings."

— Donna D.

To Every Eternal Soul
who has helped me create this book.
Feel my love and gratitude for each and every one of you.
I will honor you forever.

Acknowledgments

My publisher, Terri Leidich of WriteLife Publishing, found me out in the world somewhere and became my solid but gentle foundation for many years. Julie Bromley of Signed Books and Stuff, thank you for everything you do just to keep me going with all this high-tech stuff. Andrea Vande Vorde, you are the most patient professional editor who transforms my books into a polished level without ever changing my voice. I am so grateful to you for sticking with me through all the wild and crazy things I teach and write about . . .

I always want to declare my love to every person who reads my books, comes to my workshops, mentors with me, and takes me along in your healing journey. I cannot do this without you. It is because of you that I keep moving forward, learning, growing, and writing.

Table of Contents

Introduction

Living at the Edge of Death: My Lifelong Encounters with Nonphysical Beings

For years, I tried and tried to be normal. That didn't work out so well. Then I died in New Zealand, and that worked out much better.

In my first memory, around three years old, I stared into a Christmas ornament, a shiny red ball. I could see the reflection of my parents and the TV in the next room. I stared, entranced by the images in that red ball. I realize now that I was already becoming aware of other worlds. I remember doing the same thing again, when I was five or six years old. I studied my great-grandmother's necklace. I would stare into the depths of a tiny rhinestone, embedded in the center of a cross. I could see another world.

I always felt the magical energy in my great-grandma's house. As a child, I had no idea she was a medium herself, who gave readings, healings, and participated in séances. She even had a long, thin, trumpet-like horn that spirits would talk through during a séance. My great-grandmother belonged to the spiritualist church and the secret esoteric organization called the Rosicrucian Order. I remember how she let me look through the stacks and stacks of Rosicrucian teachings that were piled all over her tiny house. She allowed me to look through all those secret teachings.

Great-Grandma kept us entertained in many ways. My sister and I had no idea she was teaching us spiritual concepts and readings. She would place a regular deck of cards on the kitchen table, and then told us about our future lives. I remember watching hot water rise in the little glass lid of her ancient, dented percolator coffeepot. She allowed us to drink a bit of coffee, when the mystery lay at the bottom of our cups, where we carefully studied all the coffee grounds. We saw mountains, rivers, or the faces of our guides.

She was also an energy worker before there was a name for that profession. I can still hear her saying, "Swish, swish, swish," as she worked with my energy field. Forty years later, I received the first Reiki attunement. And right after receiving the third Reiki attunement, I suddenly heard my grandma's voice saying, "Swish, swish, swish."

I then began working as an energy worker. Reiki brought relief into my life. Energy work made sense to me. I could feel it and see it. Clients kept reporting to me all the ways they benefited from my Reiki sessions. The more I did Reiki, the more I felt normal . . . *my* normal. I was finally more at home with myself. Until that third attunement, I had forgotten that my great-grandmother taught me so much. I loved her. I loved her kitchen, her stacks of beautiful Rosicrucian manuals, and I especially loved the magical sparkles that always floated throughout her tiny house. I thought that was normal too.

I was around eight years old when I first surprised my family with my comments. I overheard my grandmother talking to my mother in the kitchen. Both were able to see spirit people, and yet they said there were no other beings in the Universe except here on Earth. I didn't know what the Universe was, but my eight-year-old self loudly announced, "I think there are people in other places too!"

They both were shocked. They turned to me and confidently said, "No, we are the only beings in the Universe." They thought that was the end of the story.

Soon after this conversation, I was sitting in the Lutheran church next to my grandmother, my mother's mother. I listened intently to a different minister of the church. I looked up at my grandmother and declared, "That is too simple. It's more complicated than that!"

With eyes wide in horror, she looked around to see how many people had heard me, and then she sternly shushed me and told me to lie down and go to sleep there on the church pew.

My family apparently couldn't wrap their heads around what was happening at the universal level, but they were absolutely fine with the deceased. I grew up in a family that took intuitive abilities for granted. They all experienced psychic phenomena. Both my mother's side and my father's side of my family attended a spiritualist church. Sometimes on Sunday, my parents took us to a Lutheran church, where my mother's brother was the minister. His deep voice vibrated though my body and into my soul. The longer he talked, the more brilliantly white his energy field became until, at times, I could not see his physical body at all. I felt so extremely happy when he glowed. In my childhood mind, I thought my parents and I, and the entire congregation, all went to church just to watch my uncle glow.

My family does think it's normal to see auras and deceased people, and to have premonitions. We told each other when we perceived something, but that was about it. There were no classes or discussions about the spirit realms. It was simply normal and expected to perceive these other dimensions. No one thought it was a gift, or even a special ability, or a special awareness. It was just no big deal.

Family gatherings often gravitated toward recent communications with our deceased relatives, or any strangers that happened by. For example, my family had just gathered for Thanksgiving dinner. As we sat digesting our enormous dinner, my niece blurted out for all to hear, "Has anyone had increased spirit activity in the last month? Because I sure have."

During that same Thanksgiving meal, my niece described a male presence in the hallway just outside of the children's bedroom. Her sister then described a little decorative butterfly from her grandma that had suddenly appeared on the dresser, then disappeared for a day, and then reappeared the next day. The family conversation quickly progressed, or regressed, to other memories of long ago.

My sister described being awakened by the spirit of our deceased grandma tapping on her hip, right before she received a call that her daughter was in labor. My nieces then told one of their childhood stories of the spirit of a little girl named Cindy who tickled their toes, or went up and down the staircase, or woke them up by staring at them with her chin resting on her arms, on the edge of their bed. The family laughed when someone remembered that my father had to disconnect both the front and the back doorbells because my deceased uncle kept ringing it in the night. We laughed and cried as the stories went on.

I didn't think anything about my niece's question, or the extensive conversation that followed, as we all jumped in with our latest experiences with Spirit. However, my guests, who did not grow up in this environment, later told me how unusual this discussion was, and how uncomfortable they had become. I was stunned and maybe a little embarrassed. I was powerfully reminded that my family was not considered normal, even by my friends. My family incorporates the spirit world into their lives. We expect contact with our departed loved ones, plus anyone else that happens to come around. It is just normal to us.

For example, my son's cousin had unexpectedly died at the age of eighteen. My son saw his cousin looking up at him from the bottom of a staircase. Another example happened one day, my five-year-old grandson said to his father, "Dad, Brian is looking in the window. He wants to come in." My grandson did not know it, but Brian had died just three days before his spirit stood at their front door.

My own grandchildren are now the sixth generation of intuitives and mediums. They do occasionally see things that frighten them. My three-year-old granddaughter saw the spirit of a child in a waiting room of the local hospital. She asked her mother, "Who is that?" and pointed to the corner of the room. Her mother said, "I don't see anyone." Later that week, my granddaughter quietly whispered to me that she had seen a ghost.

This was the first time she'd mentioned it to me, and I jumped on the chance to tell her that I see ghosts too, and so do her cousins. It's important to normalize the nonphysical realms alongside the physical world for children. Using a child's own natural experiences enhances their knowledge and teaches them that they're not victims of spirits, and that there is no reason to fear the nonphysical world.

My own abilities occasionally terrified me. My dead uncle, who had killed himself, would knock on my bedroom window in the night. My bedroom was on the second story of our ancient farmhouse, and we lived in the middle of nowhere. I would jump out of bed and run down the stairs, screaming. One day, I was walking down our country road. There he was again! That same uncle drove by in his old white station wagon, waving at me with a big smile on his face. He had been dead for at least a year.

I was terrified one minute but intrigued the next. We lived on a fifty-acre farm, far away from other neighbors. At night, after my parents and siblings were sound asleep, I would roam around the yard and into the barn. I experienced a great deal of peace in the quiet of the night. The dogs, cats, and my horse seemed to love my company, and so did the deceased. One night, I saw a spirit person behind the barn. He was a tall, thin man, hands in the pockets of his overalls, staring out across the fields. He glowed with a loving energy. He never paid any attention to me, and it never occurred to me to disturb him.

Although many members of my family, including my mother, were psychic or actively experienced spiritual phenomena on a regular basis, I was completely isolated by my mother's textbook physical and emotional abuse. I was kept on the farm, working constantly, never seeing another kid unless I was in school, which was mandatory back then. There was no one to talk to about auras, spirit people, or the knockings on my second-story bedroom window. My mother saw spirits frequently, especially at the foot of her bed, but she demanded they stop coming to her . . . so the deceased family stopped coming to her.

My mother is living proof that it isn't necessary to be kind, loving, or of high consciousness to be a medium. Many people think these qualities go hand in hand with the ability to connect with Spirit, but there is no connection between love, cruelty, kindness, and how intuitive you are. Our intuitive and mediumship abilities are not special gifts that only a few have. These skills are natural for everyone. What makes the difference is the interest and the yearning you have for mediumship.

Two Attempts to End My Life

At eighteen years old, I left the house as soon as possible, quickly finding that I was not "normal" in the way society defines the word. My life was rocked with crisis after crisis. I created many challenges trying to be "normal," and then created other challenges as I tried to become more of who I was meant to be. While I was deep in turmoil, I made two suicide attempts. The second attempt nearly worked because I overdosed on a large number of psychiatric pills that had been prescribed to me. Apparently, someone in the apartment next door found me unconscious in the hallway. I have no idea how many days I was in intensive care. I was told that I had barely made it through that second attempt. I was placed in a long-term psychiatric hospital for three months.

Looking back, I know these suicide attempts were truly blood-curdling screams for help. After tens of thousands of dollars in expert counseling, I finally understood that I had to live my own unique life. I moved out on my own and began college. I graduated from Purdue's nursing program and received a national board specialty certification in mental health. I worked for thirteen years in hospital psychiatric units and community mental health centers. I worked with a level of crazed humanity that very few know about. I worked with murderers, rapists, violent and psychotic people, but I also worked with the lost and depressed who had just given up.

I then moved to New Mexico to work as the head nurse for a psychiatric unit within the US Indian Health Services. I immersed myself in the Native American culture. The staff I worked with were primarily of the Navajo, Hopi, and Zuni tribes. The women taught me to weave rugs and make flatbread. (I achieved a low level of weaving, but they consistently laughed at my flatbread and told me it would be better if I just stopped trying to make it).

I also tried to learn the Navajo language and practiced some phrases as I talked to the Native psychiatric patients. Instead of, "You need to take this pill now," it would come out of my mouth as, "I am going to pull your teeth out." The Native staff members held their bellies, throwing their selves around the room, laughing until they could hardly breathe.

My Third Encounter with Death: Valley Fever

My boyfriend and I became terribly ill with valley fever, which is caused by a fungus in the Southwest portion of the US. We lay in bed for over two weeks until one day, something pulled me from my coma-like existence. I felt that I had to sit up at that exact moment. I struggled to sit up and turned to look out the bedroom door, which opened to a clear view through the living room and into the kitchen. There was a head of a long-haired man floating in the air.

Telepathically I asked, "Are you here to kill us?"

He said, "No."

But that is all he said, so I lay back down into unconsciousness.

After seeing that floating head in the kitchen doorway, we both suddenly became stronger, and finally, we were able to go back to work at the IHS hospital.

When I fulfilled my contract, I placed my belongings in storage and backpacked for six months with my boyfriend. I learned to travel and live with only what was on my back. My boyfriend opened the world to me. We flew to New York City and then to London. The first night, I slept in a tiny room within the hostel. It was full of bunk beds with six young men with twelve inches of purple spiked hair and such heavy accents that I only understood an occasional word, even though it was English. We went on to Greece and stayed a month in Crete. We had deck fare on a freighter that chugged along all the way across the Mediterranean Sea to Cypress, and then on to Israel. Sometimes we hitchhiked or took a bus, and traveled south to the tip of the Sinai Peninsula, then back north to Egypt.

We then took a train, sleeping along the way with goats and chickens, for a long, long journey down along the Nile River to the country of Sudan. Somewhere along the Nile River, a little boy ran up to me and grabbed my hands. He was literally coated in filth. I washed my hands as soon as I could, but apparently, I was not careful enough. We were now in a tiny village in either Egypt or Sudan. We had no idea where we were, and no one spoke English. We had just arrived at this tiny village, so we walked all around to get adjusted to the area. Diarrhea ran down my legs like water. I had no control.

I was exploding with an intestinal illness until I was unconscious. I woke up with a dark-skinned man rubbing oil all over me as my boyfriend talked to me. He said he walked all around this village saying the word, "doctor." Finally, someone led him to a man who spoke a few words of English and carried a small black bag. So, maybe he really was a doctor. My boyfriend said the doctor gave me an injection and told him that I may not live. My boyfriend was a registered nurse as well, so the doctor gave him a few more syringes, then left and never came back. I sensed outer-world awareness and saw many things that I cannot recall any longer.

I was in and out of consciousness for days. When I could finally stand up for a little while, my boyfriend decided we needed to return to Cairo, Egypt. There were no automobiles anywhere, so he hired a man with a horse-drawn cart. They both held me up enough to walk to the cart, then lifted me up and into it, and away we went to a railway station. The cart driver quickly left.

A few minutes later, we found ourselves terrified as we watched hundreds of men pound on each other with so much rage. We snuck away, hoping no one saw us. We somehow managed to return to our rented room and rested overnight.

The next morning, all was calm at the railroad station, so we left to return to Cairo. I had made it through my third near-death experience. When we traveled back to the US, medically trained people always said it sounded like I had shigella. No one could believe that I was alive to tell them this story.

My six-month worldly backpacking journey permanently rocked my world. No one can ever be the same after seeing such a large portion of this limitless world. I have never been the same. It expanded my mind, blew my thoughts apart, and deepened my understanding of nearly everything. There are literally hundreds of thousands of ways to live, survive, and thrive. I have now traveled to many other countries since my great backpacking journey. Each time is more remarkable than the next. Once there is an expansion of awareness through our experiences and our thoughts, we cannot shrink backward.

When we returned to New Mexico, I studied hypnosis because the mind fascinated me, and so did the powers of hypnosis. It was not until the early 1990s that people approached me for past-life regressions. I hypnotized individuals and small groups of six to ten people. I was often stunned by the experiences that people described, and even more stunned when small groups of people who had just met frequently reported nearly identical experiences during the group session. Some of these people had the exact same experience, in the exact same place, and yet they'd never met until the night of the group regression. Validation is constant, and it is everywhere, if we can allow ourselves to notice it.

In 2004, a book on a shelf stood out to me like a neon light. It was Michael Newton's *Journey of Souls.* Finally, I found another clinical hypnotherapist who, like me, knew that some of their clients actually regressed to other worlds. These clients did not experience a common life in old-world England, nor did they have a life on the plains of Oklahoma, or any expected experience. These people shocked themselves with memories of life without a formed body. They described groups of light beings and environments in space, filled with sparkles or colors that we have no name for on Earth.

I quickly read Newton's books, *Journey of Souls* and then *Destiny of Souls.* On an Internet search, I found that he was offering a "Life Between Lives" (LBL) training in the Netherlands. This is a four-hour hypnotic experience that takes a person into their most recent past life, which then leads to one's memories and experiences of the soul's life in the nonphysical realms in between physical lives on Earth.

Off I went to the Netherlands to join people from all over the world for this training. I arrived in Amsterdam alone and happy. I wandered around freely for hours and never once felt fear that I might be lost. As I wandered the older part of the city, I seemed to always know exactly where I was. My ride arrived and drove me out into the countryside to take Newton's week-long course to be a Life Between Lives Practitioner.

My Fourth Encounter with Death

At the end of the week-long intensive, I experienced my own Life Between Lives regression, facilitated by one of the other students. Once again, my awareness expanded far, far beyond all horizons. I already knew that our life and consciousness continue and never die. As I entered into my own Life Between Lives regression, I felt the sensations, visions, and a small portion of one moment in my past-life history.

I was back in Amsterdam when it was a tiny village. I found myself standing upright, tied to a post in an ancient-looking wagon, the bloody ropes cutting into my wrists and ankles. I quietly looked out across a crowd of villagers. I knew them all. Rocks pounded me from all directions. I was dying a punishing death. I turned my head slightly to my right, to look into the eyes of my past-life daughter, who is now my current-life daughter. She threw the rock that finally killed me.

As quickly as possible, I completed the requirements and became certified through the Newton Institute. I have been honored to share my client's experiences and their memories of a full, rich, and complete life in the nonphysical. During that time, I assisted clients to remember many of their own death process, their own individual existence in the nonphysical realms, and they received vital healing information to explain their suffering and ongoing traumatic relationships. Every time I guided a person through this four-hour regression, my own consciousness intensified.

Working alone in a private practice allowed me to work with freedom. Over the years, I offered mental health counseling for individuals and couples, Reiki, and clinical hypnosis, including past-life regressions and the Life Between Lives experience. I quickly discovered that I was receiving all kinds of intuitive information far beyond the usual. Reiki opened the door to an advanced awareness. I spontaneously could visualize within my clients' physical bodies. At first, I was not sure what was happening, or what on earth I was seeing. The term "medical intuition," to my knowledge, did not exist in 1991. Despite that, I always informed my client what I perceived during their session.

I began to schedule 1.5 hours for a Reiki session: one hour for Reiki, and another half an hour to give them all the intuitive information that I just perceived. The information I gave them included medical concerns, emotional struggles, and sometimes a spirit guide would tell me to give the client a specific message. One day, I heard a spirit say, "Draw them a picture!" Using lots of colored markers, I drew a picture, and at the same time, verbally told each person what I just perceived about their energy field, and how their energy changed because of the Reiki.

I began to add messages from their spirit guides, or comments from relatives who have already passed on. So much information came through me that I began to record the reading and create a drawing for the client at the same time. My clients especially loved receiving both a drawing and a recording to recall their experience but also their intuitive homework. (I always gave a homework assignment at the end of each session to send a message to each client that they are really the one who is in charge of themselves.)

I've been told that I have been many different people in the span of this one life. Many years before my private practice began, I always taught something somewhere. I taught nurse's aide classes. I taught clinicals for psychiatric nursing. I taught meditation at a women's center for over ten years. I taught new employees in the psychiatric units in hospitals. I have taught in the local metaphysical bookstore. My life and my teaching history created the foundation and framework for me to teach large numbers of people, all around the globe. At first, I wanted to teach what intuition really is, and how to be exceptionally accurate. I then went on to teach more specific, advanced courses in medical intuition and mediumship.

My Fifth Encounter with Death: A Near-Death Experience

My fifth encounter with death was officially considered a near-death experience (NDE). In 2016, I really did die in New Zealand.

I was invited back for the second time to teach medical intuition throughout both islands of New Zealand. Two hours after I brought my course to a close, my host drove me to the emergency room in Auckland. I had a hip replacement in the US eight weeks prior to this trip. The journey is quite long, flying in multiple planes to get from Central US to New Zealand. A large number of people in all the airplanes were coughing so severely they were sometimes choking.

My new hip replacement had become infected with an unusual and somewhat rare bacteria. The infection took over my entire body, and I was near death. Over a four-day period, a team of doctors did two emergency surgeries on my hip in an attempt to clean out the bulk of the infection. I just continued to grow weaker. Alone in my hospital room, I experienced my fifth near-death event. This time was different from my first four encounters with death.

I was back in my hospital room after the second surgery on my infected hip. I was septic. The infection was everywhere in my body. I was looking up at the ceiling, and then the ceiling was gone. I moved forward through a white mist or cloud-like substance. I was moving forward, past all kinds of things. I saw the faces of many, many people, none of which I knew. We looked deeply but gently into each other's eyes as we passed each other. I drifted past people of all ages, from babies to older people. And then I stopped moving forward the second I heard those special sounds people have tried to describe for centuries. Thousands upon thousands of voices rising, then oh-so-smoothly lowering, then rising again . . . all in exquisite harmony, creating waves of intricately interlaced, elegant humming. I floated in the power of angels who soothed my soul.

As gently as they came toward me, the angel song gently faded away. I was then fascinated and stopped for some reason to look into the eyes of an elderly man. We both stopped floating in the air to look into each other's eyes. I remained with him for a period of time as if I was examining him more closely. He suddenly looked at me with hatred, and his eyes turned a shocking bright red. He was trying to be scary or even evil, but for some reason I just laughed and laughed. He seemed surprised and floated past me. I turned and continued to move in the direction I was drawn to. I moved past vague, unfamiliar formations as I continued to see more adults and children move past me. Some with only faces and some full-bodied.

My drifting slowly came to a stop. I could not go any farther, so I remained floating in place. Brilliant colors suddenly surrounded me. The lights were so bright it was like I placed my face an inch in front of a multicolored neon sign. It seemed like my eyes were burning out of my head, but there was no pain at all. The colors continued to hover all around me. I laughed with all my heart and could not stop. And laughing so joyously just made me laugh some more. I felt so completely consumed with joy and elation that I had never felt before. I could even hear myself laughing. My own sounds echoed all around me. My laughter bounced off the wall of colors, while some of my laughter echoed within the colors. My own laughter kept bouncing back to me from all directions.

I was fascinated by the neon colors, because I had never seen these colors before. I noticed the brightest light of all was white, and it appeared ahead of me, to my right, and above me. The white light was blinding but without pain. The colors formed complicated geometric shapes. The shapes fit tightly together like puzzle pieces. Then the shapes changed and became one shape that duplicated itself. There were a multitude of shape changes. I remember one of a tree that kept duplicating, and each duplication fit with itself and repeated all around me. And then the form of a bird duplicated in the same way. I laughed more loudly, even louder than before. I truly felt ecstasy, and now I knew it was possible to feel that way. I was elated, and then I was in my hospital bed again.

The following information comes from the observations and experiences of three friends who are energy workers, experienced healers, and medical intuitives. For their privacy, I will call them Chris, Lola, and Mark. According to Google, Mark lives 8,419 miles away from the hospital I was dying in. Chris and Lola live in New Zealand and were about three hours apart from each other. All three medical intuitives provided me energetic support at the same time during this emergency surgery on my hip, but they were unaware of each other.

The following are Chris, Lola, and Mark's experiences that they each shared with me, thousands of miles apart from each other.

Chris

When I started the healing, I saw a light surgeon come from the light and enter the body of the real surgeon. When he opened you, he pondered for a second on what bits to do. He got a shiver down his spine and then made the decision. It was awesome to watch.

Next thing was the comment from you about your bum. I turned, and you were out of your body. I saw it happening on my left-hand side. I said, 'What are you doing out?' You said, 'I don't know, but I can float.' You started floating on the ceiling, and then said, 'Let's go visit a place.' I thought, *We can't*. We (Chris and Lola, both medical intuitives) had our (energetic) hands on you doing the healing. Then, suddenly, a double of ourselves came out. There was a double of Lola and me. I was left to heal, and the second duplicate of us went with you.

You were floating on top of the surgery room, having a laugh. You said, 'I hope my bum isn't sore after this.' You wanted to visit an ancient Pleiadian disk. That's when we found ourselves on a disk, meditating. It was a see-through disk with ancient symbols on it. We all sat on it and meditated. We had to tie a white cord on your leg and pull you back into the room and make you heavy so you sank back in. You were having too much fun and wanted to go to visit other places.

We (the two medical intuitives) knew you were light and wanted to go places. You were floaty. You wanted to go through a star gate and other places. Thank God for the white cord. We will keep it on until you are better. You were tremendously happy. I started the healing at 10:30 p.m., and it was 2:35 a.m. when I was back in my bed.

Lola

As I sent healing energy your way . . . You were laughing and had to be pulled back into the room and into your body with a white cord. It was like a comedy . . . us convincing you we had to go back, and you were sort of on laughing gas and also worried about your bum.

Mark

The morning of your surgery, I woke super early and felt strongly that I needed to work on keeping your silver cord attached. It wasn't easy either. I had trouble getting that done. In summary, it was my intention to monitor you throughout your last surgery and broadcast accordingly. The area I found that was most important to address, while the surgery was underway, pertained to keeping the silver cord attached. The cord can loosen via operations, accidents, drugs, falls, etc. The cord loosening is part of the dying process. It is quite possible, had your silver cord actually loosened, that you might not have returned to your physical body after the surgery.

> It was well after your surgery that your partner told me about the two people in New Zealand who were concurrently working to do the same thing I attempted to do, during the same surgery, via different techniques. It was also well after the surgery that you told me you had the very distinct sense, just prior to surgery, that you were not going to make it through that surgery. I had no knowledge of either of these events (the other two healers) as I was attempting the work at that time.

It seems that I am frequently at the edge of death. I have had many opportunities to "practice" dying. It's a bit of a rough road to learn the way I have been learning.

My guides pop signals into my mind to write a book and share everything I've experienced in the nonphysical realms. It was not until this moment, as I write this sentence, that a tidal wave of understanding rushes through me. My entire life has been a detailed training regarding four areas of existence:

- Humans living on the Earth's plane.
- Human transformation at the time of death.
- Human's life experience in the nonphysical realms of existence.
- Non-human existence on Earth and the cosmos.

My guides' training throughout my life has constantly involved a wide range of interactions with many types of living humans, human spirits, and non-human beings. I am constantly involved with the deceased and constantly interacting with many types of non-human beings. I am stunned at the moment to tell you that my spiritual awareness training came from my daily life experiences, my work experiences, and my own encounters with death.

Some of the deceased tell me, again and again, that they are filled with pain, unrelenting sorrow, unforgiving deep regrets, rage, and jealousy. Other deceased humans constantly tell me or show me what has happened since they left their physical bodies. Non-human beings have come to me as well for all kinds of reasons, or needs, or wants, and how they attempt to receive those things from living and deceased humans.

All while I have experienced nonphysical humans and non-human beings, the living people constantly tell me their "scary stories" about seeing "ghosts," angels, or demons. As I write this now, I realize even more deeply that the Universe is always sending me signals of information. I receive strong signals about what to teach in my courses, and what to teach in this book.

My life and death experiences over multiple decades have led to my knowledge and a heightened awareness of true life within the nonphysical realms. People who take my courses or meet with me for private mentoring sessions frequently tell me they have never heard many of the things that I teach. I keep hearing that I am progressive and at the cutting edge. Really, I give all the credit to my Divine and Sacred Guides. They are powerfully directing me to write this book, and they direct me as I teach my courses.

These extremely high-level guides frequently show me an image of a multitude of very advanced multidimensional energy healers, creating shimmering lace of energy threads all around the globe. They heal hundreds of thousands of troubled deceased, struggling living humans, and needy non-human beings. I am driven, I am focused, I am honored, and I am humbled to share these experiences and precious teachings with you.

PART ONE

Excel as a Multidimensional Thinker

Chapter 1

The Dead, Haunted Places, and Non-Humans are Real, and They are Everywhere

I am determined to guide you through the clearest, most powerful steps to excel as a dynamic multidimensional medium and healer for the troubled deceased, and all levels of interfering non-human beings. My goal for this book is to take the profession of mediumship to an enriched and phenomenal level. You are capable of being an accurate medium who talks and translates for the deceased. You can now be the exceptional medium, who is known as the healer and transformational specialist for all levels of nonphysical beings throughout all the realms.

This training manual is packed with true spirit stories from students and practitioners from all around the world. Each story demonstrates the steps that I teach to be an extraordinary healing medium. Their stories and my stories together will . . .

- Demonstrate how to have one foot in the physical and one foot in the nonphysical at the same time to create balance in your daily life.
- Enrich your keen senses to easily perceive spirit beings.
- Remove any fears or worries about the nonphysical realms.
- Describe each situation step-by-step to heal and transform the troubled deceased.
- Be the powerful, safe healer for interdimensional entities.

- Create fascination with spirit beings of all types and levels of awareness.
- Teach you exactly how to care for your energy field and physical body.
- Lead the way for you to work only with the most progressively aware wisdom of specialty guides.

I share this sincere and deeply touching story with you:

Johnny chose to ride along in the front seat of my car. He recently appeared whenever I drove past the huge swamp on my way home. I was quiet the first few times he jumped into my car to help him feel comfortable. Then I started a telepathic conversation with him. I asked for his name, and "Johnny" leaped into my mind. Immediately after giving me his name, he excitedly said, "I flew out of my body! I flew out of my body!" As he said this, he telepathically showed me his spirit being flung out of his body. He did, indeed, arch high into the air as the car plunged into the swamp.

We had long talks over the next few days. His story began to sound deeply familiar to me. As he talked to me telepathically, I saw one of my new counseling clients in my mind's eye. She told me a similar story. She was involved in a car crash with four teenage boys. Later into her story, she mentioned the same road and the swamp, where Johnny showed up in my front seat.

Johnny had brought the three of us together to help this woman who was profoundly tortured for causing the wreck that had killed Johnny. He directed me to tell my client about him, and how he came to me; how he brought the woman to me for grief counseling, and to tell her how happy he was. Then, because I am a medium who heals the deceased, I assisted sixteen-year-old Johnny to cross over into the light.

This teaching manual will help you understand all possibilities and all stages of spirit phenomena without worry or fear. You will be the director and will know the exact dynamic actions to take for yourself, for the living, and for the myriads of spirit beings all at the same time. Here at your fingertips, you have detailed steps to take regarding many types of beings, many types of issues, and situations within the massive nonphysical realms. You will also have the most powerful, invincible specialty guides at your side every moment. This book is about you becoming a confident, power-filled multidimensional healer for the troubled, the lost, and the confused.

I have been in the professional intuitive and mediumship world for over thirty years. I can confidently share with you that no one ever describes assisting, let alone healing, the deceased. Mediumship has generally focused on communicating with the deceased and providing evidence that you are communicating with someone's deceased family or friends. This historical training was a crucial step to prove to the doubting public that speaking with the dead is not a freak show. It took evidential mediumship to repeatedly show that this ability might be real and not a carnival trick.

As a counselor in private practice, I often found myself sitting with my living client, listening to the stories of their grief and remorse about their unfinished interaction with their deceased family member or dear friend. My clients described great arguments, misunderstandings with harsh words flying back and forth between them, and then the other person suddenly died. The living person was left in shock and guilt.

It took me quite a while to realize that I was doing so much more than counseling. More and more, I was suddenly the translator between the living and the deceased. I sat with my living clients as they cried and sometimes screamed. I heard every word that they said and every emotion they expressed. And, at the same time, I observed my other struggling client: the deceased. Yes, now I suddenly had two distraught human beings in the room with me—one considered alive, and one considered dead. Both needed to communicate, and both needed to heal. And both were just as alive as I was.

I finally got the message. Intuitives and mediums can be so much more than interpreters. This is your opportunity to be the healer for the deceased and other beings throughout these realms. Deceased people really are everywhere, and many of them feel a powerful need to communicate or connect with their living humans. Every one of these spirit people expressed a strong need to speak about something in their life.

Here are a few examples of locations that I unexpectedly discovered, communicated, and brought a healing with the troubled deceased. When I travel somewhere for a vacation, I have found deceased people sitting at their kitchen table in an old cabin that I rented. I also came across hundreds of deceased slaves coming up through the floor of a refurbished barge I was traveling on in Europe. I once had a long conversation with a man standing next to his mummified body in the Egyptian Mummy Room in a famous museum. I visited an antique store and instantly found an elderly man sitting on a red velvet couch. Apparently, both he and the couch had spent a lot of time in a prostitute's brothel. He was smoking a cigar and told me to come sit with him. Spirit people have appeared in the passenger seat of my car as I drove past a current auto wreck.

People in Spirit have approached me in hotel rooms, throughout the hallways of an ancient ten-story hotel, in my doctor's exam room, in my living room, in restaurants, and in airplanes.

The nonphysical world is full of life and, yes, beings are everywhere. They are sometimes in our homes or rattling the front door to our house. They are often at intersections of streets where they died in an automobile wreck, or sitting on their favorite chair that is now for sale in an antique store. Deceased people are often seen in full uniform and standing in what is now a historic site where a great battle took place. Even museums sometimes become a type of new home for the dead. But the deceased may also be discovered in unexpected places too, such as your grocery, your school, or even on vacation in the hotel. They might choose to ride along with you in your car or sit at your kitchen table.

I have witnessed the most blessed, brilliant, bright, loving beings of many types, many colors, and in many situations. Gentle, kind deceased people have come to me asking if I would give their loving messages to their family. I would also come face-to-face with people in spirit who continue to be confused, enraged, obsessed, controlling, mean, and hateful. I have had many encounters with gentle non-human beings, and I have encountered very ugly, hateful non-human beings. You already have this ability. But now you will know exactly what to say and what to do. You will know exactly how to heal and transform both the gentle beings and the aggressive beings.

Validation that the nonphysical world exists is constant, and it is everywhere . . . if we allow ourselves to notice. The nonphysical world of beings is right here, right now. They are next to you. They are around you. You are already part of the spirit world, and your soul naturally intermingles every second of your life with the spirit world. You are a spirit right now, and the Spirit that is you is always intertwined within the entire nonphysical world.

VITAL POINT

> Nonphysical beings are part of the normal world, We alive physical beings are part of life with them. We are a natural part of each other's lives here on Earth.

Everyone talks about seeing auras, but most limit their descriptions of human auras as simply different colors. The aura is actually the soul, and the soul is much larger than the human body. The soul is within the physical body, around the body, and extends outward and upward. The portion that resides outside of the body and extends upward is commonly called the higher self. Many mistakenly think it's called the higher self because it is more knowledgeable and more advanced.

I was surprised when my guides clearly told me that it was named higher self because a large portion of our soul extends upward and into the heavens. The higher self simply is referring to the position of the greater part of the individual's soul that cannot fit into the human body. Even as I write this, my guides reminded me that many of my past-life regression clients frequently stated that they did not bring in enough of their energy to support their current body. While others occasionally commented that they brought in too much of their energy, which has made life difficult in the opposite way.

None of us have ever left the Divine. There is no returning to God because we have never left God in the first place. We are extensions of The All. We are bits and pieces of the Creator, cocreating through experience and sensation. We humans are cocreating with the God force. Each of us is a tiny bit of the whole, and each of us creates the expansion of awareness though our experiences.

There is an ingenious form and design in nature around us, and within our own bodies. This design seems to function with intelligence and balanced creativity that surpasses anything our mind can wrap itself around. This intelligence is closer than the tips of our fingers. Our senses are constantly picking up information, but until you register this information into your awareness, you are missing the most precious, significant, and helpful aspect of life: your intuition. Allowing yourself to notice your natural intuition will begin to smooth life's bumpiness because you are functioning with valuable and more complete information . . . the information of the cosmos.

Intuitive information intertwines like delicate fibers, creating a matrix of energy systems and wisdom that builds and extends throughout the Universe. We humans are also made up of that universal energy, and are already connected to that knowledge and insight. We are not just bodies with minds struggling to make contact with God, or with something that is so elusive that it's impossible to receive. It's paramount for us to recognize that our intuition is a natural ability given to us by Source. It is a skill to develop. You constantly receive enlightenment in a continuous flow of informational signals. You simply need to become aware of it.

Not only are we receivers of information, but we are also participating creators in the development of The All. Our mind, the organ of our brain and our body, is a walking, talking antennae already connected to the matrix of the Universe. The Divine, Source, and Infinite Intelligence is not separate from you, and never has been. We are creators, created by the Creator, to continue the creation of all that is, and all that is about to be.

More and more, I sense there is no barrier. The physical experience and the nonphysical experience vibrate together hand in hand. All of life is a vibratory frequency forming wave patterns. Sometimes the wave is high and deep, and sometimes it's fast and fine, but it always moves and flows. Everything is connected and interconnected with everything else.

VITAL POINT

> We are creators, created by the Creator, to continue the creation of all that is, and all that is to be.

A mentoring student shared this simple example of how deceased people are truly everywhere:

"I remember one day, in my local library, I was talking to a mother at my daughter's kindergarten. Suddenly, a family in spirit walked past us and did a double take at me, as I did a double take at them!

They presented themselves as being terribly burned. They all stopped and came over to where I was, in mid-conversation with the other kindergarten mother. I tried to ignore them, but as they would not be ignored, I tuned out of the conversation with the kinder mum to help the family cross over. To my surprise, they had a tiny dog with them also. Once they'd moved on, I tuned back into the conversation, not having any idea what the lady in front of me had been saying.

"Awkwardly, she looked at me, and I just smiled. I realized she must think I was "off with the fairies." She was not far off. Sometimes it feels hard to balance this way of being in the world. I found it hard when I was young and had a busy social life. I asked Spirit one day if I could only see spirits while I was in session and when it was very necessary. I was amazed to know that this was an option, and that it worked. Take control of it."

Deceased people are not far away, and are not separate from the physical realm. There are two experiences happening at the same time, intertwined together. I see the two realms existing and moving together like waves touching the shore. Again, everything is energy, and energy is in constant motion, constant vibration, and constantly alive.

The deceased are often eager to contact us. Most of them have been making attempts to contact us since their passing. The living ignores these contacts and blames it on their unruly imagination making it all up. We are spirits with physical bodies, perceiving other spirits without physical bodies. We are naturally able to perceive each other, interacting and communicating with each other. We are natural mediums, and many of the dead still have something important to say to us, and they want or need to be heard.

My plan for this book is to go step-by-step with you into a deeper and distinct awareness of intuitive mediumship and healing troubled nonphysical beings. Many say the spirit world is out in the sky or the heavens. I say the spirit world is right here, shoulder to shoulder with each one of us. The nonphysical realm is not a place or a space. We living humans and nonphysical beings are interwoven together in this multifaceted, complex creation.

The multidimensional thinker knows that the air around us is literally filled with very complex patterns of interconnected waves of information. I ask that you never see the air in the same way again. It is not empty. The air is full of life, intelligence, and wisdom.

Many students tell me they yearn to be a professional intuitive and medium for others. But in the same breath, they look down at the floor and confess they do not ever want to see dead people. Then they declare, "Seeing spirits is just too scary for me. I want to be able to do everything else that an intuitive does, but I do not want to see any dead people."

What's All This Fear About?

Beliefs are not necessarily truths. Beliefs are commonly learned from others. Many negative beliefs are based on nothing but fear. Fear of the invisible. Fear can become a powerful frequency of energy. It can become more powerful than we humans are.

Over the years, I have heard so many rules and so many fears about intuitives and mediums. I listen respectfully, and then quietly wonder why people create such alarming stories in their mind, and why do they make their own debilitating and scary rules, and then allow those rules to rule their lives.

Notice yourself as you read some of the more common quotes from people:

"If you contact the Spirit world, you are opening yourself to Satan, and harm will come to you!"

"I was taught as a child that Satan is real and will get me if I don't go to church."

"I am terrified that if I become more intuitive, I might see spirit people. I don't want to even think about that happening. It freaks me out."

"Deceased people are going to get me if I'm not careful."

"The minister always told me that I am going to hell. My minister told us that every week, so it must be true."

"There is no such thing as ghosts."

"Everyone knows that everyone goes to heaven."

"Everyone dies, becomes angels, and then go to heaven."

"We humans are the only life in the Universe. My parents said so."

"The church told us all the time that we are sinners."

A belief is not a rule, but it easily becomes a life rule that might be false. Many beliefs that are taught to children, and to adults as well, are ideas to control people's minds and their behaviors.

A Practitioner Shares a Story

The first thing I want to share on mediumship is that no one has taught me mediumship so beautifully as Tina Zion. She has so much love for every soul from the other side who shows up in a session, and it's heartwarming. Whatever their story is, and no matter why they haven't found the light yet, she helps them transform into the light, where they can be free. Tina taught me how to do it. Today, I often help souls transform into the light, where they belong. It's one of the most beautiful things to do. It is so pure, so far away from ego, and it makes me cry every time.

My first experience I had with souls on the other side was when I was very little. As a child, I felt all these energies around me in an empty room. I knew they were souls from the other side. It often felt so crowded that it was distracting for me. Seeing or feeling energies was not normal in our family. I had no one to explain to me what was happening. I was scared of them, and I knew I needed rules to be able to cope with them.

So, I started to talk to the souls around me. I asked, "Why are you here?" "What do you want?"

The answers I got were usually, "We need help. We know you are open to feeling us." But at this point in my life, I was too scared to interact with them further.

I agreed with the souls on the other side that there's a space around me that only belonged to me. Outside of this space, they could hang out and do whatever they want, but this space was only mine. It worked. They respected my space, and we left each other alone for a long time with only little interactions about keeping boundaries.

It didn't feel special that I had my little interactions about boundaries with the other side—and it really isn't, because everyone can do it. For a long time, nothing more ever happened.

When my stepfather died in 2020, I totally lost my fear of the other side, because I now had a friend there. After he crossed, he became my gatekeeper to make sure the souls from the other side didn't overwhelm me. Today, this is not necessary anymore, and like I said, Tina gave me so much confidence that there is nothing on the other side we need to be afraid of. If something seems off, it's only a sign they need our help. So, this is what I do today: I help them.

I talk to my stepfather on the other side almost every day. I often meet him next to the sea, where it looks like Cornwall and Scotland in the United Kingdom. He sits at a table and looks out to the sea with our dogs, who have also crossed over. He is so happy there. It's who he is, one with nature with our dogs at his side. I miss him every day, and it's so good for me to meet him there consciously, and relax with him in his happy place. Other days, he comes to me and makes funny comments about things I'm doing. He makes the same comments he'd make as if he were still here. He makes me laugh, he makes me cry, and he makes me love. He is there for me when I need him most.

People who are dying are not leaving. They're just transforming into their purest form. Once we realize this, we can connect with them always and at any time. We are all connected. Everyone can connect and speak to the other side. We just have to do it and shut our brain off, because we have the ability to connect. For me, the other side is part of the whole; a part of the fact that we are all one. We all belong together. I realized that a tiny bit of me is in each of you on this side and on the other side. Knowing this not only brings us closer to the people who are living on this side, but also to the souls on the other side.

— Sonja Frey
www.sonjafrey.com

If you're feeling drawn to the spirit realms and working as a medium for family, friends, or even professionally, here are primary reasons to drop all fear.

10 Reasons to Not Be Afraid of Nonphysical Beings

Fear is the primary block that hinders our intuitive abilities. Each person has a fear, and they have that fear because they learned to be afraid, or they had a previous experience before they received any intuitive training. Here are ten reasons to not be afraid of nonphysical beings:

1. You are approximately 70 percent nonphysical spirit and only about 30 percent a physical human.
2. You are already a multidimensional being with one foot in the physical and one foot in the nonphysical at the exact same time.

3. You can learn to instantly distinguish a positive being from a troubled or negative being.
4. You are the boss. Deceased humans and non-humans will do exactly what you tell them to do. If you mean what you say, either telepathically of verbally, you will get results.
5. Even now, as you are having an Earth experience, you are also an eternal living spirit.
6. A belief is not a truth. It is only a thought you were told or taught to think when you were younger. You can now decide what you think and believe.
7. You are not vulnerable, nor a victim, to nonphysical beings.
8. You are truly the commander of deceased people and non-human beings.
9. The more you are in charge of yourself, the more you are in charge of nonphysical beings.
10. Negative beings cannot tolerate a living human's bright light and cannot stand the emotion of love.

I will do my best to take the fears away and to teach you how to be a confident, powerful medium specialist for the living, the deceased, and the troubled non-human beings.

This book is full of true stories that are also lessons to learn from. Some of the stories are from my own experiences, and others are from the students I mentor around the globe.

Here is the story of the "Nasty Man" who came into my home without an invitation:

A male human figure stood just inside the doorway of my home office. I saw him quite unexpectedly as I sat on the couch, watching TV. He did appear thick with a smoky darkness. He seemed a little sinister. As soon as I noticed him, he disappeared. I mentioned this to my family, and they said the house was full of sounds again, especially downstairs. We had been hearing snaps and pops, and bangs and thumps. It also sounded as if someone was going up and down the stairway. My family actually went downstairs earlier that day because they were convinced we had an intruder. There was nothing out of the ordinary.

I asked that no one bother me for a few minutes while I checked in with this spirit man. I sat and mentally scanned the house. Even though I sat in my bright sunroom, I was drawn to the darkest back corner of the basement, and there he stood.

I immediately said, "I welcome you with all of my love."

I asked him what was going on, and why he was here at my house. He simply responded by saying he felt nasty.

Yes, he said "nasty." *I feel nasty.*

He continued to say he had been a nasty person all his life. He said the fear in the house last evening drew him here. (I must explain that the next-door neighbor had called us the night before to tell us they were robbed the previous night by two men whom they'd found breaking into their barn.) This situation in our neighborhood shot enough fear through the family, and as a result, the energy of fear drew this spirit person to us.

Instead of remaining in fear, I began to talk with him. I asked for his name, and George Michaels leaped into my mind. Then he said he was nasty. I did not ask about the nastiness but focused on his feeling better. When he seemed interested, I continued by telling him he is not alive now. I told him he can change things right now because he does not have a dense, physical body. I asked him to notice a light inside of himself that everyone had, no matter how nasty they were. I then asked him to look all around to find his guides. I told him they would be much brighter than he'd ever noticed before.

He quickly turned his head to the left, seeing someone who had come for him. I told him, "This guide will show you how to feel better and better."

I noticed that the dark, smoky color of this spirit person began to lighten into grays, and then lighter again. I also told him that I was sending him waves of love energy to assist him. I watched as he faded away, looking off to his left. I wished him well.

We are not vulnerable victims to spirit people. I was in charge and kept directing him step-by-step. Do you see how I treated this spirit like he was a real person? He was, and still is, a real person who needs to be treated with respect and honesty, but I was in charge of each step. We did not see, feel, or hear this spirit person after that. The living and the deceased share this world together.

I hear this nearly every day: "Tina, I want to be more intuitive, and I want to do medical intuition and mediumship for myself and for others . . . but I don't want to see any dead people!" (It made me chuckle even as I typed this.)

Participate: Every time we check in with ourselves, we also learn about what makes us tick and what is blocking us from reaching our goals. Here is another opportunity to learn more about yourself.

1. Measure your fear as you read this real experience with a negative deceased man.

   What number pops into your mind from 1–10?

2. Name the fears that might have stirred within you as you read this true story.

3. Notice yourself as a very physical human having a physical experience right now.

4. Notice yourself as a spirit, seeing spirits, talking to spirits, and helping spirits.

We are not at the mercy of other alive or deceased people's poor intentions. Focusing on appreciation, joy, happiness, love, non judgment, abundance, and yes, the brilliant light, which creates an energy level at its finest frequency. Lower energy cannot match or even connect with the energy of higher thought. (More details regarding self-protection and self-healing in chapter 3).

Television shows regarding ghosts seem to be quite popular. As a healing medium, I can hardly bear to watch them. In general, the "ghost hunting" shows do find traumatized deceased people. Most of the TV celebrities try to get a spirit to speak up on their audio machines or blink some lights or appear in videos.

I have no qualms about searching for proof to show that "ghosts" are everywhere. The so-called ghosts seem to be found in locations that are known for violence and suffering such as ancient insane asylums, abandoned prisons, and deserted orphanages. Remember, science is finding that human thoughts and emotions tend to linger. So, horrendous thoughts, emotions, and actions, due to the extreme behavior of humans in these settings, will linger much longer due to the density of severe negativity. Not only will negative thought energy remain, but it will also keep hold of the deceased who suffered under these torturous conditions.

Now, notice how most, but not all, the "ghost hunters" tend to communicate with the deceased. They yell out taunting remarks, they say disrespectful words to them, and they constantly challenge the "ghosts" to act out in some way. The "hunters" are then surprised when they are scratched, pushed, or become ill enough to vomit. And then the ratings go way up when the ghost hunters declare that the deceased are evil demons.

These shows promote terror in unaware people, and they also teach that living humans are vulnerable and even victims of the troubled deceased. The people on these shows place themselves in every situation possible to allow extremely traumatized dead people to lash out. The hosts of these shows usually taunt the spirit people in an attempt to get a strong reaction for the cameras. Again, to create higher viewer ratings.

As the ghost hunters describe in detail how demons are dangerous and could potentially harm or kill the living humans who are trying to live in this old house, I'm totally witnessing the opposite. For example, I would see an elderly deceased woman who is, indeed, furious about all these strangers in her home taking down her walls to make an "open floor plan." (Yes, I am giggling too as I write this.) She is not a demon or a killer spirit. But apparently, angry deceased women do not raise the TV ratings.

Now try to imagine a ghost hunter TV show where the celebrities go into these historical deserted places in the daytime. The alive humans call out to the deceased with kind, loving information, explaining that they have come to assist everyone who is there. Then strongly direct these tortured souls to come forward to make themselves known in only positive ways. The celebrities then explain to them that everyone is dead, even if they do not think they are. Then the celebrities explain to them that they are mediums who heal. Then they state out loud, "We will now release each of you from this bondage. Specialty guides will release you from this horrible place and take you to a special location to rest, heal, and learn in a loving, caring place . . . just for you."

Try to imagine that.

Please do not base your personal understanding of the nonphysical realms around these ghost hunting shows. Again, I must declare that so-called ghosts are real people, and they are just as alive as you are. Treat them as humans, and treat them respectfully.

Do not be fooled. Do not be afraid. Be educated.

Training to be an intuitive medium does blast open the channels for energy to surge through us on a physical, emotional, and spiritual level. People invariably report that dead people are suddenly approaching them. That's because they need something, and what they usually need is help, understanding, or to communicate a message to someone. Many students report they are suddenly more intuitively aware and know things that are about to happen even before it happens.

The following story is offered to you by Barbara, one of my long-term mentoring students. For a long time, she struggled to even identify as a medium. She didn't think she was seeing or hearing the deceased. Nearly every time we met, she would deny she had any mediumship abilities and refused to even consider practicing those skills. Then she sent me this story of her mediumship experience . . .

A Practitioner Shares a Story

My eighty-three-year-old mom fell in the bathroom, fractured her hip, and needed a replacement. It was shortly before bedtime when my mom decided she should quickly tend to her one toenail that had a rough corner. As usual, she put one foot on the toilet ring and bent over to take care of her troubled nail. Without any warning sign, she found herself on the floor in immense pain. She lay on the tiled bathroom floor for over ten hours until she found the strength to crawl to her cell phone, which was charging in the kitchen. The immense pain and nausea were clear signs of a fracture. 911 brought her to the hospital, and she received a new hip joint that same evening.

I flew back home to help her out and moved into her apartment while she was still in the hospital. I was super sick during the first three days and felt miserable. On day four, I was lying on my side in her bed, watching a movie on my laptop. I suddenly felt an energy or dark shadow rush behind my back. It felt so real that I turned my head to see what was going on. My eyes stopped at an empty corner, where my inner eye perceived a spirit. It was a female, humanlike energy in a dirty old dress with a hoodie. I just saw her face and her bare feet. She looked like the character in Edward Munch's painting, *The Scream*. Her hair was grayish blonde and not very well taken care of, her face once pretty but now old and neglected.

I asked her what she was doing here, and instead of an answer, I had a sensation of anger and frustration. She did not give me an answer but mentioned that she was very upset. She was forgotten in that zone between life and death for years. Her beauty wilted away, and she was frail and old. No one cared about her. She used to be so beautiful. She was hanging around my mom's apartment for five years. She told me that even the eighty-three-year-old lady who lived here was in better shape and had more energy than her. The dead woman couldn't take it anymore and pushed my mother over in the bathroom.

She dislikes all vibrant female beings. She was clearly aware that she was dead but felt stuck and was never able to move on. I called in spirit guides who specialized in that task and asked her to pay attention to those ten energies who came to help her. They wrapped her in radiant light full of golden sparkles and carried her away. She loved the attention, softened, and smiled, and she got carried away to the edge of the Universe to a place where her beauty was restored.

I asked my guides to heal and clear my mother's bedroom and fill it up with harmony, peace, clarity, and vitality. Soon afterward, I felt less sick. I decided to tell my mom about that spirit. She agreed that it felt like she'd been violently pushed over. But now she was worried about coming back home because she could easily visualize that lady still standing in her bedroom. She voiced concerns about sleeping there again and was terrified.

I repeated those same steps one more time together with my mother. That made a big change for her, and she felt safe and in charge afterward. The quality of my mom's sleep improved drastically. She still needs to go to the bathroom but falls easily back asleep afterward. Her sleep had been a struggle for years.

My sister was visiting last December for fourteen days and was sick the whole time she was there. She only felt better when they went to a ski resort for a few days, but got sick again as soon as they returned to my mom's apartment. I did not see those connections before, but I see and understand them now. I will try to be more aware of negative spirits in the future. They seem to have a huge impact on people's lives!

— Barbara Liniger
www.barbaraliniger.com

Notice that Barbara did not question herself or think she was imagining the troubled deceased being. She did not hesitate to take action. She directed her Divine and Sacred Guides and did not do the work alone. Barbara's actions immediately healed the hostile dead woman, healed her mother, her sister, and her mother's home as well. Barbara owned her power and her abilities to heal the deceased. This is how powerful you and your team of highly advanced guides can be.

Many people do not have this detailed training that Barbara described above. She could have chased away the hostile deceased woman, but she did a healing instead. I frequently hear false and uneducated statements such as the following nearly every day. Here is one example of a common statement from an untrained medium.

"There were ghosts all around my friend, and all around her house. I went in there and chased them all away. My friend is doing better now, and everyone is so much calmer too. I am so glad I could do this for her."

This is not the solution, and it is not assisting the deceased to heal and go into the light. The solution is to create a healing for the troubled deceased that releases them from being stuck in that place or situation.

This is only one example of how people think they are helping their friends and loved ones by chasing away people in spirit. I hear versions of this same story over and over again. Both practitioners and laypeople are so proud to tell me details about their accomplishments of forcing deceased people out of homes, buildings, and off the land. I listen intently to every single story. As I listen to the details that all these people describe to me, I receive so much more information that no one else seemed to be aware of.

While listening to the people telling me about different ways to chase spirits around, I observed each situation in my mind's eye. The deceased were energetically pushed out of the house, apartment, or building and into the yard or the grounds around the building. Sometimes it was one disgruntled spirit person, but I often would perceive small to large groups of spirits being pushed outside through walls, windows, and doors. Then I almost always perceived the deceased calmly drifting back into the house that night or within a few days.

When a deceased being continues to remain in a certain area, it's always a sign that they are troubled or stuck there in some way. Forcing the deceased to leave an area is not the solution. From this point forward, it should now be a powerful signal to you that healing steps are needed. My hope is that you now begin to realize that forcing deceased beings is the opposite of directing a healing for them. You can become a powerful healing medium rather than an exorcist chasing them away.

Chapter 2

Four Steps Toward Becoming a Medium Healer

One of my students described a time when she was speaking to her client on the phone. Her client explained that she was in the emergency room at that moment, saying: "The nurse has been sticking me over and over again. They cannot find a vein!"

My mentoring student immediately directed her guides and said to them telepathically, "Help this nurse get my client's vein now!"

Her client immediately said, "They just got it!"

This is just a tiny example of how this training quickly opens up your abilities and your positive power to communicate and work across time and space.

We are bombarded with sensory input all day long from our everyday world. We see our world, taste it, hear the sounds, and physically touch the world during our waking day. We also tune out a great deal of that information to prevent an overload, which could overwhelm us at any moment. For example, when we sit to pay the monthly bills, we often tune out the dog barking, and the neighbor mowing the grass just outside the window. If we focused on all that, we would not get the bills paid!

We as humans seem to actually be quite good at filtering information out of our awareness. It's one of the ways we protect ourselves in this frantic world we reside in. This protection, however, also blocks out the intuitive information that surrounds us. We have become action-oriented humans rather than sensing humans. In many ways, our life has become more of a struggle because most of us do not take a split second to notice the intuitive information that constantly comes to us.

As a result, we take the wrong step in the wrong direction, or take too many unnecessary steps to achieve our goals. If only we would stop for a split second to notice intuitive information that is constantly there for us. If we pay attention, intuitive wisdom is there, as loud as the dog and the mower just outside the window.

Our Source is truly at a higher level of understanding and intelligence than we can ever imagine. I cannot, for the life of me, tell someone that I healed them or another individual. Medical intuition, energy healing, and spirit communications and healings have brought me to my knees, in humbled awe, repeatedly. Who am I to say that I did this? I cannot. As mediums, psychics, or energy workers, we are merely representatives, a spokesperson, an ambassador, or an open pipeline for the unseen world of healing. That unseen world is made up of all sorts of humans and all sorts of other beings.

When you look around the world, watch the land and animals that create the nature of Earth, and then look at the intricate workings of the human body, one might recognize these complex systems and the order that presides throughout these systems. Humans are, indeed, a tiny speck of the entire intergalactic system. We are creators of our lives by the thoughts we have. These thoughts lead to beliefs that create our emotions. Our thoughts and emotions literally create the vibratory level of our physical body and the life we lead. Your thoughts will lead you to be a medium who heals the living and the deceased. It all begins with your thoughts. Think now that you are in charge of you. You are the director of your life.

We humans are one of the physical expressions of Source. As you help humans and non-humans, you are developing and advancing. But we're not alone in this expansion. Many authors describe the physical and nonphysical world as a hierarchical structure containing levels of importance. I prefer to describe it as realms of awareness, understanding, and compassion. There does not seem to be an area or realm of the nonphysical that has a higher rank than another. The entire cosmos learns and expands every time we learn and expand. Each person has a choice with every second and every moment of time. We cannot make anyone advance.

VITAL POINT

> Have you noticed yet that we really cannot make anyone change or advance or heal? We cannot make anyone do what we think is right for them. Each person is ultimately responsible for their own life, health, and awareness.

The next step is to take charge of you. It's time to get out of your way in every way possible. Here are the strong qualities for the medium who heals the nonphysical.

- Using common sense, clear, and direct words when communicating with all nonphysical beings.
- Noticing the nonphysical with accurate awareness.
- Expanding your specialty skills to determine whether there is a spirit in need around you.
- The ability to determine whether the nonphysical human is causing harm to the living or the environment.
- The ability to determine whether a spirit has crossed over into the light or is earthbound.
- The ability to discover the cause of spirits remaining earthbound.

My client shared his process with me:

> My path has been led by spirit . . . this I know. I have been challenged, encouraged, and initiated by spirit guides to learn and develop as a psychopomp my whole life, whether I knew it only on reflection, or was actually awake to it at the time. I was lucky enough to be guided slowly in safe and knowledgeable ways. I would experience something I thought was bizarre, and I would never dare share, as people would think I was mad, only to research and find teachings in spiritual literature, mystery schools, occult teachings, and science modern and ancient, to explain or validate what I had experienced. I'm glad I learned this way, as I can be quite skeptical, and experience has been the most important teacher for me.

Our personal thoughts create the most powerful obstacles. Once you are aware of this, you can get more in charge of yourself. Here are the first steps toward becoming a medium healer:

Step 1: Immediately Release All Your Old Blocks

Living people continually tell me there is a veil between them and the spirit world. A veil implies a border or boundary of some type. I know the only veil that exists is due to the density of fear created by the living. Fear is a slow and thick energy. The daily grind of life, our hectic thoughts, and the burden of our emotions tend to build the barriers between us and the nonphysical realm. We humans are actually quite fantastic in creating our own barriers. You are the only one who can change you. Learn more about yourself as you continue to read about blockages that stop you from excelling as an accurate healing medium.

Block 1: Fear

Our greatest barrier is our thoughts that lead to emotions, and the emotion that creates the most solid block is *fear.*

Participate: Notice yourself as you read the most common fears mentioned by many students in my courses. Notice which fears you have been struggling with. Notice which fears you have advanced beyond. Notice which ones you do not struggle with at all.

- Fear of being blamed for something.
- Fear of knowing things I do not want to know.
- Fear of looking like a crazy person.
- Fear that it is only imagination.
- Fear of the unknown.
- Fear of seeing dead people.
- Fear of being wrong.
- Fear of family and friends disapproving.
- Fear that I will be overwhelmed by spirits.
- Fear of my primary job disapproving.
- Fear of spirit people coming to my bed at night.
- Fear of opening my home to spirits.
- Fear of spirits interfering with my children.
- Fear of carrying this much responsibility regarding other people.
- Fear of loving the spirit world so much that I will not want to stay here on Earth.
- Fear of attracting evil.
- Fear of ridicule.
- Fear of change.
- Fear of failure.
- Fear of performance.
- Fear of success.

Block 2: Expectations

What will mediumship be like when it happens? Will it look a certain way? Will it come to you in a certain way? What do you expect will happen? How will it happen? What will it look like?

Participate: Notice yourself as you think about these questions. How do you define intuition, healing, and mediumship? "Expectation" really means that if it doesn't come to you as you expect it to, then you will probably miss it. So, what have you "decided" about intuition in your life? The best example I know of is this: If you have developed a belief that you must see all deceased people with your eyes open, then you are missing all the deceased that have less density. Most spirits, and even non-humans, tend to be more visible in your mind's eye.

Block 3: Limiting Rules

The Spirit of God is not limiting, fearful, or critical. It is only people who condemn each other that create limitations. Anything that is limiting, fearful, or critical is not coming from the voice of the Divine Spirit. What rules have you created in your mind that have become limiting to your success as an intuitive healer?

Participate: Notice any sense of limitations that your thoughts have created. Do you have a rule that you must be in a certain room to have a session with someone? Do you think you cannot offer mediumship to people over the phone or Zoom? Do you have it in your mind that you can only work with people in your local area? Deeply examine yourself now and search for any hidden limiting thoughts that are holding you back.

Block 4: Be Aware of the Focus of Your Thoughts

Before or during an intuitive session, any thoughts about yourself will hinder your intuitive accuracy regarding your clients. Focusing only on your client requires that you place your life, your worries, and your issues aside. To do this, you must be in charge of your thoughts and be in control of your focus.

Common signals to know if you are focusing on yourself:

1. Are you worried that you might be wrong?
2. Are you wondering if your guides are real?
3. Are you afraid the guides might not answer your questions?
4. Did you instantly think about your own life issues or struggles?
5. Did you suddenly feel something about your own body?

If you are thinking about yourself in any manner while you're trying to connect with your psychic abilities, you're in your own way, and you are your own block. You cannot ignore that block. You must relax and surrender the self, shift your focus, and turn your complete attention to your client, or your meditation, or the information you're trying to receive. The Universe never stops communicating with you. Are you noticing?

Participate: Reflect on any anxieties you may have. Do you become worried or nervous about yourself just before or during a session? What are you worried about?

Block 5: Powerful Emotions

Any strong emotions you have of love, hate, or fear will completely block your accuracy. Do not practice mediumship with your living family, or with anyone you care deeply about. Do not practice with people you care about who are deceased. Negative or even deeply positive emotions will always interfere with receiving accurate intuition. The best way to understand this is that intuition is a piece of information. When the medium truly receives a fact, there is no emotion. You can't stop feeling emotions, but you can steer away from trying to assist your loved ones, and instead, send them to a professional that you trust.

For example, I do not have clear intuitive information for my family or my friends because my hopes and desires for them have a louder voice than the voice of my intuition. The information is more garbled and less distinct when any level of worry or concern exists within you about the subject you're trying to get information for. In other words, our instincts cannot get through the muddy field of emotions.

Block 6: Hiding Your Abilities

Hiding or minimizing your intuitive and mediumship abilities will interfere with your own confidence. You do not need to flaunt what you're able to do. However, if you're hiding it, you're smashing down your confidence as a medium. You're also missing many opportunities to help people understand how normal the nonphysical realms are in the living human's life. Speaking more openly about the nonphysical realms will allow you to become the teacher. It takes the scariness out of seeing spirit people. It also gives others a chance to share that they might have already had an encounter with a spirit but were afraid to tell anyone, so they keep it a secret. Keeping secrets is never good for the soul.

Block 7: Negative Emotions

Negative thoughts will always create negative emotions. Negative emotions take energy away from us and deplete our life force. We become exhausted mentally, emotionally, and physically. This type of thinking creates the emotions that subsequently block our intuitive ability to perceive Spirit. You cannot perceive the nonphysical if physical awareness is dominating. Negative emotions are vibrationally heavy and will pull our awareness into the physical and farther away from intuition.

Step 2: Create Your Code of Ethics as a Powerful Medium

Many people do not seem to have their own thoughts. Do you have your own thoughts? Take a few moments to digest that question. Do you tend to follow all the thoughts you heard from authority figures in your childhood? Do you go along with the beliefs you heard from parents, grandparents, teachers, and bullies? Do you still follow the thoughts they gave you during your upbringing? Whose thoughts are you really thinking? I will repeat that: Whose thoughts are you *really* thinking?

If we adults simply accept everything we hear from authority figures, then who is really in charge of you? I cherish my grandfather, but if I blindly accepted the one hideous thing he would occasionally say, I would be a totally different person than I am now.

VITAL POINT

> What you allow, the choices you make, and what you say aloud to others is what makes you who you are today. Are you truly in charge of you, and are you truly who you're meant to be?

I have told this true story in my previous books, but I must tell it again because of its teaching power. Every time I share this story, I am again stunned and mortified at the unethical actions this professional intuitive took with an innocent client. She described this moment to me during a phone conversation. As I look back on this event, I realize the conversation provided an important example of how and why we must maintain a standard of excellence and conscientious care for our clients.

This practitioner seemed very pleased to share with me that she recently facilitated a guided meditation with a group of students. However, she went on to describe to me how strongly attracted she was to one of the men in the group. While she did not name the man, she did go into detail about his qualities and why she was so attracted to him. This woman then described that after she guided everyone into a deep meditation, she then energetically approached that man sexually while he was meditating. Be aware that she did not physically walk over to him and do so. She did so by visualizing in her mind's eye but also projecting her energy to that man, creating the physical sensations of what that would be like. The imagery, the sensations, and the energy of sexual contact is what she sent to this man.

Now, initially, you might think, "Well, what's the harm in that? She was only fantasizing!" I will explain the harm that was done. This practitioner then described that the man, who had been in an altered state of meditation, immediately moved in a restless, uncomfortable manner, so she stopped and focused back again to facilitating the meditation. When she brought the session to a close and the group sat up to discuss their experiences, this particular man did not participate in the discussion as he usually did, nor did he make the usual eye contact with her. She knew immediately that he was aware of her advances. As I listened to her story, she became apologetic and knew that she had violated a sacred trust between a practitioner and a client. Her story sent me back to a similar experience that happened to me.

I was living in New Mexico at the time and had been participating in numerous traditional sweat lodges with a Native medicine man from a nearby state. One night, as I sat with ten or so others in the complete darkness of the sweat lodge, I couldn't figure out why I was having such a difficult time reaching a meditative state. I felt so restless and anxious that I opened my eyes to give myself a break and release all the effort that I was so caught up in . . . or so I thought.

I held up my hand in front of my face, testing the hot darkness. I could not even see my hand an inch from my face! Although I knew this from eleven other sweats, it increased my anxiety. Looking for some relief and comfort, I turned my head to the left, where I knew our medicine man sat. Fear rushed over me. In the complete blackness of the lodge, I saw glowing red eyes looking right back at me. I broke the stare and quickly closed my eyes. I felt tremendous fear but decided that I must have dreamed it up. I opened my eyes again, held my hand out in front of my face, testing the darkness and trying to distract myself. I still could not see my hand, nor the person sitting next to me. I glanced again to my left. The burning red eyes continued to hang in the dark air, staring my way.

"Oh my God," I said to myself. "Those eyes are really there! What has happened to this medicine man?"

The sweat lodge finished late in the evening. We crawled out on our hands and knees, and stood together, quietly whispering to one another. The medicine man walked up to each person, gave them a quick hug, spoke a few words, and moved on to the next person. As he stood in front of me, I felt something push against my groin area. As he embraced me in what appeared to be a loving hug, I was also sexually violated. I was so shocked that I could not respond, let alone protect myself. Later, as I drove the 2.5 hours home, I was depleted, exhausted, and raped!

For years after that, I always thought that I had just fabricated the entire incident. I questioned and blamed myself. "What on earth was the matter with me? Why did my imagination create something like that regarding a man that I highly respected?"

As I learned more and more about the power of energy, I slowly began to realize that I hadn't imagined that episode. Our thoughts, emotions, and sensations have an energetic substance. Spiritualists call it ectoplasm. Now it is usually called astral projection. It is the actual manifestation of energy into a substance. In other words, energy can congeal into a level of density that a physical human can see and feel. These two practitioners used their training in a negative manner and crossed a professional boundary. They violated a code of honor.

Here is another ethical issue. I am constantly asked this question: "Is it okay to go up to a stranger or someone I know in a public place and tell them that a deceased human has a message for them?"

At the time of writing this book, a student directly asked me to include this ethical issue in my book. I immediately realized that many people ask me this question, and now a student directly asked me to include this issue in my book. I knew the student was a messenger of Spirit. So, here it is . . . I want to alert all you well-meaning mediums to not approach people in public settings to suddenly tell them that a deceased person has a message for them. It's not only a surprise but a shocking, emotional moment for most people, and it happened in a public setting.

Keep in mind that intuitives and mediums will always know things on multiple levels everywhere we go. Knowing or witnessing things in the nonphysical realms does not demand that we tell everyone around us. Most people do not understand our abilities, and many people are terrified by it. Instead, communicate with the deceased and inform each one of them that it isn't appropriate for you to approach the living, and it will only terrify them. I often teach the deceased to approach their living person while they are sleeping, because the living are more open to receiving them at that time.

People who come to practitioners for any type of guidance do so with hope or a sense of trust. Clients are often quite vulnerable to the guidance of practitioners. That trust can never be violated! What we do is powerfully real.

Your Code of Ethics for All Physical and Nonphysical Beings

Here are ten guidelines that I follow as my Code of Ethics. I hope you use this as your professional guidance, but you can also add to this one or create your own. Either way, live every moment of your life ethically, respectfully, and carefully with kindness and love. Be the multidimensional professional who applies these guidelines to all physical and nonphysical beings throughout the galaxy.

1. Never force your empowerment to make someone do what you think or believe is right for them.

2. Never use your intuitive or energy skills to force a healing modality without permission.
3. Be completely confidential at all times and in all circumstances. Never share what happens in sessions with the client's family, friends, or other clients using their name or any other identifying information.
4. Always think or speak aloud with conscious awareness. Your thoughts and emotions are powerful signals to individuals and to the Universe.
5. Do not pray or direct Spirit or your energy against anyone. Always pray, or direct Spirit and your energy, for a positive outcome.
6. Always receive permission intuitively or verbally before working energetically with clients.
7. When working with very young children or handicapped people, intuitively ask the child or the handicapped for permission to work with them.
8. Never astral project or remote-view into a person's body, their life, their home, property, or any environment they are associated with, unless you have received clear permission to do so.
9. Do not approach the living in public places to give them a reading.
10. Treat all deceased and all non-human beings as if they are real and alive, because they are real and alive.

No one should ever have to experience anything like the examples I described here. When people come to us for intuitive guidance or education, they are opening their energy and their hearts to us to learn, to receive, and to heal. We must never, under any conditions, feel vulnerable to a leader that we have placed our trust in.

As practitioners and professionals, we must first hold ourselves to the highest professional standard and act accordingly. As energetic leaders, mediums, and healers, we must value and hold the integrity of that position for all of our multidimensional clients. Healing living humans, deceased humans, and non-human beings affects each of us globally, and then affects the entire cosmos. We all must constantly learn and raise ourselves to the most outstanding level of humility, understanding of the world, the humans around us, and to love without any conditions or rules.

I can ask you, and I can beg you, but I cannot make you hold yourself at a master's level of integrity.

Step 3: Discover the True Meaning of Healing

We living humans are focused on our physical lives on this physical Earth. So, we are accustomed to think and act on a physical level when we struggle with our mental and physical health. Most people tend to think of pills, supplements, doctor visits, hospitals, surgery, physical therapy and counseling. How many people do you think might first consider healing their eternal soul?

We are not just a physical body with a thinking brain on top of it. What does healing truly mean, and what does it entail? Is it even okay to attempt to heal a soul? Is it okay to heal a struggling nonphysical human? What about healing and assisting all types of non-human beings? What is healing for non-humans? Should they even be assisted? And who are we, as mere humans, to assist them anyway? Who are we to make those decisions and take those actions?

For quite some time, I was obsessed with trying to figure out what the word "healing" really means. To me, the word seems indescribable and vague; and yet, energy workers all around the globe casually use the word throughout their day. Physicians, nurses, and nurse's aides, along with every health care worker in the world, use that word constantly and strive to make healing happen. How could a word possibly be used constantly for every patient, and how could it be used every day by all types of practitioners trying to help other people?

After contemplating this word for a couple of years, my guides continually popped information into my searching mind. I finally listened. My Divine and Sacred Guides kept repeating two statements repeatedly for a couple of years . . .

"Healing means to bring some level of relief to yourself or to another being."

"Healing means to help yourself, or another being, to release a burden that is in the way of advancement."

And I would respond to the precious Divine and Sacred, "It can't be that simple! There must be more to it than that!"

So, I would wait a couple of days and ask again and again, but they did not give up on me. They just kept repeating those two statements again and again, with unbelievable patience.

We humans seem to be skilled at lugging around intense emotional burdens. Thoughts and emotions are key to the mystery of our suffering. Each thought we have is really a blast of electrical energy that carries a specific signal of information. So, every thought we think blasts through every cell of our human body, then it surges outward into our energy field and continues to blast into our environment and into the Universe.

Our emotions either empower or weaken each electrical blast of thought energy. Consider this: How many times a day do you repeat that same thought? The repetition of each positive or negative thought increases its energy in one of those directions.

For example, holding on to negative emotional burdens tend to lead to physical pain. Physical pain is a signal of thoughts and emotions gathered into an area of our bodies. A burden could be an illness or a repetitive negative pattern. Burdens come in all shapes, sizes, situations, and forms.

Participate: Allow these words to enter your awareness:

I am in a physical body now, and at the same time, I am a spirit being now. I am even more a nonphysical being than a physical one. The aliveness in me is my eternal soul.

Notice the feelings of these words in your mind and body.

Step 4: Notice That You Make Choices Every Second of Your Life

Every living human, deceased human, and non-human is a client. Yes, they are clients! I hope I say that one hundred times. Each human and non-human has a story, and that story lies within our being, or our soul. The healing medium discovers truths that are hidden within multidimensional patterns, vibrating in complex relationships between all that is. The healing medium accesses that connection and retrieves the story, and that story is often complex. As a medium, you constantly have many choices to make regarding the depth of what you accomplish for your clients. As a medium, you can be the spokesperson for the deceased, or you can become a powerful healer for the living, the deceased, and the non-humans as well.

My guides tend to get louder and louder, as if yelling at me to speak about the word "allowing." They began yelling to discuss this word in my live and recorded courses. They wanted me to describe how "allowing" strongly applies to the world of mediumship, and now they're speaking out again, to again examine "allowing" in this book. The word "allow" is really just another word. It is the action of allowing that will make all the difference in your mediumship skills. The guides tell me to emphasize to students that "allow" is a power word and a powerful action.

Participate: Slowly read through the following list and notice what you think and feel:

- Will you allow yourself to be, and feel, that you are absolutely worthy, and that you absolutely deserve to be an excellent, accurate healing medium?
- Will you allow yourself to be a medium in the first place?
- Will you allow yourself to be in charge of a session that may include a living client, a deceased client, or a non-human?
- Will you allow yourself to truly be the boss and the director to take the session into a healing for everyone involved?
- Will you allow yourself to be in charge and listen to the nonphysical without ever allowing them to enter into your own body?
- Will you allow yourself to be proud and full of joy that you live with one foot in the physical and one foot in the nonphysical at the exact same time?

This is a very important and powerful section of this book. Your choices and what you allow are valuable key factors to your success. Look back and review the "Will you . . .?" list. Slowly feel the sensations of all this happening to you, and for you . . . if you let it happen.

PART 2

Take Care of Yourself First

Chapter 3

Self-Care Begins with Learning From the Nonphysical World

> "We are all vibrational beings. You're like a receiving mechanism that when you set your tuner to the station, you're going to hear what's playing. Whatever you're focused on is the way you set your tuner, and when you focus there for as little as seventeen seconds, you activate that vibration within you."
>
> — Abraham channeled by Esther Hicks
> Facebook post on December 22, 2014

You are receiving much more intuitive information from people, buildings, the land, the world, and the Universe than you allow yourself to notice. Nonphysical beings are with us, and we alive physical beings are with them. Nonphysical beings, of many types, are a natural part of our lives here on Earth.

Intuition Will Forever Feel Like Your Imagination!

For every intuitive, the highest hurtle to leap over is realizing that what you receive will forever seem, feel, and look like your imagination, and it will never stop. The accurate healing intuitive is accessing different realms of reality. You are perceiving the reality of other levels or planes of existence. Intuition leaps or pops into your awareness as if out of nowhere, and it is truly real.

I will try to describe "impressions." We mediums are always interacting with the world of the nonphysical. We physical humans have defined forms. It's like each of us has an outline or a defined edge of our body, and that outline is filled in with substance, and then clothed with material. All of this creates the strong experience of a human being. The deceased are only energy. So, spirit people will appear mostly as an impression, which is defined as an idea, feeling, or opinion about something, or someone.

Deceased people will appear to you as an impression. This is why most people think they're failing to be a medium. People consistently tell me they're not *seeing* the deceased. They are so surprised when I say, "You will not see a dead person like you're seeing me right now. You will receive a shimmery or shadowy impression of a human form. If you let yourself notice, then you will also receive a wave of knowing." It is simply delightful to see the looks on their faces. The natural medium within comes leaping forward and ready for action.

Consider what I just described as you read Heather's description of a beautiful healing that seemed beyond reality. Her story ends with a surprise validation:

A Practitioner Shares a Story

> I had not seen one of my regular clients for a few months. When she returned to my office, she said she was feeling very scattered and distracted. She had a sense something external was disrupting her energy field and wanted to see what could be done about it. I'm always grateful for people who have the confidence to put their energetic sensations into language and voice them. Many societies are not generally encouraged to do that.

I began the healing session with my Reiki Master. In just a few minutes, I saw a female figure who looked like she was made of a white feather boa. She was flailing around and felt chaotic. I could see how this was exactly what my client had said about the disruption to her field. I was just about to begin an extraction when a large, warrior-type man showed up, stood with arms folded across his chest, and forcefully sent her away. It happened so quickly that I simply watched. I was fascinated by this male Asian warrior spirit with a beard and a distinctive hat. I looked closer at the vaguely familiar hat, trying to connect it to a culture, and then suddenly, I was looking at a yak, of all things.

This warrior being, my client, and I all had powerful intentions. We were all supporting each other with powerful intentions that made it happen at that time. Intentions are so powerful. Intentions are direct, clear, and focused thought energy. Every thought we think is an electric signal rushing out to the Universe.

After the session, my client felt much calmer, more centered, and relieved to be free from the scattered sensations she'd felt earlier. I felt comfortable sharing with her what I'd seen and what had happened. Now here is the surprise. I described to my client the warrior, the hat he wore, and then that he turned into an animal called a yak. She had such a strange look on her face. She declared that she had just received her DNA testing and discovered that she had traces of Mongolian ancestry.

As soon as she said "Mongolian," I realized that is exactly who the spirit warrior looked like. But my client is a very pale Italian, so it would never have crossed my mind that she had Mongolian roots. When I got home that night, I googled "Mongolian warrior," and the images that popped up further validated our assessment. Then I saw the hats and looked more into them. Turns out, they're often made of yak skin.

— Heather McCutcheon
Author of *Connecting the Dots: From Ad Exec. to Energy Practitioner*

I was scheduled to do a phone reading the next morning at 9:00 a.m. I thought about this session off and on, which is not unusual for me to do. This time, however, I simply couldn't remember my client's name. I cannot tell you how many times I went back to my calendar to see her name once again in order to etch it into my brain. I feel and sense a greater connection with my clients when I repeat their name over and over in my thoughts. Our name has its own unique vibrational signature that reflects a great deal of information about us as an individual.

I checked my calendar over and over, trying to remember this woman's name. I decided that I must be more exhausted than I'd originally thought. That night, I woke up, thinking about this client. I immediately saw an owl wearing a pair of opaque glasses, and the owl could not see through them. I then saw a group of birds that flew up from the ground and scattered in all directions. I took note of those symbols to inform her in the morning, and again, I could not remember her name! As I prepared for the session, I decided to write her name on the top of a piece of paper to help me remember it.

Notice that I was still focusing on my failed memory, and nothing else. I was completely focusing on me and what I perceived as my limitations. The instant I said hello to her at the onset of the appointment, a wave of "knowing" came over me. I realized that my failure to remember her name was where I needed to begin the session. This was *big*.

I told her that I simply could not remember her name, and she seemed elusive and disconnected. I told her she seemed to go in all directions and without a focus for herself in her life. I went on to say that she seemed different from the actual person that she used to be. My client declared that this was the most powerfully significant information that she could ever hear. She described hating her last name, and was embarrassed by it because of her husband's behavior. She had long ago changed her first name. We then had a long discussion about the significance of her name, and who she really was.

If you remember, I mentioned that I had also seen an owl with opaque glasses on. I shared that image with her, stating that the owl is an ancient symbol of wisdom and the ability to see even into the depths of the darkness. I discussed that there were many things in her life that she was trying to ignore and not even see. I told her about the birds scattering in all directions to symbolize her energy having no focus. I added that she was finding it difficult to even acknowledge who she was as an individual, let alone accomplish any of her goals. The client completely agreed with me, and then shared with me that her husband was having an affair that she had known about for quite some time but couldn't bear to deal with right now.

These are interesting and dramatic examples of learning to trust the signals coming to you. When the same thing repeats over and over again about a client, take note. It is not about you. It is spirit coming in from many different angles, and many different avenues, attempting to get your attention. I was not imagining anything. That repetitive pattern was information coming to me about my client. It felt like my imagination, but it was real, and with accurate information.

Let's break down this example of trusting myself and my imagination:

- There was a repetition of a pattern. I couldn't remember the client's name, even after looking at my schedule over and over before the appointment.

- I realized the pattern was a huge portion of the reading, so I described the pattern in detail to the client to show her it was the exact information she needed.
- I described images, the owl with smoky glasses and the birds scattering, even though it sounded and felt like my imagination.
- What I perceived made absolutely no logical sense to me. That should never matter to the intuitive medium. What deeply matters is that it makes complete sense to the client.
- I described whatever came to me, and in whatever form the information appeared.
- The information kept repeating in four ways: My own behavior, in my sleep, in symbolic images, and in waves of "knowing."

Most people are conditioned from birth to ignore our intuitive nature and then declare it as just our imagination. Most children and adults are laughed at, ridiculed, told that we have vivid imaginations, that we are psychotic and need drugs and a counselor, or that we are outcasts of reality.

I am psychic, and you are too. My life has constantly benefited from this inborn ability to receive abundant information that is offered in each moment of life. Your life will benefit as well. It is up to you.

VITAL POINT

> Intuition wisdom is within the very subtle, tiny, everyday stuff of life. Stop looking for the splashy, flashy moments.

One of my dear family members described intuition in this way: "I do trust my intuition and messages from Spirit. They just seem so ordinary and quiet to me, in contrast to the splashy stuff I read and hear about. The main point of it all is that I do feel certain that I'm directed to people who need me."

Don't look for the splashy stuff of intuition. It will occasionally, but rarely, flash and splash. Focus on the tiniest bits and pieces of information that come your way. Especially notice the things that just seem to pop in from nowhere. Be aware of the quietest thoughts that linger down in your stomach and will not go away, or the ones that whisper in the back of your mind.

Physically Touched by Spirit

It was after midnight in the old-growth woods on the grounds of Lily Dale, New York, the oldest Spiritualist community in the US. With tiny flashlights in hand, my dear friend David and I walked down a path through the great trees of these woods.

We were looking for a place called "the Stump." Mediums have stood there since the middle 1800s, giving Spirit messages to throngs of onlookers. We found the old wooden benches that faced the Stump and sat down together. We had planned it just right. We scanned the area with our flashlights. No one else was there. The stillness of this old-growth forest surrounded us, peaceful yet eerie. We quieted ourselves and settled in for a short meditation.

Just moments later, we both jumped and turned to look at each other. "I just felt a hand on my shoulder!" We both declared this at the exact same time. I experienced a man's hand on my left shoulder, and David, sitting to my left, felt a hand on his right shoulder. The hand had placed a little pressure on my shoulder, and then gently squeezed in a welcoming gesture. David reported the same sense that the spirit person was male and had welcomed us to the Stump. We quickly turned on the flashlights to see who had snuck up on us, but no one was there. Only one lone night bird gently called out in the black stillness.

I have found that we only feel the sense of touch by deceased humans when they carry amazingly strong emotions. By strong emotions, I mean any and all emotions. It can be the loving, welcoming touch of a spirit man greeting you in the depths of a woods at midnight, or it can be something negative. The sensations of being physically touched by a nonphysical being can be anything between love and adoration, to jealousy and hate.

What seems consistent about the sense of touch from a spirit person is the strength of any emotion that the deceased human is deeply feeling. That emotion will continue to affect the person even beyond their death. The longer and more intense the person felt that emotion during their life, the stronger that person carries that emotion with them into their death process, and then into their nonphysical spirit life.

VITAL POINT

> A powerful emotion felt right at the moment of death will usually continue with the being in their nonphysical life. Powerful emotions that had consumed a living human over time, will also remain with them into the nonphysical.

When They Enter Your Dreams

Are you aware of a deceased person coming into your dreams? Deceased people tend to come to us in our dreams when they haven't been able to communicate with us during our awake times. We living humans are so busy, or sometimes so overwhelmed in our waking day, that we miss the subtle signals the deceased give us. As we relax into sleep, our defenses relax, and we enter into different brain waves. Theta is our lightest level of sleep, and our deepest level of sleep is called delta. Most people say they were approached by a deceased loved one just as they were going to sleep, or as they were waking up. When we are in that theta brain wave, we are more open and aware of the deceased communicating with us.

This is an important detail to remember. Our deceased loved ones usually come to us in our dreams because they have given up trying to communicate with us when we are awake. I frequently hear the deceased tell me: "I finally gave up trying to talk to them, because they never answer me!" It often causes confusion for the deceased who do not realize they have died. They are deeply frustrated, and even sound hurt sometimes. It seems this is when they resort to making loud sounds or moving things around. When they give all that up, they show up in our dreams.

Self-Care Depends on Receiving Accurate Information

There is another primary struggle with communication between the dead, the living, and your guides. Living people keep talking and talking to the dead, the living, and our guides, but no one stops talking long enough to listen to what anyone else has to say. I know this because every time someone tells me they don't get anything back when they talk to their deceased loved one or their guides, I always ask this question: "I hear that you're talking and talking to your deceased person and your guides, but I do not hear that you stop talking to receive their responses. Do you pause to give them a chance to answer your questions, or hear their responses, when you inform them of something or ask them a question?"

With a shocked look on their face, living people always say, "No, it never occurred to me to stop talking to receive their answers!"

In my experience with thousands of clients and students, there seems to be three primary pathways to communicate with the deceased or our precious guides. They are telepathy, clairvoyance, and astral projecting. We living humans tend to ignore these primary pathways of communication. Please do not dismiss these three abilities as nothing but your imagination. It will always feel like you just imagined everything that you just received. Do not ignore thoughts that pop into your mind.

Pathway 1: Telepathy

The first path is telepathy, which is described as communication from one mind to another. Telepathy is the exchange of words, but it's also receiving words or images, like photos or movies, that pop into your mind. You must be both a talker and a listener to accurately communicate and receive information from the deceased. When you say something aloud or telepathically to the deceased, you must pause, then notice whatever pops into your mind in words or images. That is the way the deceased send verbal information to you, and it is the key to your accuracy as a healing medium.

Accurate back-and-forth communication is also the most vital key to your own health and well-being. For excellent self-care, you must telepathically send directives to your team of Divine and Sacreds. If you truly stop and listen to your guides, you will remain healthy as you continue to work and heal nonphysical beings.

Pathway 2: Clairvoyance

The second primary pathway to receive information from spirit people is by receiving images. Everyone can see within their mind's eye. If you think you're not visual, you have only convinced yourself that you cannot see. A belief is only a repetition of a thought. Repeating a thought does not make it a truth. Create your new truth now. Repeat and repeat again: "I now see images in my mind's eye."

Clairvoyance is a great pathway to receive a great deal of information all at once. Seeing with your eyes open, or seeing with your eyes closed, is clairvoyance. You are witnessing information within your mind's eye, which is located within the area of your forehead. This ability offers the medium detailed information. You will notice images, symbols, brief moments of a scene, just like a clip of a movie that is being promoted on the television. One tiny moment of a scene gives the medium a wealth of instant information for your own well-being or your clients.

Always remember: You did not imagine it.

Steps to Enhance Your Clairvoyant Skills

1. Remember: It will forever and always seem like you're imagining everything.
2. Notice that your eyes are seeing right now as you read these words on the page.
3. Now look across the room or out the window. Find one object to focus on. Study that object and memorize its details.
4. Feel playful as you experiment with these steps and learn about yourself.
5. Close your eyes. Instantly notice that the object you just memorized will appear somewhere in your mind even with your eyes closed. Repeat this multiple times. Again, study and memorize one object. Close your eyes and notice a location within your head, or even somewhere around the outside of your head. The object will show up within you, or around you. It will have a location.
6. Now look at something alive. This could be a plant, a tree, or an animal. Study and memorize the alive thing that you chose.
7. Close your eyes and check out where the physical image is located.
8. Practice with something different each time. Does the animal or the plant appear different in any way? Playfully look for any differences or similarities.

9. When you have the opportunity, ask one or two people to volunteer. Memorize the person, then close your eyes and notice whatever you notice without judging yourself or your volunteer.

10. As you practice with your human volunteer, scan your inner mind for colors, shapes, patterns, or any other forms. Forms may be very vague or very distinct.

11. Look for the following:

    - **Human Forms:** Seeing a human form in your volunteer's energy field will usually be a deceased human. What is the human form doing? How does it position itself to your client? Intuitively ask the deceased questions that are short and to the point. What words from the deceased pop into your mind?
    - **Faces:** May be a spiritual guide, family, or friend who has passed on.
    - **Eyes:** These are common forms to see. Notice if the eye is wide open, partially closed, or completely closed, and in which direction they are looking.
    - **Animals/Birds:** They provide information that birds or animals are important in your volunteer's life and symbolic of something or someone.
    - **Earth shapes such as trees and mountains:** Might be where they're going for vacation, or a past-life memory.
    - **Angels:** Appear as winged beings, different from guides. What is the angel doing? How does it look? Ask the angel multiple questions.
    - **Cartoon characters:** Often symbolic. Watch its actions.

- **Ladders, ropes, chains, windows, buildings, or other inanimate objects:** These are symbols that tell a short story about the person.
- **Short action movies:** Pieces of information regarding the living or the deceased.

Do not wear yourself out or wear out your volunteers. You will not perceive anything if either of you becomes tired. If that happens, you may think you're failing again. Allow yourself to play and have fun.

Pathway 3: Astral Projection

The human ability to astral project opens new and sometimes surprising opportunities to heal the living and the deceased across a short distance or around the globe. For example, I have used astral projection to do remote healing for a tiny infant in a plane. That baby and her mother sat six rows in front of me. All was well and quiet until the plane took off and the air pressure in the cabin changed. The screams were not of an irritable baby. It was screams of stabbing pain. Nothing could soothe her. So, first I asked the infant for permission to help her. I felt the frantic, "Yes!" I then looked into her body and head. Her left eustachian tube was completely blocked with a bright-red mucus. My guides pulled on the mucus like a vacuum, and immediately, the baby became silent and remained quiet to the relief of the parent and everyone on that plane, including myself. (For more information on healing the living, see my other books, *Become a Medical Intuitive* and *Advanced Medical Intuition*.)

Our thoughts are energy, and energy also follows our thoughts. We humans can be in complete control, and in complete charge of our own energy. Your thoughts focused in a certain direction create an energetic beam to stretch outward in that direction. Astral projection is simply controlled thought energy, focused in a certain direction.

You can astral project accurately, with a laser-beam focus, for multiple goals. First, you can astral project all around your own body, energy field, and home to assure yourself that a negative deceased human or non-human is not interfering with you or your health. You can astral project into a living client's energy field and their physical body to assess whether a negative being is interfering with them. As a healing medium, you can project outward to a certain address or physical location to assess if the area is harmed by negative beings. You can astral project to a home, land, an entity, or to a living person located anywhere. Because we healing mediums are so very, very powerful, we can then positively alter and heal any situation located anywhere in the world. You are capable of astral projecting and remote-viewing instantly across a small room, to the other side of the world, or beyond this world.

Steps to Astral Project and Do It Ethically:

1. Always ask the person for permission to begin. This keeps you functioning ethically.
2. Stop all thoughts about yourself. Get "you" out of the way.
3. Direct your Divine and Sacred specialty guides to completely and permanently guard and protect you in all ways now. (This way, you are ready for anything you perceive.)
4. Focus all thoughts and all your attention on the client, home, building, land, animal, etc.
5. Think and feel that you are stretching outward to the place, object, or person. Allow the guides to direct you. You are *not* to work at this. Allow the guides to take you.
6. Think and feel that you have hypersensitive sensors at the end of your extended beam of energy. These sensors are alive, alert, active, and noticing everything.

7. Pause and receive all the instant pops of information in words, images, feelings.
8. At the end of receiving the information, direct your Divine and Sacred Guides to create a powerful cleansing filter around you. Pull your energy field back through the filter so that only the pure you comes back into you.

Astral Projecting to Receive Information on Deceased or Nonphysical Beings

Your personal well-being and safety will be enhanced by astral projecting outward and all around your body, home, or work.

1. You have just noticed a general sense that a spirit person has arrived near you.
2. Important: Do not search or try hard to find anything. Only passively notice.
3. Notice if words, phrases, thoughts, or images pop into your mind. It will feel as if those things come out of nowhere. Thoughts from a deceased person will not feel like your own thoughts. Things that are said by a deceased being will not be said in ways that you would say it.
4. If you do not hear sounds, words, phrases, or see images, do not be discouraged. Keep yourself in the position of noticing, and do not take any action.
5. When Spirit does speak words aloud, the words will either be soft whispers or a booming voice. Messages from friends and relatives who have passed may be brief, sound muddled, or they often repeat the same statement over and over.
6. First listen and receive their information. Then talk to them! Have a conversation. Ask one question or make one statement in your mind. Then pause to receive the "pop" of their answer. Give

the spirit person time to respond to you by speaking or showing you images.

7. If you struggle to understand their message, you simply give them some common-sense directions. For example, "Slow down," "Speak louder," "Tell me more details," or "Send me a picture of what you are telling me."
8. It's up to us to focus our complete attention on receiving. Do not try hard to do anything, and do not take action. Passively receive.
9. Inform your living client exactly what you perceived from the deceased, and exactly the way you received it, even when it does not make any sense to you. *Never* paraphrase the words of the deceased. Repeat every word or action exactly as you received it.

One of the best examples I can recall is the Jumping Jack Man. I was offering fifteen-minute sessions for the local metaphysical bookstore. A young woman sat down and said she was open to anything that I received about her. I instantly felt a rush of energy come through the door along with the man in spirit, who rushed in and stopped beside my chair. I was a bit new to this, so I ignored what had just happened, and I went on to describe other things I was perceiving. The deceased man then began doing the exercise called jumping jacks. I still thought this couldn't possibly be right, but I decided to tell her what I was perceiving. She leaped from her chair in tears and declared that was her favorite uncle, and he did jumping jacks all the time.

Do you see the point I'm making? Tell your living client everything you get, and in the way that it happens. Do it without holding back a single detail.

18 Ways the Universe Constantly Communicates with You

The Universe is a living organism. The Universe communicates with us constantly, but most people don't notice. Do not work hard, try hard, or actively search for signals from the Universe. Simply and constantly notice the world around you. Notice what keeps pulling or drawing your attention to it. Notice things that repeat or frequently come into your awareness.

Here are the primary pathways the Universe uses, along with a few simple examples.

1. Your Name: A name is more than a name. It's a frequency of information. The name that we are given at birth sends a signal throughout our lifetime. When women change their name to their husband's name at marriage, they are doing more than a name change. It alters the person's energetic signature. The key is to notice the feel of the change. Does it feel right and positive, or does it feel like something else? Sometimes people change their names to deliberately send a different signal. Notice now the feel of your name.

2. Your Environment: The environment is not just space around you. You are an integral part of your environment. What you see around you has been created by your energy signals. One client sent out a thought that if her Divine and Sacred Guides were with her, then show her pink vehicles. Pink cars, vans, and trucks suddenly began to pop into her world.

Have you had a book literally leap from a shelf and land at your feet, only to find that it was the perfect book for you at that time in your life? Notice an object that keeps drawing your attention. A friend realized he was constantly seeing antennae everywhere. He asked Spirit to tell him the meaning of antennae, and a situation at work immediately popped into his mind. He realized he was not communicating, or especially listening, to a coworker. Spirit sent him a symbol about improving his communication with the coworker.

3. Clouds in the Sky: People send me photos of clouds that look exactly like angels, or an eagle, or many other images. I was in an airplane just above the clouds when I glanced up ahead to see the exact form of Santa Claus sitting in massive chair. He had a great smile on his face. He was so massive that it took the plane a long time to pass by, so I had a long time to perceive every detail of this signal of information. Santa was a signal of information that was, indeed, a gift to me at that time in my life.

4. Dreams: So many adventures happen within our dreamtime that it would take an entire book to explore what I'm now aware of. We are astral projecting around the globe, and way beyond our Universe. We communicate with our deceased loved ones who are trying so hard to reach out to us. We are processing our day and our life. Guides are directing us. These are just a few examples of the activities that happen in our dreamtime.

I do teach internationally in my awake state, but I also frequently teach internationally in my dreamtime as well. Sometimes I wake in the morning knowing that I was teaching in a certain location, or in a specific country. Within two days, I will receive emails from people in those same countries where I'd just dreamed I was teaching. The people emailing usually ask for mentoring sessions with me, or they request that I come to teach in their area. What a powerful confirmation that we are truly traveling throughout time and space within our dream state.

I received an email from a woman telling me that I was in her dream last night. She said that I was standing at a podium in an ornate golden building, lecturing to a class. She arrived late and hesitated to enter, but finally did so. She said that I immediately stopped talking to the class, looked directly at her, and declared, "Do not ever be late again!" This woman had no idea that I really am a stickler for being on time. Again, more confirmation of the realities going on in our dream state.

5. Internet/TV: A woman in Wales emailed me one day. She stated that she was on her son's computer randomly clicking on things, when suddenly my photo popped onto the screen with the words "medical intuition." I began laughing as I read on. She stated that she was not searching those words at all, but there I was, smiling at her on her son's computer. She reached out to me and took my classes, and she is now a powerful medical intuitive medium held in high esteem in the UK.

6. Déjà Vu: This is real and not your imagination. Again, we are not trapped or confined beneath our skin. We are energy beings experiencing a world of energy. We tend to openly discuss our awareness of past lives, but most people have little understanding that we have the ability to travel away from where our body is currently located, and we also can travel forward in time. We can, indeed, project forward in time to moments, locations, events and to other dimensions. Time is not linear. We humans attempt to control it in our minds with clocks and calendars, but time is not under our control. We are energy beings flowing throughout realms of energy.

7. Deceased People: We are all mediums. Yes, you are too. We all have the ability to perceive, and to communicate telepathically, with dead people because they are just as alive as we are. So many of the dead still have something important to say, but they also want to be heard by the living. The deceased cannot lie to us. Deceased people must respond in truth. They will become silent or try to distract you by verbally rattling on about nothing, rather than lie to the living.

Are you aware of a deceased person coming into your dreams? Deceased people tend to come to us through our dreams when they haven't been able to communicate with us during our awake times. The primary struggle is that living people keep talking and talking to the dead, but no one stops talking to listen. Talk to them aloud or in your mind. Ask a question first, then pause. Pausing allows you to receive their eager responses. People in spirit will usually communicate in two pathways. Either thoughts will pop into your mind, or images will pop into your mind's eye. To receive their responses, you must become a listener and not just a talker.

8. Synchronicity: I found this definition: "A remarkable occurrence of events with no deliberate cause but significantly related." There are no accidents, and there are no coincidences. The Universe is organized, complicated, and powerfully responsive to our thoughts and our emotions. When we think and when we feel, we send out signals that communicate to the world around us. The world around us responds to our signals, and at the same time, the Universe sends us signals. Synchronicity is a perfectly timed, meaningful union of information.

I was driving down a busy road, and at the same time, I was powering my toroidal field. I finished running each separate color of the rainbow, and then filled myself with the violet flame to cleanse and purify my body and my field. As I wondered if I was using the most powerful shade of violet, I saw up ahead that a large panel truck was coming toward me. It was painted a brilliant violet color that was the exact shade I was cleansing my field with.

9. Nature: I was walking alone in a large woods nearby. It had been amazingly still and beautiful for an hour or so. I knew the trees, the elementals, and my guides were listening to my thoughts and ideas. I stopped on the path and asked the Universe a clear question within my mind. Instantly, a strong wind rushed through with words riding along in the wind and entering into my mind. Stillness returned immediately and remained for the entire walk. Nature responds to our thoughts, our emotions, and our questions. Notice now that you will always receive an answer. It is only a matter of noticing in a different way.

10. Birds: Birds of all types are the messengers for Spirit. My friend called me in a panicked voice. She had just pulled into her long driveway to see twenty vultures sitting along the entire length of her roof. Her first response was fear. She immediately thought it meant certain death was about to befall her.

After listening to her words, I asked her a couple of questions. My first question was, "Do vultures actually kill people, or anything else?"

She responded, "No, they eat what is already dead."

I agreed and added, "Vultures are the 'cleaners,' removing something that has already come to an end."

My friend declared, "That makes so much sense!" She then went on to share her story of a long, painful relationship that had just ended, and she felt such a relief regarding it.

I then said to her, "Twenty vultures are also a personal symbol of information for you. What does the number twenty signify for you?"

She told me that she had struggled for twenty years due to a certain relationship, and now she ended it.

I replied, "You see, the number of birds on your roof symbolized the number of years, but it also showed me that a huge and thorough effort is going on to clean and remove the negative that has just ended for you."

11. Animals: People often say to me, "How on earth am I supposed to know the exact information I'm supposed to get when I see a certain animal?" We humans need to first look at the way the animal survives in the world. What are the natural characteristics of the animal, and how do they live? Are they aggressive or passive? Do they tend to hide, be loners, or do they live in a pack? How do they receive their nourishment and what sustains them? What actions are they taking when you see them? For example, a movement out the window caught my eye. There was a massive coyote in my yard. He was alone. He was leaping in the air, stiffening his front legs to stomp on a mouse.

Coyote characteristics are that they run alone, but they also meet in large groups. When they come together in groups, there is a lot of loud yelping and greeting each other. People tend to be afraid of them and think they will attack their horses, etc. In fact, coyotes prefer to eat mice and rabbits. They are loners, but they also need to make meaningful connections with others. They love to communicate, and loudly, but they happily share information among their peers. They are powerful, sometimes scary, but they are not aggressive at all. At that moment in my life, that coyote gave me an amazing number of details regarding an issue I was dealing with.

12. Accidents: There are no accidents when there is an accident. My dear friend had a series of medical issues that prevented her from going to the office to see her clients for nearly two months. She frequently commented that her physical problems were a surprise to her. She would say, "I didn't see this coming." On her way to work that first day after a lengthy illness, she pulled out in front of a car, resulting in a terrible accident. Her car was totaled, and she was injured again with a concussion.

Our daily thoughts and subsequent emotions are constantly

sending powerful signals of information outward into the cosmos. The signals may be positive and light, or dark and dense, or anything in between. The cosmos is structured to respond to us by matching our signals. Accidents tend to happen when there is great upheaval in our emotions. When our emotions are rumbling and churning, the world around us begins to rumble and churn in response.

13. Numbers: Numerology is real. Numbers are everywhere. Each number and combinations of numbers vibrate with meaning. Numbers tend to show themselves to us by repeating that same number over and over until we notice the signal. You might see the same number repeating over and over again in different locations, such as on license plates, then on a billboard, and then on the receipt at a restaurant.

An example of one of the most common numbers that appears is 1-1-1-1. This number sequence commonly means the gates of heaven, or the passage to higher awareness, or a doorway to the next step in your life. One day, my uncle commented that for months he woke up every night at 2:22 a.m. I was startled, then shared with him that I, too, had been awakened for months at 2:22 a.m.

Now notice the numbers that keep repeating in your everyday world. Each individual number contains a meaning. Each combination of numbers has meaning. Each pattern of numbers has a meaning.

14. Repetitive Life Patterns: Everyone has repeating patterns in their lives. Some are very positive, and some are negative. Look back over your life and notice a pattern or theme that keeps recurring in your life. For example, do you keep finding yourself needing money? Do you keep finding yourself in an abusive relationship?

Are you trying to head a certain direction in your life, but nothing works out?

A pattern will keep repeating throughout millennia until we develop a deeper awareness of our soul's mission. A negative repeating pattern itself is not just a signal. It is another chance, or another offer from the Universe to:

1. Learn and understand something vital about your development.
2. Heal unresolved, traumatic past lives.
3. Heal and release a current life event or trauma.

The more we ignore the repetition of a pattern, the more it will repeat, and the more severe the negativity will become. The severity of the pattern strengthens because the Universe is trying to get your attention. Each repetition is another chance to learn, to heal, and to change toward the positive.

15. Meditation: A mentoring client told me recently that she was deep in meditation when suddenly, out of nowhere, an image of one of my books popped into her mind's eye. She then said she had never heard of me or my books before that, but still, the correct image of the book was clear in her vision.

Meditation is prayerful time, and yet, we are not praying. Meditation trains us to stop chattering, stop wishing, hoping, yearning, or begging the Universe for something. We are given meditative moments all throughout our daily life. Rather than blocking out time to meditate, now bring meditation into your active or even hectic day. The most accurate intuitive is merely an excellent receiver (listener) of information.

16. Photos: The moments Spirit communicates with us is often a great surprise. The Universe seems to adore children. So, I taught the grandkids to call out to the Universe for orbs to show themselves. Together, we called out for orbs to appear to us. Then I handed them cheap cameras. Off they went, out the door and into the night, clicking away with their cameras. I, on the other hand, strolled out the door with my expensive camera, and I clicked at the nighttime air around us. I got nothing, but the children's photos are full of orbs and fairies! Spirit communicates with us through old, old pathways, and now Spirit is utilizing cameras, the Internet, and social media to open awareness that nonphysical realms do exist. It's hard to deny when you're looking at a smiling face within an orb in the center of your photo.

17. Music: The Universe loves music, and many of our guides love to use music to communicate with us. People often complain that a song has been stuck in their head all day, and they cannot get it to stop. If that happens to you, or even if it happens occasionally, I ask that you examine it in quite a different way. Notice the exact song in a deeper and more detailed way. First notice that it is usually only a piece of the song that is "stuck" in your mind and not the entire song. The piece that is "stuck" is really only a short portion of the lyrics. That stuck music in your head is truly only a section of the song's lyrics. What exactly is the section that repeats over and over? Then what exactly are the words in that section? Here lies the message meant just for you. When you receive the message, the song gently subsides.

18. The Living People Around You: Living people around us are often unaware messengers for us. A stranger will sometimes direct a comment to you, in a very casual way. That comment is filled with the most enlightening, profound wisdom that you needed in that exact moment. That comment poked a hole through a block that you could not get through on your own. And then that stranger just walked away, having no idea they just changed the direction of your life forever.

VITAL POINT

The Universe is there for you and speaks to you today, tomorrow, and always.

Chapter 4

Develop Your Elite Team of Six Specialty Guides

The nonphysical spirit world is made up of different types of entities. Some of these entities are, indeed, human, and some are not human. All entities, some human and some not human, have individual characteristics or personalities. They all seem to have a conscious awareness among each other.

Deceased humans are only one group of spirit beings. There are beings from many different realms, also existing as an expression of Source. The saying, "As above, so below," is accurate. On Earth, there are nasty, hateful humans, and there are deeply kind humans. It is also the same in the nonphysical spheres. Some entities are harmful while others are precious.

This might be difficult for you to read and consider, but I must say it: I often hear people declare that their deceased grandmother, or another relative, is now their guide. While this grandmother, or other loved one, might have lived a very loving life, they have not advanced to this high level of wisdom. Just because we die, it does not mean we are now a guide. Some deceased, but certainly not all, seem to have a broader view of things on the Earth plane, which is often helpful. They are certainly our personal life helpers, but only for our personal life. Human or non-human, it does not mean that everyone who resides in the nonphysical is enlightened or advanced. It does not mean that everyone is a guide or an angel, no matter how much you loved them.

Masterful, highly developed, and complex guides do exist. They exist to directly steer humankind to achieve higher standards and live with an unshakable understanding of what our current life path is meant to offer us. The ascended masters are a small group of the Divine and Sacred too. You may find that most of your team of Divine and Sacred are not known as ascended masters, but there are usually a few that are part of your team.

There are not many, but some spiritual masters did achieve an impressive level of understanding and awareness. At their moment of death, they literally ascended to an elevated status. Jesus, Mother Mary, Mohammed, Buddha, Kwan Yin, St. Germain, and a few others are considered ascended masters at the Divine and Sacred level.

True Divine and Sacred Guides have nothing to do with any religion. Clients are often perplexed when Jesus or Mother Mary arrive. Clients declare. "This can't be right. I see Jesus! I'm not a Christian, I'm Muslim, or Hindu, or Buddhist!" The same surprise happens when Mother Mary arrives. People exclaim, "I'm not Catholic! This can't be right. Am I making this up?"

My response to these surprised mentoring clients is this: "Now think about it . . . If you were making this up, you would have come up with some being that you thought would never come to you. In other words, you would never be surprised. The fact that you are surprised should tell you that you did not make that up or imagined it. It is even stronger evidence of how real this particular guide is for you. The ascended masters and the Divine and Sacred have nothing to do with a certain church or a certain religion."

Do not dismiss a true evolved guide that is an Ascended Master or a Divine and Sacred just because that being was not part of your childhood training.

The clarity of your intuition will increase exponentially. Your abilities to heal others will burst open as you actively and conscientiously work with an elite team of highly developed, refined level of specialty guides.

VITAL POINT

A deceased person with a broader view is no comparison to an elite, advanced specialty guide created by Source.

Please realize that some deceased will have a broader view of an Earth plane situation due to being in spirit form. However, having a broader view is still a very long way from holding a position of purity, wisdom, and functioning as expert specialists that the Divine and Sacred have achieved.

I used to work with any deceased human or non-human that said they were a guide. I accepted what any of the nonphysical beings told me. Little did I know that I was learning the hard way. I stopped accepting all nonphysical beings that casually floated around me, declaring they were guides. Be aware of these fakes.

Suddenly, many years ago, I was bombarded with two words. I woke up in the middle of the night hearing two words: *Divine* and *Sacred*. Then, throughout the days and weeks, those words popped into my mind no matter what I was doing.

I cannot remember how long this continued, but it stopped when I finally blurted out this question: "Tell me who you are, and why you keep repeating the words 'divine' and 'sacred?' You are making me a little nutty!"

This deep voice replied, "I am Divine and Sacred, and so are many others. You are ready to work with us and take your healing to advanced levels."

Yes, that is how this all began. I gradually learned that most people work with any loved one that has died, or any other type of being just because they say they are guides. When I developed a deeper connection with the Divine and Sacred, I released all the other beings who said they were guides. I thanked them but firmly told them they couldn't work with me again and that they must leave. You are not required to direct the current guides to leave, but I strongly recommend it. Many of my mentoring students, at first, refuse to release their current guides, but they quickly experienced a phenomenal difference as they slowly began to work only with the Divine and Sacred.

Struggling to Deserve the Divine and Sacred

At the time of writing this book, I was working with a new mentoring student. While she was new to me, she was not new to perceiving deceased people. She did not identify herself as a medium. She was not sure what to do with her abilities, and she was often afraid of what, and who, she was perceiving. She immediately put my steps into action with wonderful results. This is her description of an event that included her angry, deeply religious, deceased relatives.

A Practitioner Shares a Story

I have been in a big funk in regard to feeling like I lost my family. I was the golden child who complied with my role as the smart, capable, caring, responsible one to carry on the family legacy. Now they (two grandmas, an aunt, Coco, etc.) are angry, and I am on the outs. (I had to bring in specialists to help them cross over, as my Grandma E was raging at me, and I needed peace.) It brings up so much questioning in me of what was even real in my life with all of them. Did they ever really love me? How, or where, do I fit into the family structure now?

I was feeling so much emotional pain in my body, so I called out to my Divine and Sacred Guide who specializes in that type of pain. For some reason, I felt wary of him, so I asked if he was truly at the Divine and Sacred level. I received the vague, sheepish answer of "no." This was surprising to me, because I had interviewed him when he was first called in a few weeks ago! (This particular specialist took five tries back then).

Evidently, I had another fraud today, and I kept getting frauds for several more tries after this.

I then asked my other guides why this was happening, and why I couldn't hear them. It was like their voices were muffled. When I asked them to tell me or show me now why I couldn't hear, I sensed immediately that I was dealing with a non-human entity. He grabbed me from behind and covered my eyes and ears. I asked how long he has been with me and when he connected to me. It was right after my first car accident when I was rear-ended forty years ago. (Right after the impact, I remember feeling energy exploding in the bottom of my skull and seeing a bright light.)

I have not yet gotten to the part in your book that deals with non-human entities, but I remember seeing a summary of the steps to remove and transition these types of spirits. I asked my guides if I should move forward with that process. They said to move forward. I commanded every step exactly as you wrote in your book. What happened next was that the Divine and Sacred specialist who knows about that entity removed him from the backside of my body, but they both remained on the right side of me. I saw many dark cords—especially at the base of my brain and my sacrum.

I went through the steps to remove cords *and* asked my team for help with the process. The struggle continued on and on, and I felt fear creep in. I powered up even more with love and compassion. I read the commands and finally saw them

> leave (the entity and the guide). Immediately, scores of angels rushed in to bring healing to me. I lay down on the ground as they worked. Right in front of me, I saw the face of a guide with kind, blue eyes reassuring me.

Actively making a clear connection with this quality of guidance from the nonphysical will amplify your state of awareness and your level of effectiveness as a medium and healer for the deceased. This honorable, virtuous classification of guides will take your intuition and mediumship to new and exceptional levels.

Participate:

Take a moment to notice your inner self.

1. Notice sensations of any self-doubt.
2. Notice any sense of inadequacy.
3. Notice if feelings of unworthiness are rising up within you.
4. Notice any feelings that you might not deserve to work with this grand level of Divine and Sacred beings.

Within this last year, my Divine and Sacred Guides have again pounded a certain word into my awareness. I finally realized they want me to ask you about your willingness to *allow.* Many people tell me that no one shows up when they put out their invitation. Nothing can happen if you do not *allow* yourself to experience the nonphysical world. We humans are the only thing that ever gets in the way. These Sacred Divines are extremely eager to work together with us. So:

1. Will you allow yourself to accept the wishes of the Divine and Sacred?
2. Will you allow yourself to deeply feel their eagerness to work as a team with you?

3. Will you allow yourself to notice they will never judge or criticize you?
4. Will you allow yourself to feel their blissful joy to working together as a team with you?

People share their unusual stories of how they came to know my work. I have heard that my face leaped upon someone's TV screen in Wales. Others have shared that my books dropped from a shelf onto the floor of a bookstore, while others have said that my name came up three different times from three different people in one week. My books, my courses, or my website would not have appeared to you if it was not the right time. This is how it works. Divine and Sacred beings constantly request that you accept them and accept that you deserve to work together with them. If you were not ready, or did not deserve to work with the Divine and Sacred, you would not be reading this book now. So, get over it and jump in!

Exceptional Communication with Your Team

Because they are wise, mystical, supernatural beings of the highest stature, they cannot, under any circumstances, take action for us, nor will they take action for our living or deceased clients. You must direct them to take action for yourself, or on behalf of your clients. So, the more you clearly direct them, the more they can take clear action.

When they first told me this, I was mystified. When I asked them why they don't leap into action to aide us in this earthly life, the Divine and Sacred specialists clearly said these words:

"We stand in honor of every human making choices every second of every day. We cannot act until we are given a directive to assist. It is paramount to the human experience that you have constant choices every split second of your earthly lives."

Then I said, "What about the practitioners like me directing you to our clients?"

They responded, "You are speaking on their behalf because they are not aware at this level, and you have acquired their permission to do so. Never work at this level without the human's permission. We cannot take action without each human's permission. You must also hold honor for each human's choice."

Every word we think is an electrical surge of energy rushing through our body, our energy field, and then out into the Universe. Your thoughts are more than thoughts. Each thought is an energy signal. It is your right, as a light-conscious worker, to send out your requests for yourself and your clients in a powerful, exact, and compelling manner.

You must direct each guide with clearly worded action commands. Please immediately realize that I do not mean you are a boss, and you are bossing them around like slaves.

The misuse of our words is an open invitation for beings to attach or interfere with us on a deeper level. Choose your words and thoughts wisely when calling out to the cosmos. Consider using precise words and phrases, such as "in the name of Christ," "in the name of Almighty God," "in the name of the Holy Spirit," "the Holiest of the Holy," "the light of Source," "the Compassionate Heart light," "sacred light of All," "held in the light," "the most Sacred of All," "the highest divinity," "pure," "hallowed," "consecrated," "ultimate good," or "divine."

Commanding, in this case, means that you use clear, exact words because thoughts are energy. If you put out mush, then they can only respond with mush. To do well in life in every way, we must direct our thoughts in more specific ways. Commanding only means that you are thinking and sending out precise, powerful, and positive word signals, and at the same time, you feel like you really are the "commander of your ship." By calling these "commands," you can feel more in control and sense that you are truly the commander of your body and your life.

When you feel and know that you are communicating clearly and powerfully, the Universe will respond to you in profoundly positive ways. The Universe and all of its beings for some reason simply cannot or will not lie to us. I am always amazed by this. The most hostile or troubled nonphysical humans, as well as all other nonphysical beings, will not lie. They might begin to chatter away in an attempt to distract you, but they will not lie to you. They will go completely silent, or will quickly send distracting topics into your awareness, but they will not lie. I have noticed this for decades now. Beings of the nonphysical realms must be held to a law of only speaking the truth.

This is putting the Law of Attraction into action for your personal life. When you think in clear, specific words to your guides, they will answer you with exact information or actions. The key for commands is to concentrate on the words and let your emotions feel their power. Do not hesitate to tell them what you need or want regarding communication.

Direct these guides to be more specific, to talk louder or more distinctly, and to send the information as images, or to give you specific details or directions in words.

When you direct your guides or ask a question, then *stop* and receive the *pop* of information. It is imperative that you do not dismiss it as just your imagination. Your ability to communicate with precise words will make all the difference in your accuracy and your effectiveness.

VITAL POINT

> The key to excellent communication with each Divine and Sacred specialty guide is to ask many questions but only one question at a time, then receive their wisdom in words or pictures in your mind.

We living humans frequently tend to feel as if we are totally alone as we go through our daily lives. We are not alone, and we were never meant to live or work alone. We do not need to struggle in all the ways that humans struggle. This is a planet of choice. You can invite this distinct level of specialty guides to assist you in any situation. There is a specialist for each person and each situation. This communication can be out loud, or telepathic from deep within your mind and heart. You must first invite these gifted guides to join you, then constantly inform each one of your needs or wants. It will always feel like your imagination, and it will never stop feeling like your imagination.

Develop a Working Relationship with Each Guide

Talk to your guides right away, and do not wait until you're in a session with a person you're trying to help, or who needs your intuitive and mediumship abilities. Communicate with your team all throughout your day. Get to know each other and learn how you will all work together before you assist people. To achieve a deeper relationship with them, begin to ask them important questions. Ask one question at a time, pause, and receive the telepathic pop of words, phrases, sentences, images, or little movies. Here are some great questions to begin with, but also ask your own questions too.

Questions to Get to Know Your Guides:

- What name can I call you by?
- How do you qualify as a specialist in _____?
- What do I need to do to work well with you?
- Do I need to actually see you as we work together?
- What should I notice when you contact me?
- How will I know you're there?
- How will you help me with intuition or mediumship or healing?

- What is the first step I should take to work excellently with you?
- What is the first step you will do to work excellently with me?
- How often can I ask you questions?
- Tell me one thing I need to do to work with you better.
- What should I notice when you contact me?
- How often can I ask you questions?
- What signals have I been missing from you?

Remember that every thought you think, and every emotion you feel, creates an electrical rush of energy throughout your body, energy field, and out into the world around you, and then into the galaxy. There are many words and phrases that will never be useful in your communications with the nonphysical. Many words are not useful for commanding. The Universe and spirit beings of *all* levels, including the Divine and Sacred, are absolutely literal, because the thoughts or words we say out loud are simply energy. They receive your thought energy as a signal of information.

The Divine and Sacred are very literal, and it is of utmost importance that you never say things like, "Give to me now the disease that is making my client sick." You really meant to give you the information or the cause of the disease. What the guides and the Universe literally receives is a request from you to get the disease: Give me the disease." The careless use of words is one of the primary causes of energy workers' demise. Very few understand that our thoughts create our life, our health, or our lack of health.

Watch your thoughts and commands, and STOP using ones that are not useful due to:

- A meaning that is too general.

- A meaning that is too vague.
- A word used in a broad manner throughout society.
- A word that does not direct guides to take an action.
- A word that suggests you are only asking the guides if they can do something.
- A word that tells them to give you something negative that is also hindering your client.

The primary words that should NOT be used in directives or commands to your guides due to the issues listed above are:

- Wish
- Hope
- Want
- Help
- Can
- Ask
- Need
- Heal
- Trying
- Take care
- Would you
- Will you
- Could you
- Give me

Examples of Unclear, Weak, or Vague Commands:

- Give me the (name of the issue) this client is struggling with now.
- I wish for some guidance to increase my abilities.
- Can you show me the meaning of that symbol.
- I hope you will bring kindness to his heart.
- I ask that the negativity changes.
- I want you to help me.
- I need to know what is wrong with (client name).
- Help me please.

- Heal this client.
- Take care of this client's knee.
- I am trying to be intuitive.
- Would you give me intuition?
- Could you increase my abilities?
- Will you tell me the first steps to take?

Proven Steps to Develop Your Team

As you live the life of an intuitive medium healer, you will invite the most advanced, beloved expert guides who will remain at your side. You are stepping into the position as the director for your specialized elite team. Your team will grow over time based on your needs, and the needs of your living and deceased clients. The six specialists to begin with are the following:

- Your Divine and Sacred Guardian Warriors
- Your Divine and Sacred Healer for Yourself
- Your Divine and Sacred mediumship specialist
- Your Divine and Sacred Healer for Living Clients
- Your Divine and Sacred Healer for the Troubled Deceased
- Your Divine and Sacred Healer for All Non-Human Beings

Notice that the first two guides, the guardian warriors and the healer for yourself—will always be focused on you. Your job is to . . .

- Take care of yourself first, to hold the power of your health and the power as a healing medium.
- Never use your own energy for any healing situation.
- Direct your Guardian Warriors to excel at shielding and defending you twenty-four hours a day.

If you do not care for yourself first, then there may soon be nothing left of you. This is why you must hold the position as the director of this noble team. Do not use your own personal energy to heal the living or the nonphysical. There is only one of you, and there is an uncountable number of those in need of healing.

As you begin to gather these six specialists, use precise words and *feel* the request deep within your heart as you send it out into the Universe. If names are important, then ask for a name to assist you in making a strong connection with each of your guides. Guidance from the nonphysical will instantly be there for you. Let yourself be aware of it and do not place any judgments on how they present themselves to you, or how strange the name may be.

Here Is a Brief Summary of the Steps You Are About to Take:

1. Telepathically send out a powerful invitation to the Universe.
2. Notice who instantly arrives and where they are located near you.
3. You will then, telepathically, send the guide one interview question: "Are you *truly* at the Divine and Sacred level?"
4. If they do not give you a strong "Yes," you then demand that they "permanently leave now." You then repeat the steps until you receive a powerful "Yes," signaling that you truly are communicating with a Divine and Sacred being.
5. The more you communicate with each guide, the more you develop a working relationship *with them.*
6. Important to Remember: Once you have connected with a Divine and Sacred specialist and have received a strong "Yes," they are always with you, and you never need to invite them again.

We all deserve to work with this level of guidance, and that truly includes you. They tell me that helping humans is one of the greatest things they can do. My guides especially want me to tell you that the more you allow them into your life, the more they develop. We are never bothering them. Always remember that the invitation is only an invitation.

Here are the guidelines to invite Divine and Sacred specialists to join your team:

Step 1: Your Divine and Sacred Guardian Warriors

The Invitation: I, (your full name), invite now, the most powerful Divine and Sacred Guardian Warrior who will powerfully protect me, my physical body, my energy field, my spirit, and my soul on all levels, all dimensions, and all timelines now.

Question: Are you *truly* at the Divine and Sacred level?

Examples of Action Commands:

1. "Create for me now the most powerful protection for my body, mind, and soul."
2. "Create for me now a complete sacred space around me, my clients, my energy work, and your clients."
3. "Keep all negativity away from me, and keep me away from all negativity. Stop all attacks, and all sources of all attacks, toward me now."
4. Inform your warriors: "I am worthy, I am safe, I am free. I am powerfully protected. I am the master of my body and ruler of my mind."
5. "Stop all attacks, and all sources of attacks, toward me now. Keep all negativity away from me, and keep me away from it."

6. "Surround me now with complete protection in all levels, all timelines, and all dimensions as I assist the deceased."

Step 2: Your Divine and Sacred Healer for You

The Invitation: I, (your full name), now invite in the most powerful and potent Divine and Sacred Healer who will work perfectly to heal my body, my mind, my energy field, and my soul.

Question: Are you *truly* at the Divine and Sacred level?

Examples of Action Commands:

1. Completely and permanently extract all negativity out of me now.
2. Extract from me now all negativity from the person I just assisted.
3. Fill me today with vitality, cellular health, and stamina.
4. Work with me to strengthen my toroidal field together now.
5. Remove and extract all needy or negative cords out of my body, mind, energy field, and soul now.

Step 3: Your Divine and Sacred Mediumship Specialist

The Invitation: I invite in now only the most authoritative Divine and Sacred Guide Specialist who will be excellent in working with me, (your name), in communications with all deceased humans.

Question: Are you *truly* at the Divine and Sacred level?

Examples of Action Commands:

1. Tell me, am I missing any communication from this deceased person?
2. Tell me now exactly what has caused this deceased person to remain on Earth and not cross over.

3. Did I receive this deceased person's message correctly?
4. Is this deceased person causing the illness in my living client?
5. Bring to me now the deceased person causing the problems in this house (or land).

Step 4: Your Divine and Sacred Healer for Living Clients

The Invitation: I, (*your full name*) invite in now a Divine and Sacred Guide who specializes in healing living humans negatively affected by the deceased.

Question: Are you *truly* at the Divine and Sacred level?

Examples of Action Commands:

1. Completely and permanently extract all negative cords and all roots from (name of the living client) and return them back to the deceased sender.
2. Fill every single space and place where the negativity used to be with vitality, love, and light.
3. Tell me now the best way to inform my living client that the cause of their struggles is a negative deceased person.

Step 5: Your Divine and Sacred Healer for Troubled Deceased

The Invitation: I, (*your full name*) in now the most authoritative transform-ational specialist who specializes in this deceased person.

Question: Are you *truly* at the Divine and Sacred level?

Examples of Action Commands:

1. Wrap this deceased person in a glowing white blanket of comfort now.

2. Tell me or show me now what this deceased person needs to know to release the Earth plane.

Step 6: Your Divine and Sacred Healer for All Negative Non-Human Beings

The Invitation: I, (*your full name*) invite in now the most authoritative and forceful Divine and Sacred Guide who knows how to handle and control all negative non-human beings.

Question: Are you *truly* at the Divine and Sacred level?

Examples of Action Commands:

1. Contain this entity now. Wrap it up tightly in a white light of comfort now.
2. Tell me now, is this being causing my client's sickness (disease or emotional issues)?
3. When did this being first attach to my client?
4. What is the first step to bringing a complete extraction and a healing to this being?

VITAL POINT

Always remember that the invitation is only an invitation. You must daily direct each guide in what you want or need from them. You never need to repeat the invitation again.

Notice if you are struggling in any way regarding working as the head of an elite team of Divine and Sacred specialists. Take a moment to notice yourself without criticism. Notice yourself now.

I truly deserve to invite in, and to work with, the most progressive level of guides.

I feel profoundly worthy to be in the presence of Divine and Sacred beings.

The answer is absolutely *yes.* They have been waiting patiently for you.

Chapter 5

Always Heal the Healer First: What Causes the Healer's Struggles?

Practitioners are known to focus so deeply on their alive and deceased clients that they rarely take care of themselves. There is only one of you and an uncountable number of them. Always, always, always take care of yourself first.

As I write this chapter, I just received information about an energy worker who just died. That now makes the tenth healer I know who has died within the last year and a half. Some I know personally, and some I know of them. What I do know is that I am older than most of the energy workers who have now died. I know this tenth death happened as I write this chapter to get your attention, and to take this chapter seriously.

What does "save your life or save yourself" really mean? For many decades, I have worked with clients who are holistic practitioners, intuitives, medical intuitives, mediums, and energy workers trained in all types of energy-healing modalities. They are working with me because they are suffering in some way and don't know what to do about it. Most practitioners are not taking care of their own health at all, so they are certainly not saving themselves. Every energy worker I've met has shared with me at least one of the following struggles:

- "I am totally drained into exhaustion after I do energy work with my clients."

- "I am dedicated to helping my clients even though I am struggling."
- "I do not have time, and I'm not sure what to do to help myself if I did take the time."
- "Even though I often feel bad and drained, I cannot stop helping others."

Then I say, "You are the only one who can save you. If you keep giving to others and do not take care of yourself, you will collapse and never be able to help yourself or your clients again. When you drain your energy field, you are draining your soul. If you keep repeating the same things that deplete you, then no one else can keep restoring you at the same rate you're draining away your own vitality. You need to stop doing whatever you're doing that's constantly devouring your essence. When you collapse, you will not care for anyone."

There are one or more of these things happening. Read these one at a time and notice what truly applies to you:

1. You might be an empath.
2. You might be sending your own personal energy into the situation or the person.
3. You might be forgetting to direct your Divine and Sacred Guides.
4. You might not be giving back to yourself and invigorating your own energy field.
5. You might be unaware of clients draining you during a session.
6. You might be unaware of clients continuing to drain you after the session.
7. You might be triggered by old trauma from a past life or earlier in this current life.

8. You might be interfered with by a negative deceased person or a negative non-human being.
9. You might be missing or ignoring valuable signals from the Universe.

Work with Your Personal Healing Guide Daily

There are many causes for an energy healer to become ill in some way. While there are many causes, there are three common causes, leading the healer to become ill or severely drained. The three primary causes are:

1. Using your own energy to build up the energy of the person you're healing.
2. Working and living as an empath.
3. Allowing needy people to cord into you, then absorbing your strength until you're empty.

No matter what has been causing your illness or life struggles, you must do healing steps every day to keep yourself vibrant, aware, and healthy at a cellular level. Most family members or clients have no idea that their neediness or their desperation can harm you. They will simply see you as their healer, their all-knowing guide, or even their savior. You need to be an expert for those people, but first and foremost, you must be an expert healer for yourself.

Remember in chapter 4, you invited in a specialist just for your own healing and to keep yourself well. Please hear me: There is no reason for you to come to any level of illness or harm as you work to heal others. You must allow your specialty guide of healing to be an integral part of your daily life as a healing medium.

Hopefully, as you read chapter 4, you already invited the Divine and Sacred Healer who specializes in your health and all levels of your well-being. Again, you do not need to keep inviting the same guide.

Once they arrive and you demand to know if they are Divine and Sacred, you *never* need to invite that particular guide again. But you must always ask each guide a question, or direct your healing specialist with specific commands.

If you do not have time between sessions, then *always* direct your specialist at the end of your working day. It is vital to discover the cause or the source of your health struggles. Here is an example of a few strong commands to discover the cause:

- "Tell me or show me now the exact cause of my illness."
- "Tell me or show me now the exact moment that caused my exhaustion now."

Next, create commands to direct the actual healing. Here are a few examples:

- "Completely and permanently extract all causes of the illness within my body now."
- "Completely and permanently extract all causes of exhaustion now."
- "Completely and permanently release and transform all negativity from my body, mind, and energy field now."

VITAL POINT

Take Care of You First. When anything is removed or extracted from you or your clients, you must immediately direct the healer to: "Fill every space and place, where the negative used to be, with (powerful, positive words defining what you want to be filled with. For example: cellular vitality, surges of energy, positive thoughts, love and light.)"

Are You Using Your Own Energy to Heal Others?

I began to realize there's another reason that energy workers are suffering with illness and devastating exhaustion. This came to my attention during one of my courses. Many people who attend my courses tell me they are Reiki practitioners. I am always so pleased to hear that, since I taught Reiki many years ago. During one of my medical intuitive courses, one student asked me why she was so horribly tired every time she did a Reiki session. I quickly responded, "You should never be exhausted, or even tired, in any way while offering Reiki. You should be energized."

I began to ask her some questions and discovered that she was sending her own vitality and her own life energy into each of her clients. I want to carefully explain now that energy practitioners of any modality should first of all fill themselves with the healing energy of the Universe and not their own energy. It is the same with Reiki, and with all modalities.

Practitioners must first fill themselves with the energy of Reiki or for other modalities, the most blessed energy of the Universe. To do this, you simply think of Reiki, or the most blessed energy, or the Universe, and inhale many times into your own body. You will naturally begin to feel fuller, lighter, and even happier. That is what you send into your clients. Never use your own energy again.

Are You an Empath?

On a positive note, empaths are phenomenal intuitives because they are quite intuitive, and they instantly pick up the energy of other people and animals. They are so sensitive that they pick up anyone suffering near them, as well as any anguish that is shown on TV. They will describe picking up on people's anger, depression, or sadness, and especially someone's trauma. Many people have come to me stating they are empaths and there is nothing they can do about it. They go on to say they can no longer go to the grocery store or watch TV anymore. They often describe the need to stay at home more and more, and watching TV less and less.

Empaths often tell their story with a certain sense of pride. They say it's the way they connect with other people. Many times, they refuse to change. They do not wish to release the agony they carry for others, and I cannot make anyone change who does not want to change. What I can do first is teach empaths what is really taking place in their bodies and in their lives.

Empaths are extremely intuitive and very sensitive to all energy. First, they are attracted to the most negative situations because they are so sensitive. Then they feel the agony. Next, the empath identifies with the situation, but even more harmful, they actually astral project outward toward the painful event and the people involved. When we astral project toward someone, or a certain location, we are literally standing in that location, and the tragedy is truly happening around us. When we humans astral project, we are stretching our energy body outward and land in a certain location. We are actually there in that moment, and then the empath experiences the trauma and makes it their own experience.

Esther Hicks, who channels Abraham, stated at a conference I attended: "Of course, it is a wonderful thing to help others, but you must do it from your position of strength and alignment, which means you must be in alignment with their success as you offer assistance, and not in alignment with their problem."

This absorption of suffering never helps anyone. It only harms the empath. It not only harms them emotionally but harms their physical health as well. There is so much more that the empath can do to handle their intuitive skills in a more knowledgeable way. Merging and suffering with others does not change, transform, or heal any situation. It is especially not healing anyone either.

As a mental health counselor, I have heard horrible, gut-wrenching stories from thousands of people over the decades. People cry, scream, and some even vomit as they tell their stories. The energy of all that emotion is right there in the room, and yet I do not absorb it into my body or carry it into my life as if it's my own. I would not be able to function as a counselor if the burdens of my clients clung to my body, mind, or my energy field. Try to imagine the amount of tragedy building up inside of you day after day, and over many decades.

And yet, I am right there 100 percent for the people I serve. I listen intently to every word that is said, and yet I take it in only as information. I do not absorb or carry the dense energy of raw emotion that is around me. Empaths, however, soak up the pain, grief, and shock of the world around them, but this level of trauma does not belong to them at all. If this anguish is not happening in your own personal life, there is a reason. Your life contract hasn't been set up for you to learn from trauma in your own life. Please hear me when I say this: You are deeply harming yourself. Identifying with the suffering of others only adds to the suffering and does nothing to heal the suffering.

Participate:

Do these steps very slowly:

1. Notice exactly what happens as you feel yourself take on other people's emotions.
2. Examine other people's energy as it enters your body. Notice the specific locations where your body receives it.
3. Notice how your body feels as it fills up with the grief and sorrow you see around you.
4. Now decide to take charge of yourself and your abilities.
5. Teach your mind and body that you are in charge now as a healer.
6. Direct yourself to receive emotions only as important information.

7. Inhale deeply many times, strengthening your own energy and your power.

Energy Cords are Everywhere

I always hear two statements regarding energy cords from long-term energy workers, newer students, and anyone else who is even slightly aware of cords:

"They are terrible, negative, and harmful."

Healing practitioners proudly declare, "I cut cords with nearly everyone I work with!"

Now I will declare . . . Chopping an energy cord between two or more people is not a healing! The receiver of the cord still has a piece of that negative cord within them. That is not a healing. I beg you to never cut an energy cord again.

Energy cords connected to a client are very complicated—too complicated to just chop it somewhere in between the two people involved. As an intuitive medium, you're constantly creating positive energy cords with the living and the deceased clients. And, as an intuitive medium, most of the people needing your help have, unknowingly, created energy cords into you without realizing it. Most of those people will continue to draw energy from you long after the meeting with them. And there are still others who will deliberately cord into you and use you like a battery for their own selfish needs. For your own health, well-being, and stamina, you must evaluate your entire energy field, then take the correct actions to take care of yourself. You cannot help anyone at any level if you're drained down to nearly nothing.

Positive cording happens between positive people connecting in a relationship of any type. Take note: Positive cords will feel and appear more like threads. The cords will be thin, shimmery, and sometimes will even sparkle. They will appear in different colors, depending on the thoughts and emotions that created the cord. For example, a positive cord is often connected between the hearts of individuals. They can also appear in other areas such as the shoulders as they "shoulder life together." Positive cords might also appear in the groin area in a positive sexual relationship. Sometimes positive cords connect the hands of two people because they frequently hold each other's hand. I never alter positive energy cords in any way, but I do inform the client about them, where the cord is located, and why it is there.

Here is an example of a positive cord that still caused a client physical discomfort. A woman came to me with a severe feeling that her neck was pulling to the right. She had already been to doctors, clinics, and physical therapy without any success. No one could find why this was happening. I intuitively astral projected a few feet outward to where she sat in my office and found a rope around her neck. The rope extended out toward her right. The rope was actually an energetic cord. The rope was not dark in color at all, but it still pulled on the woman's neck, causing her pain. I followed the cord to the end and found a man holding the other end. I described the man to her, and she said in alarm, "You just described my husband exactly!"

I wasn't sure how to address this situation, let alone begin a healing process. So, I did what I always do. I asked my guides an extremely clear question. "Tell me or show me now, the exact steps to remove this cord and heal this woman."

I received telepathic information in words leaping into my mind, and at the same time, images appeared in my mind. I told the client, "My guides told me to tell you to follow the rope back to your husband. When you get to him, the two of you are to talk things over."

She quickly agreed and was quiet for a few minutes. I waited. She suddenly began to speak. "We talked it over. He says I've been changing. He told me he was worried he might lose me because I'm getting into this spiritual stuff so deeply. We held each other and talked it over, and we're good now."

I then said, "Let me check that rope," I still saw it around her neck and told her that I wanted to ask my guides why the rope was still there. She agreed. I asked that direct question to my guides. They said, "You are capable of removing it; however, do not remove it for her. Tell this woman she is to remove it herself and give it back to her husband. This will send her a message of how healthy and powerful she has become."

Negative cords are a completely different situation and can be very complicated. These cords tend to be thicker, dense, and will seem to be a dark muddy color. They appear this way because negative emotions created them, such as jealousy, anger, hate, revenge, or the desire to control someone. They also syphon the receiver's skills, or their popularity, or serve as a battery to save the energy of the cord's creator.

It's important to intuitively watch the flow of each cord. The flow will tell you if your client was the actual creator of the negative cord or the receiver of it. The slow direction of the cord's flow will identify who created it. Be aware that your clients are not always the victims. They could have caused it without knowing the power of their own negative emotions, or they could be the perpetrator who created it on purpose. It's possible that your client created a negative cord; however, when a person comes to you for help, they are usually not the creator.

Because of the extreme complexity of negative emotions causing cords, I can only give you some examples of what you might discover. Negative emotions, while slow, dense, and sluggish, are also powerful in their control, and their ability to drain and destroy an individual's energy. Negative cords tend to appear ropelike due to complex emotions, while positive cords seem more simple, light, and threadlike, created by affection and love.

VITAL POINT

There are negative cords, and there are positive cords. Know the difference.

One of my mentoring clients gave me permission to share one of her life's stories. She and I both knew that her story would touch each reader and would help so many people.

This client had recently left her husband due to severe verbal and emotional abuse.

Due to his increased drinking, he became scary, and she was now afraid of him. When drunk, he was even more threatening. She asked if I would remove all the cords from her, because she intuitively felt there were negative cords attached to her body and field. I asked for permission to scan her body. She quickly agreed.

Before I even began the scanning process, a deceased male moved toward me. He first presented himself with a mask covering his face. The mask was in the shape of a horse's head. Even I thought this was a bit strange. He appeared as a thick, dark, blackish-brown human form as he stood low to the ground. The mask, while an unusual form of a horse head, immediately told me he was out to do harm but could not face me.

I asked if he was connected to my client's husband.

"Yes."

I asked, "Where and when did you begin to be with him?"

"I followed him out of the bar. He's drunk a lot. I really like that feeling, so I've been following him around."

Intuitively, I saw this mean, drunken deceased man had corded into my client's husband, and then, due to the husband's rage toward his wife, the deceased had also corded into my client. This deceased man siphoned drunk energy from the abusive husband, but he also took advantage of cording into my client to interfere with her as well.

When I described this dead male with a horse mask on his face, my client said in a surprised way, "I have been seeing a spirit man around me!"

With a little guidance, the female client invited in a Divine and Sacred Guide who is a specialist in extracting negative cords. She followed my steps to first extract the negative spirit man's thick, dark, ropelike cord from herself.

I witnessed three more negative cords that originated from her abusive husband. All three were in her backside. (Cords embedded into someone's back signifies a deep level of sneakiness.) I informed her that one cord was plugged into the base of her neck at shoulder level, and it was pushing her face down toward the ground. She immediately said she had been having a terrible time holding her head upward and kept finding herself hunched over, which, of course, was causing her pain.

The second cord from her husband was implanted through her back and into her heart. Again, in an attempt to hide his intentions, the husband attempted to control her emotions and her heartfelt decisions. The third cord created by his harmful emotions went into the end of her spinal cord, which is also the second chakra. That energy center is about home life and relationships.

Please note this important detail: I did *not* remove the cord for her. I only offered this client each step to remove these cords herself and give them back to the wrongdoer. I taught her how to direct the Divine and Sacred, but she took charge and directed the guides into a wonderful extraction and a positive healing.

VITAL POINT

> Cutting negative energetic cords is never a healing. Directing your guides to extract the cord from your client is a healing.

My guides did not tell me to address the energetic cord between my client and her husband. Apparently, that was not the primary focus in healing this situation, but it would need to be addressed in the near future. Sometimes the specific removal of energetic cords is a critical factor in the healing experience. Cords can exist not only between a needy spirit person and an individual in the physical, but also between two or more physically alive people as well.

Needy humans and controlling humans will drain you. So, do not hesitate and think you will work on yourself later. You deserve one minute of immediate self-care. Here are the instant steps to take to remove negative cords from yourself:

Steps to Extract Negative Cords from Yourself

1. Completely and permanently extract all negative cords sent to me from needy or controlling people. Give all the cords back to the senders now to help them realize they have their own power.
2. Completely and permanently fill all places where the cords used to be with cellular vitality, glowing health, and amazing energy now.

Accurately Scan Yourself

Constantly scanning yourself is the first step to maintaining your ability to successfully heal others. Scanning oneself is fun and can be done in the shower, or standing in line at the grocery store, or waiting for the train to finish crossing the road in front of you. It's deeply important to scan your body and energy field without judgment or criticism. Scanning yourself is not searching for flaws. It is about being fascinated and trusting your intuitive self each day. Discover every day where your body and energy field are strong. Also discover any weakened areas of your body and field. With the assistance of your guides, you can understand the cause of the weakened areas by asking your guides detailed questions. You can then direct your guides to do the steps to bring those areas back to their healthiest to maintain the powerful healer within you.

Your Daily Scanning Steps:

1. Your focused thoughts become like hypersensitive sensors. First send your ears, eyes, and fingertips all around your energy field, then inside your physical body. Notice your sensors scanning 360 degrees throughout and around you. Remember to scan your backside, under your feet, and above your head.
2. Notice the instant images or thoughts that pop into your awareness. Take note of the words or images that pop into your mind.
3. Notice where your field and physical body is rich with energy.
4. Look for areas that seem, feel, or look different from the rest of your field. Look for areas that are thin, weak, dim, open, torn, discolored, and any tunnels or leaks. (Leaks can appear anywhere from bubbles rising upward to gushes of energy leaving you like a fireman's hose, or even larger.)
5. Look for objects or impressions of objects in your field or body. Do not be alarmed if you discover objects such as dark cords, knives, arrows, spears, or other objects. Take it as important information of the cause of your struggles in a certain area.
6. If you become aware of objects, then notice the exact location of foreign objects, or other things within your physical body and your energy field.
7. Always notice the pop of images or thoughts that leap into your mind.

There is no way to do this wrong. Notice whatever you notice. Write down all that pops into your awareness.

Scanning is all about discovering. The next step is to attend to your own very personal healing. So, let's begin . . .

Cleansing, Healing, Protecting, Grounding, Empowerment, and Self-Love

I was enraptured by a psychic named Marian Stearns. She was giving a public talk to approximately sixty of us about Earth changes and the energy of love. As I sat there, overcome with waves of love for this woman and what she represented, I literally felt one of those "waves" from inside of me rush up to her like I was giving her a long hug in the middle of her presentation. But instead, I banged into an invisible thing around her.

I felt the bump as if I slowly walked into an invisible, large screen door. The screen seemed to give just a little, but then I bounced back and away from her. At that same split second, she stopped mid-sentence, turned my way, and stared straight into my eyes. I turned scarlet. She regained her composure and began her talk again. I didn't hear another word she said. I spent the remainder of her talk trying not to bang into her force field again.

When I look back on this moment, I now realize that I actually bumped into the protection that Marian had created. I sent my energy field out to this woman because of my admiration. I have always wondered what might have happened if my adoration for her was not blocked and walled off, but allowed to touch hers? I was merely sitting still, listening to her words and feeling waves of positive feelings, and yet something happened. She knew it, and I knew it.

We do affect each other with our words, actions, thoughts, and emotions, but all those things are within our energy field. Our human energy field, or aura, has substance. My crashing into her had substance to it. The aura contains every thought, every feeling, and every action that has happened in our life. The energy of all we are, is always there, in us, through us, and around us. Marian had control of her energy field with her powerful thoughts. Our intent is merely focused thought followed by the emotions associated with the thoughts.

We will now look deeply into all aspects of our energy field, how to use it, and what it does for us.

Cleansing and Healing Qualities of Each Color

Color is so much more than color. Human energy is often perceived as colors. Most people discuss colors of the human aura but seldom discuss colors within the body and field as having significant and powerful meaning. Your aura is more than colors shining out from your body. Each color emanating within a human or non-human offers the medium:

1. An instant piece of information.
2. The client's health in general and specific details.
3. The level of awareness at which each client is living.
4. Instant knowledge regarding their negative or positive intentions.
5. Immediate ways to improve your own health.

Let's first begin with you using color as electrical healing frequencies for your own health and well-being.

Red: Gives heat to an area, builds up energy, draws in strength and vitality at the cellular level.

Orange: Positive for kidneys, bladder, and eliminating or releasing toxins.

Yellow: Strengthens self-empowerment and confidence, energizes physical life, sends Energy to power up like the power of the sun. Positive for skin and bones.

Green: Detoxes, decongestion, disinfectant, breaks up blood clots.

Blue: Decreases inflammation, decreases infections, soothing, cools, decreases overheating.

Purple: Builds and empowers all levels of healing, cleanses, breaks up density, transforms negativity into the positive.

White: Building up the spirit to more clearly connect with the Universe.

Violet: Transforms, transmutes negative energy into positive energy.

The Transformative Qualities of Violet

As I began to write this section regarding the violet flame, I instantly felt uplifted. Violet is not just a violet color. It's known for its extraordinary ability to purify and transform negative energy into pure positive energy. This powerful transformation usually takes the form of violet flames. I was first introduced to the violet flame and to the ascended master, St. Germaine, nearly forty years ago. My partner at that time told me tales of a human who became an ascended master known as St. Germain.

If you wanted to paint a picture using violet, you would mix purple, red, and white to create the color. Look back at the healing traits of each of those individual colors. When colors are mixed together, an interweaving of those characteristics blend into one energy. Take a moment now to sense how powerful violet is, and then perceive it as fiery flames.

The violet flame is known for its ability to transform anything negative into the positive. Its power is to purify whatever it touches. I'm not sure how it came to be perceived as flames, but it makes total sense to me. Its flames do not kill, and energy cannot be killed. It can only transform into another form. So, the violet flame is the transformer, the reconstructionist. It transforms the energy of anything from the negative into the positive. It's a flame because it burns away negativity, transforms, and transmutes the heavy density of negativity into positive, bright purity.

Allow this information to heighten your sense of how important, and how powerful, it truly is. The violet flame is so important to me that I googled it and found an image of it I use as the background display of my phone. Negativity of any type, size, shape, or density cannot tolerate this fiery transformative frequency. Imagine, see, sense, and feel the power of the violet flame rushing inside of you and completely around you.

The Empowering Qualities of Brilliant Clear-White

People tend to be fascinated with the brilliance of the stars and how they seem to sparkle throughout the sky above us. Each and every star is light within the darkness. Clear-white empowers the spirit within your body. Imagine placing a star inside every cell of your physical body. Now consider how star energy would make the billions of cells in your body glow brilliantly bright. Negative or dark energy cannot tolerate or even exist in the brightness of white light.

The Precious Qualities of Gold

Oh, the energy of gold. First, take a moment to notice what you think and feel about gold and its golden energy. On the Earth plane, gold is considered precious, cherished, and treasured. Energetically, gold creates precious, cherished, and treasured value within your field, your body, and your soul. Allow your body and energy field to overflow with golden energy. Allow yourself to actually be precious.

Your Toroidal Field is Your Powerful Link to the Universe

Your toroidal field is you. You are a toroidal field. Every cell of your body and every cell of the Earth, animals, plants, trees, and the entire cosmos is a living, moving toroidal field. Your toroidal field is recognized in sacred geometry as the form of eternity, of life, of death, and is our personal eternal interconnection that weaves throughout eternity.

There is a phenomenal interconnectedness in our lives. You, as an alive individual, link the Earth and the Heavens together continually. And as that continuously happens, you also extend outward horizontally to be part of that interlacing with daily Earth life. Can you picture and feel your important position here? We humans are phenomenally important as the nexus or core link within the entire system of the Universe. You are important and have an opportunity to advance, or not to advance.

Your toroidal field is . . .

1. Your vitality.
2. Your own cleansing tool.
3. Your own energy healing mechanism.
4. Your own thoughts and emotions.
5. Your connection with the world around you.
6. Your own personal protection from any and all levels of negativity.

Your toroidal field is the electrical energy of your body, aura, and soul continuously intertwining. Many people think it's only moving upward, but it's so much more. It's constantly vibrating and rotating at the same time as it moves in absolutely all directions. It flows horizontally, vertically, sideways, and at angles. It moves inward, downward, and upward. But it is vitally important to know that your toroidal field spins and rotates as well as extends throughout your body and into the Universe.

Protecting yourself is another serious and controversial topic. I am about to discuss and describe the opposite of what most people are doing to energetically protect themselves. I include myself when

I say that most people who have taken any type of class on awareness or energy have been directed to place something around themselves for protection. That something is usually a crystal ball, or something similar. So, I did that for years and never experienced any protection at all. If anything, it seemed to block out the bad *and* the good.

I mentioned earlier that when the Divine and the Sacred finally got through to me, they asked me to stop placing something around me. I was startled. I said I certainly cannot stop doing that because then I would be even more vulnerable than ever. This level of guide is so patient and so kind. They just kept saying the same thing. "Stop placing things around you."

I finally asked, "Then tell me how to protect myself."

That is exactly what the guides were waiting to hear. They responded, "Fill your body and your energy field with different light frequencies until you are so full you shine outward like a light bulb."

So, I googled that, and there it was: the human toroidal field. Some scientists had already figured it out.

The following steps are again about the energetic qualities of different color frequencies, but now with the focus of protection, grounding, and empowering who you are really meant to be.

On the following page is a simple image showing you as a fountain of vibrant energy. Directing your energy in this natural toroidal field pattern results in the following:

1. It teaches you to be in command and *empowered* by who you truly are.
2. The more you are in command of your own energy field, the more brilliant you shine outward. This brilliance inside you that shines outward is *protecting* you.
3. You *ground* yourself by receiving Earth's energy upward, then sending your energy down into the Earth to rise up again through you. This builds your natural toroidal field form.

4. The more you direct your toroidal field, the more the energy form builds strength. So, you're actually going down to the center of the Earth, and when you rise up through your body and out the crown of your head, your energy connects with the cosmos. We can become a powerful *link in the system of the Universe.* It's your choice.

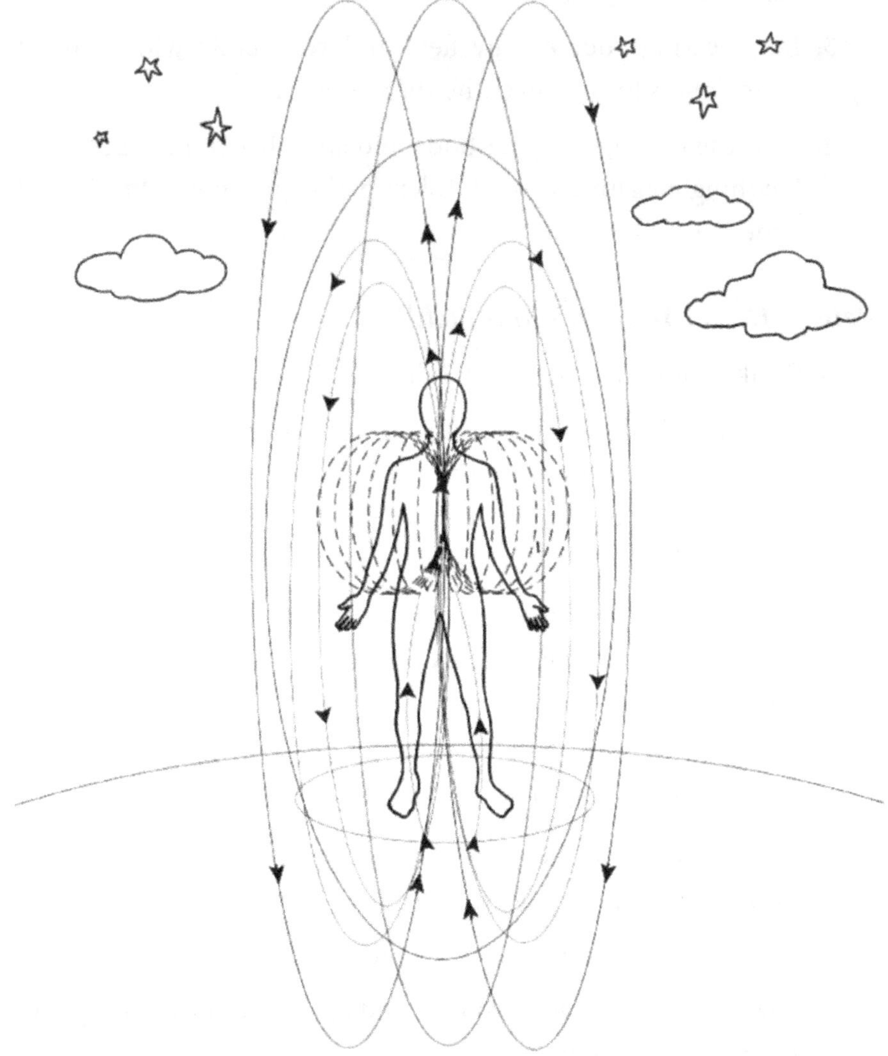

Tips on Directing Your Toroidal Field

1. The healing qualities of each color are related to the natural human energy centers known as chakras. Deliberately directing each color frequency throughout your body cleanses and strengthens your body.
2. The important use of the violet flame is to transmute and transform the negative into the positive.
3. Empowering your energy field and your body with brilliant white light is to shine like the stars above us.
4. Send the message to your body and soul that you are precious. Anything negative cannot tolerate the precious vibration of golden energy.

Steps to Direct Your Toroidal Field

- Think it, and the energy will follow in this order.
- Imagine inhaling upward through the soles of your feet and filling every cell. Imagine breathing in and upward, *each color, one at a time*, in this order: Red, Orange, Yellow, Green, Blue, Purple, White.
- Then breathe into the soles of your feet and fill every cell with fire-like energy of violet, burning off all negativity within and around you.
- Then breathe into the soles of your feet and place a brilliant white sparkle inside of every cell in your body.
- Then breathe into the soles of your feet and fill every cell with precious, electrified golden energy.
- Feel as if you are a brilliant light bulb.
- Open the crown of who you are and allow your brilliant light to shine up and into the cosmos.

- Ground yourself. The cosmos notices your new brilliance and sends energy wisdom downward into your field and your physical body, then back down into the Earth. Then repeat all the above steps, pulling energy back up into your body to ground yourself.
- You are training yourself to constantly be empowered.

Here are two of the most high-powered methods to keep you protected, healthy, and empowered.

Opening and Closing Each Session You Do for Others

1. At the beginning of each session, direct your specialty guide: Create the perfect, sacred, and safe space for the work that's about to happen. You may feel it, or you may be able to see it. Intuitively invite each client to join you in that space.
2. At the end of each session, or at the end of each day, direct your specialty guide who excels in cleaning and clearing your energy field: "Create the ideal cleansing filter for me now."
3. Command: "I bring me, and only me, back to me, clean and clear through the most perfect filter provided for me."
4. Inhaling deeply, draw your energy back into your physical body through your thoughts. Sometimes you might see a thick substance clinging to the filter. You will be pleased to know you're not bringing that back to yourself or into your life.

Valuable Steps to Heal Your Heart

Science has also discovered that the heart has the same brain cells as one portion of the human brain. Your heart can think, feel, process, and even communicate with your body, and at the same time, with other people. It's as if it is its own being within the larger being of your body. Because of this, your heart has its own toroidal field. That toroidal field not only generates its own intelligent energy but blends into the entire toroidal field of your body and soul.

Dr. Brooke Stuart, a doctor of Oriental Medicine, states: "When we allow our conscious awareness to be in our heart center, we can begin to shift our perspective from what is, to what can be and realize what is actually possible."[1]

Practice: I Give Back to My Heart Now

1. Place both hands over your heart.
2. Command: "I give love back into my own heart now, equal to all the love and care I have given to others."
3. Allow yourself to send and feel the energy of love going deep into the organ of your heart and its energy center.

My Divine and Sacred healing specialists have shared multiple methods to heal and empower you to:

- Get in charge of your soul.
- Get in charge of your body.
- Remove negative energy cords.
- Strengthen and invigorate your field.
- Heal your physical body.
- Heal your precious heart.
- Heal your eternal soul.

People from around the globe continually tell me the self-healing methods I offer in this book, have strengthened their own health, their heart, and their entire life in uncountable ways. We constantly have a choice to be a powerful human or a weak human. It is vital to your

---

1 Brooke Stuart, "On the Toroidal Field," December 7, 2022, https://www.drbrookestuart.com/on-the-toroidal-field.

existence to do these methods every day of your life. You truly are worth it!

Forgiveness is Not a Healing Method

The word "forgive" is power-packed with emotions. The next power-packed emotional statement that usually goes along with that word is: "You need to forgive!"

No, you do not! You do *not* have to make yourself forgive a wrongdoer, or the moment the negative event happened. If someone states, "You just simply have to forgive someone," it usually only brings up your suppressed rage or pain that has been pushed down for a long, long time.

When someone tells you that you have to forgive, the opposite happens. We immediately think and feel that if we forgive someone, it really means something else. Deep down, we think our forgiveness will send a message to the wrongdoer. We're afraid that the wrongdoer will think that what they did was suddenly okay with you!

This is not what forgiveness is about. I ask that you share with your clients to never worry, or even try to forgive anyone, or anything. Don't even think about forgiveness, or worry about achieving forgiveness! It's about focusing on healing, and healing some more. When you focus on healing your struggles or guiding your living clients to do the same, then someday you will gently realize that you no longer hold any emotion about the wrongdoer or the event. That is true forgiveness.

You no longer carry any baggage of heavy emotions every day of your life. You, or your clients, may still remember the event, but now you recall it only as a fact in your history. You feel neutral with no reactions. It is nothing else but a moment in history, that you have learned and now love yourself even more. That will happen, and when it does, you will know that true forgiveness is the end result of you truly healing your soul.

PART 3

Take Action as a Multidimensional Healer

Chapter 6

Be So Much More Than a Speaker for the Deceased

Here is a mediumship rule: Never chase away the deceased ever again! Consider each one of them—the good, the bad, the ugly, and yes, even the mean and the sinister—always and forever as a client. There, I said it, and I mean it!

When people chase away a deceased being, that being must go somewhere because it is a real human being who does not have a body at the moment. They will always leave, but they will usually return when they think no one is looking. They will go outside, or go to the neighbors, or down the street . . . but only for a while, and then they return.

This might be a new thought, but I ask you to consider that each deceased person is just as alive as you are. A deceased person is still a real human being with real thoughts and real feelings who exists in a nonphysical state. Please understand that all nonphysical beings want or need something when they appear to the living. All deceased humans, especially those who have not crossed over, still have the range of emotions they had when they were alive. Some were kind and giving, while others were harmful or even predators. But realize that most struggling deceased people are somewhere in between kind and harmful. I consider all nonphysical beings as clients.

- Always be respectful.
- Dead people are still real people too.

- Dead people are just as alive as you are.
- Never, never, never chase a spirit person away.
- Each nonphysical being must be considered a client who needs or wants something.

These nonphysical clients and loved ones . . .

1. Yearn to communicate.
2. Want something.
3. Need something.
4. Are terribly confused and not aware that they have any wants or needs.
5. Relive the same emotional moment over and over again, completely unaware that they are dead.

Most people have no idea that nonphysical beings want or need anything, and certainly, most living humans have no idea that any deceased humans have anything to say. Deceased humans who come to us are often not loved ones. Sometimes we know them casually, but many times, we have no idea who they are. For example, sometimes the spirit person might be a great-aunt or great-grandfather, or the deceased mailman you connected with many years ago, or a neighbor down the street who died before you were born. In truth, you will not know many of the troubled deceased, and most of the time, they have no idea why they have come to you.

The deceased who come to us are often total strangers. That type of experience leads to the question: Why would a spirit person come to me if I do not know them and they do not know me? This is one of the many situations that creates a massive block for potential mediums. Many people wonder about this, and then wrongly come to this conclusion: "I thought I was seeing and hearing a ghost right now, but I do not know this person, so this is not real. I just made it up."

The deceased that you do not know have come to you for help. They want or need something, and many times, they do not even know what they want or need. They are now your client.

Less Talking and More Listening to All Nonphysical Beings

Ninety-five percent of my living clients and students consistently have one primary struggle that gets in the way of communicating with the deceased. I hear people describing this problem nearly every single day. This is what the 95 percent describe to me: "I probably cannot become a medium, because I never hear them say anything. I don't even hear my own deceased loved ones, such as my grandmother. I can't even get her to talk to me."

First of all, believe me . . . this is not an exaggeration. This is the most common problem that is described to me. My response is always the same: "When you talk to your loved ones, do you then stop and listen to what they say back to you, or do you just keep talking?"

Now, imagine the stunned looks on people's faces as they go silent. They realize it's true. Apparently, most people never stop talking to the deceased, which must mean that no one listens!

This mentoring student shared his story about what he calls a "Full-On Conversation" with his grandmother. This is a fantastic example of a balanced conversation of talking and listening to the deceased. They often have a great deal to say.

"I went to my motherland of Greece to heal for a month alone. The energy there always seems to uplift and balance my own energy and vibration. One day, at the beginning of my trip, I woke up one morning in my hotel to find every single light in my room was on—all the lamps, overhead, background lights, you name it. I knew it was a signal from the other side. This was how I learned that my main spirit guide was trying to get my attention by turning on a lamp on my desk while I was asleep. Before I went to bed, I would tell her to either leave the lamp off or turn it on. And when I woke the next day, I would find my request answered as asked. I did this for ten days straight.

"I had made the connection, and it has been strong ever since. Because of this, I knew it was her. It was my Greek grandmother and grandfather. They were telling me they were with me, and supporting me, and cheering me on. My guide was also saying "hi," and they were all cheering me on for my journey ahead in Greece.

"Toward the end of my trip. I lay on the beach when I suddenly felt a hand touch the top of my left thigh. I quickly looked up to see who was touching me, but there was no one there. I immediately knew I was contacted by a spirit from the other side. I closed my eyes, connected to the Universe, and asked who had touched me, and my Greek grandmother came through. I was overcome with emotion. I was told to hold that vibration, and to connect with her, and that by doing so, I would be able to talk to her.

"I held that high vibration and was able to connect with her, and I had a full-on conversation with her. She told me many things about my life and my journey ahead. She told me how she is with me always, and that she will help me walk my path. I had tears streaming down my face the entire time. I couldn't believe this was actually happening, and I felt overwhelming love and gratitude to the Universe for allowing this experience in my life."

I was delighted to tell this mentoring client that he is truly an excellent "listener" for the deceased, which allowed the "full-on conversation" with his beloved grandmother.

VITAL POINT

Listen and receive the pop of information in words, in pictures or little movies. Receiving information which is listening makes for the most accurate healing medium.

Many deceased are simply trying to find someone who will listen to them. They came to you in hopes of communicating and expressing something that is on their minds. Nearly everyone I know began to doubt themselves in this way. Deciding you are imagining ghosts and making everything up is the most dominant block hindering our abilities to be an intuitive medium. I will say this again and again . . . Dead people are just as alive as you are, and they have loads of things to say to you, or anyone who will listen. Dead people are absolutely everywhere, and many struggle to be heard. Here are a couple of examples to help you trust yourself from now on.

Just as I began writing this book, a dear friend had an experience in her home. Because she was such a good listener, I asked her if she would write this experience in her own words for my book.

A Practitioner Shares a Story: Johnny Was Lost

I was sitting in a deep meditation when, suddenly, there was a huge bang in the kitchen. It was so loud that it sounded like a hawk had flown full force into the kitchen window. Not more than ten seconds later, there was a second identical bang from the same place. I continued my meditation until I was finished, then I sent my energy field out into the house and asked, "Who is there?"

A young man, tall and thin and probably early twenties, dressed in jeans and a white T-shirt or work-type shirt that seemed somewhat dated, came around the corner from the kitchen (which is the same place the noise came from). I asked the deceased man his name, and he said Johnny. I asked him what he was doing in my house. He clearly said, "This is my house." I shifted my tone then and asked him gently, "Do you know that you are dead?" He replied with some alarm, "No! I am not dead!"

I asked him if he recognized anything in the house, he said no. I asked him if he knew me, and he said no. I asked him if he knew anyone who has been in his house lately. Again, he replied no. So, then I asked him how he got here. He replied, "I don't know," Johnny said the last thing he remembered was driving a car, and then he was just here. So, then I asked him if he'd seen a bright light, and he said sort of, but that it was really bright like daylight all the time. I told him it is time to go into the light, and that doing that will truly take him home. I asked him if that was okay, and he looked nervous. So, I informed him that I'm calling in special helper angels or guides to help him. He said okay.

I called out for a Divine and Sacred Guide who specialized in transforming Johnny into the light. I directed the guide to assist Johnny and take him to the best place for his highest transformation. Johnny and I both saw a woman come in, who was dressed like she was from the fifties or sixties. He asked, "Why is my mother here instead of at home?"

I answered him, "The world is more complicated than it seems." Then I also saw a Divine and Sacred Guide who immediately arrived. I asked Johnny to look to his left. Surprisingly, there was a second guide that Johnny recognized immediately. He went with both of them into the light. The noises in the house stopped.

My friend had listened to a struggling spirit person. She and Johnny talked things over, which created a positive outcome for both of them.

I used to live in the truly enchanted land of New Mexico. Rarely, in this day and age, do we humans ever have the opportunity to sit in meditation, outdoors, in absolute peace and quiet. We usually hear a plane or a motorcycle, an ambulance, or the neighbor's stereo, or even the wind. The desert offers a complete stillness that I have never experienced in any of my travels around the world.

One day I sat alone in the desert, miles out from the city and humankind. At first, I could not discern what was so different. I quickly realized that I could not hear a bird singing or even a breeze moving through—nothing. I closed my eyes and sighed the deep sigh that comes only with relief. I wanted to soak up this moment, so I settled into a meditative state. I have no awareness of the length of time that passed when I heard a sound: a deep, slow vibration or humming sound. As soon as I heard it, it stopped, then began again. I now know that I heard an electromagnetic frequency, the aliveness of this great planet . . . the Om.

I have never heard this again from the Earth. Occasionally, mentoring clients tell me they frequently hear an electromagnetic vibration coming from inside of living people. Some people are able to hear sounds, as their hands are on certain chakras of human and animal bodies. These sounds are only a portion of what might come through our auditory sense. Hearing the voice of spirit guides, angels, or your deceased family also falls into the sense. Music of all kinds can be heard, as well as the sounds of a certain moment in a client's past life.

"Weird, weird, it was just so weird." Energy practitioners all over the world are frequently saying that to themselves, as strange and wondrous experiences are happening during their energy work sessions. But no one is talking about it. Why is that? Is it because the practitioners try to ignore the odd occurrences because they cannot believe it themselves, or is it because no one taught them to acknowledge the magic of it all as the energy of healing is taking place? Listen for vibrational sounds as you participate with any modality of energy work and think about your answers to these questions:

1. Does the vibrational sound feel pleasant to you?
2. Is it chaotic or smooth?
3. Where is the exact location within your client that the particular sound is coming from?
4. Ask your Divine and Sacreds to tell you the exact meaning of the sound, or the exact location.

There is a whole world of intuitive information within sound waves coming from the living and the deceased, and seldom does anyone speak of it. Now you can listen for it as well.

Another Story of Listening

One afternoon, I stretched out to take an afternoon nap. The light on my large computerized thermostat began blinking. I had never seen it do that before, so I walked on by and lay down on the couch.

Then I clearly heard: "I am Sarah. I want to talk to you."

I sat up and responded telepathically, "Give me a moment so I can write this down for you." I gave her that direction because she is the deceased sister of my dear friend.

Sarah directed me to tell her sister, then she began her message: "I am sorry. I am at peace, but I am still sorry. I have done this before, and you were there. I created my own death. We go back so far together, and yes, times in the Middle East. We know each other from the depths of our souls. You have always been the most powerful. Every time, I learn a bit more from you.

"This life, I spent too much time hiding. You (her sister) hid from nothing! I see that now from this perspective. I have hidden many times before. It is so much easier, but now I have regrets. I could be a butterfly, but I stayed inside of a cocoon. Tell all the family I will blink a light so you know I'm there. Talk to me then. We all have things to say that need to be said. Tell everyone I rode the ferry away." Sarah turned toward me. "I made your light blink."

She then began to leave so I spoke out to her: "I am so happy that you found me, but I don't know how you ever did."

Sarah said with a bit of an attitude, "How could I not find you? You stick out like a sore thumb!"

Notice that I did not try to keep her talking. I quickly became the attentive listener to the message from my friend's sister.

Special Ways to Communicate with All Beings From All Realms

Communication is a general term of exchanging information. Intuitives recognize that they are receiving information in multiple ways that most people do not notice or do not acknowledge it as communication. Here are different ways to exchange information with beings from all realms, using clairaudience and telepathy.

Clairaudience

The spiritual term for hearing anything is clairaudience. I want to distinguish the difference between clairaudience and telepathy. Clairaudience is receiving sounds, such as voices or noises, that enter your ears and touch your eardrums. It is literally hearing messages from departed friends and relatives with their voices touching your eardrums just like listening to music or the TV. Clairaudience is possible, and is one pathway to communicate. Usually, it is an instant yelling of your name that wakes you up at 3:00 a.m. It could also be a loud thump in the next room to get your attention.

Telepathy

Usually when I question students, they realize they're receiving words or sentences leaping into their minds and not their ears. Then they find themselves sending words from their minds back to nonphysical beings. A description of telepathic communication is the transfer of thoughts and images back and forth between two living people or between the living and the deceased.

Once again, notice the importance of using clear, precise, descriptive words as you communicate with the deceased. Deliberately send out words and detailed, short, and to the point sentences. You must then stop yourself from thinking, just for a moment, to receive instant words or full thoughts that pop into your mind. This is truly the power of listening and communicating back and forth with the dead.

Telepathy also takes place among two or more deceased humans in this same manner. I have often woken in the middle of the night to hear multiple people whispering in my kitchen. I call out to them telepathically and command the following: "I can hear you. You must be quiet so I can sleep. Please talk to each other out in the yard, then meet me at 10:00 a.m. in the kitchen so we can talk it over."

Notice that there is no reason to become fearful. You are in charge, and the deceased will do as you ask if you are clear, and if you really mean what you say. And because they are real people, you must follow through with what you tell them. Do not tell them anything you cannot do, such as not showing up at 10:00 a.m. when you told them you would. When you do meet with them, you must listen telepathically to their wants and needs. Then take action to assist them. Listening will escalate your accuracy, which will greatly benefit the deceased and their living loved ones.

Besides receiving telepathic words or complete thoughts, you will often notice telepathic images of all sorts pop into your mind. These images may be scenes of the moment the spirit person died. They are often images of something the deceased has been yearning to tell someone, or anyone, who will listen. You may see tiny movies within your mind, or still pictures of a person, an object, buildings, land, or even a room. The dead will often say words, phrases, or speak in paragraphs as they quickly flash important images to get their point across to you.

You always need to be ready for all types of variations from the normal. There can be experiences with the deceased that are like tiny silent movies. And then there are instances like my experience with the "Jumping Jack Man." You just can't make this stuff up!

Physical Sensations in Your Own Body

The spirit person will often give you information through sensations in your own body. These bodily sensations can range from slight discomfort to severe pain. For example, you might experience a strange sensation of choking on water, or you might feel your chest painfully tighten, signaling that the spirit person died of a heart attack. You might also feel like you're limping or dragging one particular leg behind you. You clearly received evidence of how they died, or how they struggled while alive. There is no reason for you to suffer in any way. So, you must do the following:

Command your Divine and Sacred healer: "I received this information. It is not mine. Get it out of me now!"

What to Do When the Deceased Does Not Arrive to Communicate with Your Living Client

When you receive signals from the deceased, you only need to notice whatever pops into your awareness. But what should you do as a medium when the deceased never arrives to communicate with your living client?

My mentoring student told me that her client's deceased mother came in to communicate with her client. All went well, and the client was quite happy with the results. But then the client asked a very reasonable question: "Is my deceased father here? I want to speak to him too."

My student told me she looked all around and did not receive any sense that he was there. So, she told her client that he did not come forward. Slightly alarmed, the student told me she had no idea what to do when her living client burst into tears.

Deceased clients not coming forward actually happens quite frequently, so you need to be ready for the living client's deep disappointment. Here are steps that can be taken in these situations:

1. Inform the client that their deceased person did not make themselves present.
2. Tell the client that both of you will call out to the missing deceased person by name. Tell your client they can call out loud or in their mind.
3. Be honest and inform your client if the deceased arrived, or if the deceased still did not make themselves present.
4. If the deceased arrives, you can begin by asking why they did not immediately arrive for your client. Tell the client exactly what the deceased says.
5. If the deceased still has not come forward, tell your living client that you will be silent for a minute to direct questions to your Divine and Sacred Guides: "Tell me or show me now, exactly why (name of the deceased) did not appear for (name of your living client.)" Pause and take the pop of words or images and inform your client exactly what information comes to you about this situation.
6. Prepare to be surprised about why the deceased did not arrive. There is an uncountable number of explanations you might receive. It may be negative or positive, or at least understandable. The fact that the deceased is not arriving can also be a temporary situation.

Here are a few common explanations:

1. The person has just died and needs time to go through a healing process in the spirit realm that cannot be interrupted. In my experience, a three-month period of time is common.
2. The deceased is not yet aware that they have left their body.
3. The deceased is deeply focused on another issue and needs to understand something before coming to you.

Basically, state to your living client whatever your guides tell you. Explain that you directly consulted with your guides for an explanation.

Here is a touching story when the son did not appear:

My ninety-five-year-old client had outlived both her daughter and her son. Her deceased daughter always came through and was eager to talk to her mother. But her daughter would always turn to me with a frown and say, "I really don't want to talk to you, but Mother needs you to communicate." I telepathically told the deceased daughter that I understood and would do my best to use her exact words.

One day, my living client said, "Why doesn't my son ever come to see me?"

I told her honestly, "I truly have no idea. Let's call out to him together and see what happens."

As I said that to her, I had a strange image in my mind's eye. I was shown a tiny dot so far out into the Universe that it seemed like millions of miles away. We both called his name and asked him to come to his mother. The dot quickly grew larger until an extremely bright light glowed outward. In the center of this stunning brightness was a vague human form. I described this to my ninety-five-year-old client.

She responded to her son, "Where have you been, and why haven't you come to see me like your sister has?"

I repeated his words to her: "I was sent very far away from this Earth. I have been guided to travel very far away. I am on a specific path that I must take. This is the only time that I can come to speak with you. I will not be coming back for any other lifetimes to this Earth."

His mother said out loud to her son as tears flowed from her eyes, "You were always so special and so different. Thank you for coming such a long, long way for me."

I told her his image was fading and shrinking at the same time. I watched him leave as if he was being sucked backward and became a barely visible dot again. My client asked about him a couple of times after that. I checked, but I only saw his tiny pinpoint dot out among the stars. The next time my client asked about her son, I had to tell her that I could no longer even see the dot.

Many mediums who are developing their skills will quickly think they have failed to perceive a deceased person when, in fact, the deceased person simply did not come forward. Do not automatically think you have failed. Some deceased are evolving and leaving the Earth, and others are caught up in their own emotions while others are profoundly busy as if they are on a mission far, far away.

Chapter 7

Many Choices, Surprises, and Outcomes at the Time of Death

As a clinical hypnotherapist, I facilitated hundreds and hundreds of past-life regressions and Life Between Life (LBL) Regressions. LBLs are a hypnosis method created by Michael Newton in his book, *Journey of Souls*. As a student of Newton's, I will summarize his four-hour hypnotic process in these three steps:

1. The individual is guided into a past-life memory.
2. The individual goes through their death in that past life.
3. The individual continues into the memory of their life in the spirit realm before they were ever in a physical body.

These regression methods become very detailed. The living client is deliberately guided into the cause of their death in that past life. The client also remembers their experience of death, including the release from their physical body. In other words, I guided many people to remember and relive their death process, and I asked questions such as:

- What thoughts did you have in that last minute before leaving your physical body?
- What was it like to feel the release of your body?
- What did you understand in that moment?
- Where did you go after the release of a body?

- What were the next steps into nonphysical realms?
- What did you perceive as a soul in the nonphysical realms?

This aliveness we carry within us every day, is our eternal soul. The word "eternal" is key here. Your soul literally holds up your physical body. Your soul is what holds your personality, your quirks, and your characteristics, as well as your body. Your eternal soul carries what you have learned and what you did not learn. This soul information moves into our next life, and the next, and the next after that. It is our eternal soul that carries us forward. Our eternal soul:

- Contains energetic frequencies of all that has happened throughout our many past lives.
- Sends signals to our current body and mind, telling us what opportunities we have in this current life.
- Knows the next step in our personal development and sends us whispers of who we have been, and what we can learn, and who we can become.
- Has already had many precious experiences of dying throughout each lifetime.

Esther Hicks is a well-known author and channel of a nonphysical being called Abraham. This is an important teaching from Abraham, channeled by Esther Hicks:

"There are those who feel such fulfillment of life and such Connection to Source Energy, who understand that there is no separation between what is physical and non-physical; who understand that there is not even a lapse in consciousness, that 'death' is a matter of closing one's eyes in this dimension and literally opening one's eyes in the other dimension. And that, truly, is how all death is, no matter how it looks, up to that point."

Five Common Options in the Dying Process

I always tell people who take my courses that the nonphysical realms are much more complicated than life on Earth. We humans tend to describe the nonphysical in the same terms that we perceive the daily world around us. We shouldn't assume that the entire cosmos is structured the same as life on Earth. The Earth and life on this Earth is only one tiny speck of the whole cosmos. For example, I frequently hear people stating that at the time of death, everyone is greeted by their loved ones. That is simply not the case. Releasing the Earth experience and crossing over into the light seems to be a choice with many, many options along the way. Here are five of the most common options.

1. Some People are Greeted by Loved Ones, While Others Leave Alone

I, myself, was never greeted by anyone when I left my body. It didn't even occur to me until I returned from my near-death experience that I had no greeters. I simply shot out of my body with exhilaration, as if I were a joyful explorer heading off into new territory to discover whatever I discover. I had no cares . . . only an excited curiosity.

In truth, I have only personally met a few individuals who did not have anyone greet them. It seems more common to have a welcoming party. I have witnessed both experiences as I facilitated many people into their past lives, or their Life Between Lives in deep hypnotic regressions. (To learn more about this, read *Journal of the Soul*, and then *Destiny of the Soul* by Michael Newton.)

My grandma Marie, however, was always an extrovert and enjoyed parties. She is a lovely example of releasing her body to join a large gathering of deceased friends and family who adored her. Grandma Marie was in her process to pass on. My father, grandma's son-in-law, said that he would stay with her while everyone took a break in the cafeteria. Later, he told us that after everyone left, Grandma raised her arm and pointed her finger across the room and up toward the ceiling. Very slowly, she pointed and counted. He kept track as she pointed and counted to fourteen. She then became quiet.

He said, "Marie, what are you counting?"

She replied with a tiny huff, and then in a whisper, "Well, everyone who's here, of course!"

Then he asked, "Well, tell me who is here for you."

She began to say people's names. My father kept track of the number of names that she listed. She stopped at fourteen names. My father said he knew many of the people she named, but some he did not know. She always did love a party!

VITAL POINT

> Death is not the end of everything. It is the beginning of the next experience.

2. We Sometimes Choose to Die or Stay a While Longer

We often seem to have some control over the moment we discard the physical body. My precious grandma Marie, who I mentioned a few moments ago, seemed to hold on to life even when it seemed impossible for her to remain alive. One of the nurses told my parents that she must be waiting on someone. We knew she was waiting for her son. The family did not plan for her wheelchair-bound, disabled son to travel such a long way to see her. He had experienced a massive stroke, leaving him unable to walk and unable to talk, but he knew exactly what was going on around him.

My family immediately reached out to my aunt, stating that Marie must be waiting for him to arrive. Plans were quickly made. A couple of days later, he was pushed into his mother's room. Neither Marie nor her son could speak out loud anymore. They communicated telepathically as they held each other's hands. She crossed over just a short time later. My grandmother Marie extended her death for weeks, waiting for her son.

I described yet another situation with a grieving mentoring client. While some people in their process hold on to their body, waiting for an important person to arrive, many others often need to be alone in order to leave their body. If there is a group of family members around, or even if it's one person, they often keep holding on to not disappoint their living people.

It's the living people who are so horribly distraught and say, "Oh no! He or she passed, and we weren't there! We shouldn't have left to go eat! We failed our dying family member!" The living usually have no idea that it was very beneficial to the one who is dying. Lots of clients over the years have told me they were with their person twenty-four hours a day, and somebody talked them into going down to the cafeteria to get lunch. Suddenly, their loved one passed moments after they left. Over many years, I have explained to many, many people that their devotion to their loved one and never leaving their side was holding them to this earthly existence. Now many people tell me the deep relief I've given them by telling them their loved one was waiting for them to leave their side so they felt free enough to release their body and move on.

The following story is about love between two people. That love continued for many decades until they had to part at the time of death. This is a very small part of their story.

A Beautiful Love Story

I am so happy to share this precious story from a distant part of my own family.

Grandma was our family's caregiver. She took care of everyone and cooked for anyone who entered the house. She took care of bills, etc. Grandma had her stroke eight years ago. Even after the stroke, Grandpa had to run everything by her or she would get upset. Everything he did was with her in mind. Grandpa had to do everything for her, but in her eyes, she was caring for him still.

Not all of those years were at death's door, but the family called hospice on a few different occasions, and they were very surprised she didn't check out. Brenda, their daughter, worked at a hospice and had never seen anything like it. She said that Grandma should have died a few times.

"She would stop breathing, and then visibly shake herself awake and look proud of herself for coming back."

Overall, they are a beautiful example of love. I think she did stay, feeling he needed her, and he was afraid to make her feel otherwise. He always would say that he wasn't making her stay but that he didn't want her to feel like he wanted her to go. Whenever she seemed as if she was leaving, he would cry and start rubbing her arm, not always telling her he needed her, sometimes just things like, "You are my baby." But to us other family members, it was apparent that she felt he needed her.

He just refused to tell her she could go. Their connection was too strong. His daughters started telling the medical staff it was their tie holding her here. It's such a great love story, and it's what held her here. But I don't think it was a selfish act on his part, and it wasn't all him. Grandma thought he needed her, and he didn't want her to think otherwise, so he wouldn't tell her to go. He was so visibly happy every time she came back.

He spent eight years taking care of Grandma around the clock and never complained about it. My aunt described being with my grandparents during their last moments together. My aunt said, "I was sitting on the other side of the bed from Dad when I said, 'Mama, are you seeing the angels?' At that moment, my father said, 'Baby, it's okay to go home.' Within seconds, her heart stopped . . . seconds."

My aunt went on to say, "This is a story that illustrates the bond between human spirits. A bond that ties. A bond that needs closure so the spirit can leave."

3. We Can Prolong Leaving the Body Even After Death

Elizabeth is a physician. Because she is so compassionate, she has sat with many of her patients going through their death process. For years now, she has stated that many people simply leave their body immediately upon death and the body completely feels dead, looks dead, and can be clinically declared as deceased. She then describes a different situation. She has witnessed a very different experience. Sometimes a clinically dead body continues to feel and look very alive, to the point that you expect the person to sit up and talk. She states that they remain very present in the body even though she must declare them dead because they meet all the criteria of a dead body.

My friend Eric and I had a similar experience of the deceased remaining in the body after being pronounced dead. Here is the story of our experience as Eric's father died.

The phone rang late that night. I expected the call. Eric's shaky voice told me his father was near death, and would I be able to come and sit with both of them? "I'm on my way," I said.

Just a week ago, in that same hospital room, I saw the spirit of a young man standing at his father's bedside. The spirit person stood staring down at Bob with a great deal of interest and caring. The spirit man seemed, in fact, fascinated with Eric's father. I described to Eric the young man who stood by his father's bed.

Although I knew that his father was a heart-transplant recipient many years ago, I did not put two and two together. I was a close friend of Eric's but had never met his father, so I had no relationship with Bob. I described the spirit man to Eric. He said they never knew the name of the heart donor, but he confirmed that I was describing the correct age and known characteristics of the donor. The young spirit-man remained deeply focused and attentive to Eric's father. He constantly stood next to the hospital bed and seemed unaware of other living people coming and going.

A few days later, I again sat in the intensive care room with his father. I encouraged Eric to take a break and go to the cafeteria to eat, assuring him I would not leave his father. So, Eric left the room. A little while later, I thought I might as well try to intuitively talk to Eric's father. I asked his father what he needed. Did he need assistance to heal, or assistance for his transition? Instantly, a large golden male spirit guide appeared between me and Eric's father.

It happened so fast that I jumped back in my chair. This powerful spirit guide held his hand with the palm toward me in a gesture that said, "Stop. Stand back!" The spirit intuitively said to me in a stern, commanding voice: "Do not interfere with this."

I felt a strong, physical push against my chest, so I immediately removed the energy of my question from Bob and pulled back into my own body. When Eric returned to the room, I told him exactly what had happened. We discussed his father's process. I then reminded Eric of my own mother's dying process. A ring of twelve spirit guides had encircled her and sternly directed me not to intrude during my mother's dying process. Eric and I compared notes. We knew something profoundly sacred had happened with my mother five years before and was now happening with his father.

Eric's father passed on that night. There was no pulse, and yet, the nurse was not sure that he was dead. She said she just could not tell if he was deceased. The body of Eric's deceased father did not change in appearance at all. In fact, the nurse called in another nurse to get a second opinion. As Eric and I stood there, both nurses talked it over. When they both finally decided that he had passed, my friend and I sat in the room, quietly meditating for another hour or so after the nurses left. When we opened our eyes again, Eric looked at his father and was startled.

"My father still seems to be in his body!"

My dearest friend took the words right out of my mouth. The deceased man continued to look very alive.

If you have been with someone during their death transition, you will know that usually the face and the body tend to sink in, and the color drains from the skin, and a complete stillness surrounds the body. Bob did not change in those ways, nor in any manner after he was declared dead. Physicians and nurses have both experienced that occasionally a deceased body does not appear or feel like 100 percent of the soul energy has left the physical body. So, was this a choice not to leave his body completely? Was he surprised at his passing and so chose to stay attached to the physical? Was he confused and thought he was still alive?

There is another piece to this mysterious story. At Bob's funeral, Eric and I overheard many people talking about how good Bob looked and how he still seemed alive. Did his young heart donor remain with his donated heart, still refusing to release it? Might that have caused this unusual situation of my friend's father feeling and looking as if he were still alive even after being pronounced dead three days earlier? I do not know the answers to these questions, but I do know that many of us witnessed something very different, and yet, very special and sacred. Do we have a choice to stay attached to some degree to our body, or choose to instantly release the physical body?

There was something very special going on in this particular death transformation. The young male spirit was not causing harm. In fact, his presence seemed extraordinarily special but also complex. I feel deeply that I received that powerful "Do not interfere!" due to the heart that both of them shared. While I could not hear any spoken words, it seemed as if a private conversation was going on between an old man who held the spirit person's heart in his chest, and the young man who had given it away over twenty-five years ago.

4. Many Have Near-Death Experiences (NDE)

Here is a story from one of my students who had a traumatic experience that caused his death and then came back to life.

A Practitioner Shares a Story: A Healing Plumber Clearing Away Your Shit

When I was thirty-three, I was electrocuted from a commercial hot-water heater with 480 volts! After my electrocution, I encountered these light beings in my near-death experience. I can assure you, you do not get to expire! You get to transition into a form of light . . . when it's your time, of course! But I personally can't wait. I have been a plumber for over twenty years. Now I am a spiritual healer. A plumber getting electrocuted! The irony . . . what a shocker. Now I can help people to understand the Light Force within.

My experience: I was going through this white tunnel of light. My feelings exploded out into pure emptiness. Floating in light made of love. I felt I was a droplet of this white, plasmic, liquid light that was in a spaceless oneness with it all. After that, I can confidently say I know what the Light Force really is about! I got to meet the big G-O-D.

I felt fearlessly free from all the senseless living beings. I was floating in this forever oceanlike place of love. And the most beautiful part of this G-O-D was this noise. This sound of light! A loud, roaring symphony blowing this powerful wind of

> frequency and vibration! I was feeling, floating, and suspended. I was just *there*.
>
> As a plumber/healer, I'm always trying to figure out the internal problems. Like if there is a blockage, or an imbalance throughout the facility or the patient. They both have channels that either hold on or that flows. Is it all working properly? Whether it's plumbing or healing, there is a force behind it all. I've learned there are different kinds of people in this world to make it go around. Different kinds of people with different kinds of problems. These problems can be from a karmic or a traumatic event. Tensions are from your intentions. Generally, that is your life condition . . . your life force!
>
> My Boy, the Buddha, told me, "If you light a lamp for someone, it will also brighten your path." And JC once said to me, "Glow wherever you go, my guy, and let the light reflect the world around you. And that is all, my friend."
>
> — Sam Kim

My own near-death experience always seems like an amazing, unexpected gift. I am deeply aware that I have never heard anyone else describe a near-death experience as a gift. In fact, many people suffer terribly after a near-death experience. They suffer for many different reasons. Some feel cheated that they were jolted back to the Earth. Others feel so different that they struggle to step back into their "normal life," or their normal daily patterns. Others are left with a detached feeling, no longer part of the Earth-plane existence. Some constantly compare their Earth life with the wonderous sensations of the spirit realms. These are only a few of the more common experiences that these people describe.

I want to give you some more information that I hope you will really take into your heart. Even though I have worked at this deep level for many years, and with many clients, while using past-life regression hypnotherapy, my own near death was truly a different experience. If you have had a near-death experience, you will never be the same. I have never been the same. If one of your loved ones, or even a distant friend, has had this experience, they will be different. That being said, there are still many details I want you to notice . . .

We are not meant to remain the same after we experience our own death and then return. We have been given a phenomenal view of the world beyond this physical experience. We have experienced and received a phenomenal level of knowledge. Now you can:

- Share your story with anyone who will listen.
- Assist others who are afraid, or even terrified.
- Become known as the person in your community who died and came back.
- Become known as the person who will share their story with others so they will have an idea of what to expect at their time of death.
- The most important: Become the person who actively guides others during their precious transition called death.

You really are in charge of yourself. Stop yourself now from all struggles about this experience and the physical world around you. I want you to now practice seeing everyone and everything that is happening in the world in a different way. I'm asking you to never be repelled by people or their actions again. I ask that you become fascinated. You are witnessing not just horrible people sometimes doing horrible things, but you can now observe everyone as eternal souls trying and trying to learn and develop. You are observing them in the depths of emotions including hate, sorrow, grief, loss, and love.

VITAL POINT

> We are not meant to be the same after a near-death experience. We are meant to become the teacher who removes the fear of death.

Everyone's soul is learning. Many souls are new souls that have quite a long way to go to reach the level of awareness that you are arriving at now. Your near-death experience is a profound training that only a very small percent of the human population receive. You now have a choice.

You can focus on how horrible the world seems, how depressed you are, and how much you want to get out of here, *or* you can step into your position of receiving a precious learning and guide others in their lives. It truly means you have been selected to be a teacher and guide for others. It is your choice to make. You can dislike and sometimes hate the people on this Earth, or experience yourself and everyone else as eternal souls learning, and learning, and learning some more.

Yes, it's true . . . you will never be the same. And that can be a beautiful thing if you allow it to be.

5. Walk-Ins are Real

Some readers have never heard the term "walk-ins" before. Some have heard the term but do not want to know what it is. And some of you have read the most famous book about it, *Strangers Among Us: Enlightened Beings from a World to Come* by Ruth Montgomery. Basically, it is yet another experience that might happen at the moment of death.

A very long time ago, this person was kind enough, and intrigued enough, to explore her traumatic life event with me. This woman, who I will call Susie Q, shared with me that she is a walk-in. Here is Susie Q's story as I recall it . . .

Susie Q's Story

Susie Q was horribly depressed and had purposely overdosed on prescription medications. She was found unconscious. An ambulance was called, and her life was saved . . . or was it?

She told me she could not continue under the hateful control of her husband. She was literally imprisoned in an isolated house far from any neighbors. She had no car, and the husband did not allow a phone to be installed in the house. Her depression was so severe that she simply could not see another way out except to kill herself.

One day, she overdosed, and he found her nearly dead. The ambulance staff tried to keep her alive, and then the hospital emergency staff tried as well.

When she woke, she found herself in a psychiatric hospital. First, she was amazed that she felt so much relief. She asked me, "How could I have been so relieved to see that I was locked in a psychiatric unit and not in my own house?"

I truthfully said, "I have no idea!"

Then Susie Q went on to describe the many changes that she immediately felt. She said, "I knew I was not the same person. I was thinking differently. I could see I had many options. I was not a victim. I could not even find any feelings of being a victim. I looked at my husband and did not see a controlling bully. I saw an afraid young man who did not know what to do. I looked at him and said, 'I am not coming back!' "

As she spoke, I too realized she was not describing the same person she was before. The change was phenomenal. It seemed as if nothing about this person was the same. She was a different human in the same body. I looked into her eyes, and I saw and felt a different person looking out at me. This newer version of Susie Q is confident and not a victim. This new version seemed to know her power and her confidence.

Briefly, the concept of a walk-in is this: At the time of death, the soul rises upward and out of the physical body. As that soul leaves, another soul literally leaps into the body. It seems as if one soul rises upward and another soul lowers down and fills the space within the human body. The exchange seems to be immediate, which keeps the physical body alive as if there was no death. But here is an entirely different situation of leaving one body and merging into another.

A friend of mine told me about the death of her family member, Aunt Janie. At the exact moment the soul of Aunt Janie rose up and left her body, a distraught family member named Angela threw herself over the top of the body. Aunt Janie had no intention of taking over Angela's body, but Angela became a "walk-in."

Even as early as the funeral, Angela seemed very different to the family. She became very involved with the belongings of the dead family member. She asked if she could have the clothes of the deceased and began wearing them right away. Her mannerisms changed, closely resembling Aunt Janie, whom they had just lost.

Three months later, Angela became ill with the same disease that caused the death of their family member. The deceased person probably had no idea that her death had just happened, and she had no idea that, as she rose up to leave her body, she had slipped into Angela's physical body that was draped on top of her. Undoubtedly, Aunt Janie was simply trying to be herself.

The death transition is a sacred moment that can always be shared together. As you hold the hand of your loved one, do not become afraid that this will happen to you. Hold their hand and speak to them. Continue to be an integral part of this blessed experience, but do not interfere with the soul's transition.

The alive and vibrant soul energy, beyond a doubt, is rising upward and out of the physical body at the time of death. Give them room to rise up to the blessed light. This is such an important yet unknown point that I now discuss in my course. My hope is that you gently pass this on to others if they are overcome with grief, but do not cause any fear for the loved ones. This will allow the person in their dying process to rise up and be free to go to the light.

Another important point to recognize is this: The deceased human being that slides into a different living body, could be a dead person of any level of awareness. In other words, the deceased person who took over someone's alive body could have been a criminal, or a confused drug addict, or any type of struggling deceased human.

However, the stories that I hear about people who know they are walk-ins, feel they are now filled with a human who is an advanced, spiritually aware being with greater insight than the original person had ever had before. Many walk-ins have a more profound wisdom and knowing about life, which then leads them to helping the world in a deeper way.

Chapter 8

Guiding People in Their Dying Process

I listened and witnessed each person reliving their death experiences while facilitating past-life regressions and Life Between Life regressions. Each one was a sacred experience. But the most powerful and meaningful experience of all is to assist someone who is releasing their current body from their current life and to do your best to guide them toward a positive pathway for their soul. As you read, I ask you to notice the different steps, methods, and guidance used to assist each person in their unique moment of passing.

A friend gave me permission to share a precious experience she had with her mother.

A Practitioner Shares a Story

> I want to share this with you . . . This past Friday night, my mother passed away. I was there with her all day as her soul was transitioning. I was her death doula, coaching her, calming her, reminding her where she came from and where her soul was returning to. We sang together. It was a surreal experience. There is something so powerful in witnessing the disengagement of body and soul. So spiritual . . . so sacred. What an honor to be in the mindset to guide and escort her soul in this way.
>
> I feel like I never really knew my mother, and that's a strange feeling. As she was being prepared for burial, I sat with

her body as her soul hovered. I heard myself saying, 'Mommy, I look forward to getting to know you now.' How poignant that it's only now, through death and in soul state, that I can connect with her and get to know her. I recognized on a very deep and meaningful level that all was exactly how it was meant to be. I understood how I chose this journey and all the lessons to be learned. It is through her shadows and through childhood pain and trauma that I was encouraged to find myself, to reconnect with my soul, to remember who I am, and to reach higher consciousness. It was a divine plan, stunningly orchestrated to perfection.

At the burial, I honored the body that contained her soul for the seventy-six years of her life—the body that was the channel that brought my soul to Earth. I got to thank her for agreeing to give birth to me. I am here today because of her agreement, our contract.

It's hard to lose a mother. So many contradicting emotions and memories surface as I process. I honor them all. We've journeyed together in this lifetime, my mother and I, and we've come full circle. To recognize this is such a gift and a blessing!

And so, I moved from resentment to acceptance, to compassion, to forgiveness, to gratitude, and to so much love and respect . . . not only toward my mother, but toward myself as well."

— G.G.

We humans are known for hanging on to our bodies and prolonging the death process. I want to emphasize that the stories you just read, and the story you are about to read, are beautiful examples of three processes that occur for the medium becoming the healer:

1. Mediums can be active healers, assisting people to make the best choices as they release the body and move on to the best place for their transition into Light and Love.
2. The medium healer can astral project from the other side of the world to come to the aid of someone struggling to release their body.
3. The medium can bring profound levels of healing to a relationship between a deceased person and an alive person who is struggling and delaying their dying process.

This is the story of my colleague's auntie lingering for over a week, and no one could understand why she was not making her transition. Please note that at the time, I was located in the US and my colleague, her auntie, and her family were all located in Europe during this process. My colleague's auntie and I were communicating telepathically.

Colleague: "My Auntie is going through much the same thing that my other relative went through. It is my auntie. Cancer is so cruel. It could be any day now."

TZ: "Tell me her full name please, and I will check to see how I might help her in her transition. But I will only do this if it feels right to you, and I will also ask your auntie for permission too."

(My colleague told me her auntie's name.)

TZ: "I asked your auntie for permission to see if I could help her with her transition."

Auntie: "Yes, indeed."

TZ: "How are you doing, and how do you feel?"

Auntie: "I feel very heavy, and I feel like I cannot get my breath."

TZ: "I am calling in assistance to bring you more comfort right now. I am calling in a Divine and Sacred Guide who specializes in you, and to assist you now, and to assist you in every way for your transition. I want you to look around and find the most brilliant, brightest being that is there with you now."

(She immediately lifted her arm and reached out to that being. This angelic being reached out to her at the same time. They touched their fingertips together. Auntie's spirit soul instantly sat up but then her spirit laid back down into her physical body.)

Auntie: "I am not quite ready, but now I know what to do."

(She did not feel like she was carrying emotional baggage. She had seemed quite ready but stopped and lay back into her body.)

Auntie: "I am waiting to see someone."

(She did not tell me who, so I asked my colleague.)

Colleague: "Her husband, David? He passed sixteen years ago. He was her one and only true love. Her sons and both of her daughters-in-law are here with her. We know she is ready. She was ready last week when she was able to speak clearly to us. She has everything in order and has said goodbye to her sons. It's this limbo that has gone on for a week now that is so upsetting."

TZ: "Auntie, are you waiting on your husband?"

Auntie: "Yes, but I do not see him."

TZ: "I want you to call out his name and then look all around for him."

(I suddenly saw her husband, but he was standing way back away from her.)

Auntie's Husband: "I am standing back because she was so good and so special that I often felt I did not deserve her."

TZ to Husband: "Please move forward and toward her, because she needs you now."

(He moved very close to her right side.)

TZ to Colleague: "Does this make any sense to you that he would be hesitant to approach your Auntie?"

Colleague: "Oh, yes. He was a lovable rogue . . . Tina! She just passed over! I am shaking. I truly believed you helped her! My heart is pounding!"

TZ: "Oh my . . . she was simply waiting for him. I am so happy to help your auntie, her husband, you, and everyone in your family."

Notice that Auntie crossed over as soon as I asked her deceased husband to stand next to her, where she could clearly see him. That is all she was waiting for.

My Family's Story

Betty has been my ex-mother-in-law for many decades now, but here we are, still together in her living room. I reminded Betty that I have known her since I was in the fifth grade.

She looked directly at me and said in a whispering voice, "We have gone through some rough times, haven't we?"

I said, "We sure have."

She was still, with her eyes closed for a few minutes. She slowly opened her eyes and said, "I saw Jesus a few times. He was standing there." She pointed to the floor a few feet in front of her. "He had really long, very dark hair. He was wearing a white robe and a brown sash. He didn't say anything. He just stood there. He had a large light behind him. He showed me something like a big card that opened like a book. His picture was on one side of the card and the other side was black. Maybe the black is hell. I think he's telling me that I'm going to hell."

I gently responded, "If he was telling you that you are going to hell, he would not show you his picture on the other page of the book. He is showing you that you have a choice. He is showing you his image and his light. He wants you to choose him and the light and not to go to the black."

She was quiet for a moment, and then said, "Yes, I think that is right." Then she said, "You know, there are not many people that I can talk to about these things."

I said, "Yes, that is sure true."

I heard my son chuckling in the kitchen. She died soon after our talk.

I sat in the pew, looking all over the church for Betty. I didn't see her anywhere. At other funerals, I see the deceased standing next to each person standing in front, speaking to the audience, or I see the deceased moving super fast all around the room. Sometimes I see the deceased standing in front of different individuals that have come to their funeral. They stand in front of them, trying to communicate even though their funeral is happening at that moment.

I kept looking for Betty and finally saw her sitting in the pew next to her son, my ex-husband. She had lived like a recluse, so she would never stand in front of everyone. As the service continued, she finally went over and stood next to her grandson, then slowly stood at different places with people in the first couple of rows but didn't try to talk to anyone. And then I saw something I'd never seen before. I watched my ex-mother-in-law stand at the head of her own casket. She slowly leaned over and kissed the forehead of her body. I heard her words, thanking her body for doing so well.

In all my life, I had never observed a spirit person do that before. She returned to the pew and sat down with her son. She then faded away.

About a week later, I was nearly asleep when she rushed down the hallway and came to the side of my bed. She was terribly anxious but did not speak to me. So, I said telepathically to her, "Remember, Jesus showed you to go to him and the brightest light." She instantly lifted straight upward through the ceiling, and just as she flew through the ceiling, there was a super loud pop like the ceiling broke open, and then she was gone.

I later asked my guides about her actions. They said, "For a week, she has been going around to be with her family and friends. She had just come from seeing her son, your ex-husband. Then she went to say goodbye to her grandson, your son. She suddenly felt a great rush to go, but she came to you just before leaving the Earth plane. She needed you to remind her that she was not going to hell."

I watched her lift upward through my bedroom ceiling.

My Friend Shares a Story

During COVID, my biological father (whom I had only known for four years) was diagnosed with pancreatic cancer. He was given less than a year to live. He had an operation, which didn't make things any easier. Nine months later, he was hospitalized, and if we wanted to see him, we had to stay with him in the room and not leave (because of COVID). If we left, we were not allowed back in. We didn't have anywhere to sleep. We had to rely on nurses to bring us food and drinks. We were exhausted but couldn't bring ourselves to leave him.

At this point, he was sedated for the most part, and very restless. On the fourth day, he was moved to a hospice suite. This is when Tina reached out to me. She knew something was wrong. Over text, I explained to Tina that my father had another daughter who was only seventeen and didn't know what to do. I was supporting her the best way I knew how. I had never been in this kind of situation before. Tina told me, "Tell your sister to say goodbye to her father. Tell him it's okay, and that she will be okay. I will speak to my guides and help him too."

Tina got right back to me and said, “I help people when their family member is close to crossing over. Even if he’s unconscious now, or in the near future, please say everything to him that you want or need to say. And say it out loud. Science has found that people still hear everything even when they are unconscious or in a coma. Think about this as a healing for yourself as well.”

At 6:00 a.m., I sat down with his daughter and told her what Tina had told me. She agreed. I made sure that everyone (four other family members), were out of his room to give his seventeen-year-old daughter the privacy she needed. He passed at 6:35 a.m.

A Practitioner Shares a Story

I was meeting with Brandi for a mentoring session. She began the session by quickly describing how her client’s mother was nearing her death process, and she was trying to help. As she sat at the older woman’s bedside, the grandmother was talking out loud, but she was not making any sense because the woman had been diagnosed with dementia. My client Brandi, began to describe this moment in more detail. She said that as the older woman slowly babbled, clear thoughts were leaping into my client’s mind. She said it felt like the clear words were coming from the dying woman. My client was convinced that she was failing as an intuitive and was struggling to understand what was happening.

I explained that literally two things were happening here at the same time: the older woman was talking out loud but not making any sense, but at the same time, my mentoring client was receiving not only individual words but also full sentences that leaped into her mind. These clear words were coming from the grandma's soul energy and not her brain struggling under dementia. I then asked Brandi to direct a question to her own guides.

I said, "Ask your Sacred Divines this: Was I truly hearing the clear statements from (the dying woman)?" She received a strong "Yes."

We then proceeded to take some first steps to assist the grandmother in her transition process. I directed her to invite Divine and Sacred Guides who specialize in (dying person's full name) transformation. She noticed that a very special guide appeared.

I said, "Ask this guide, 'Are you truly at the Divine and Sacred level?' "

"Yes."

I then suggested for her to ask this specialist, "What does (grandmother's name) need now to assist her in her transformation?"

Suddenly, Brandi looked very distressed and blurted out, "This is a very sacred time. What if I am interfering and not helping her at all?"

My response was, "Directly ask your guides right now if you are interfering with this woman's death process."

She hesitantly said she received a "No."

I then suggested, "Ask your guides this: 'Am I able to help (elderly woman's name) with her struggles in her dying process?' "

She heard, "Yes."

I directed my client to notice the elderly woman now and notice if she was struggling in any way.

"Yes, she has anxiety rushing out from her abdomen."

I asked Brandi, on the elderly woman's behalf, to direct her specialty guides with these words: "Please remove and heal the anxiety within her body now."

Brandi witnessed a profound calm come over this dying woman.

I said, "The calm you are sensing now is not an interference with her process. You just helped her to deeply relax and feel at peace."

She replied, "This is Holy!" When she said that, with so much awareness, it felt so special that I began to cry.

The fact that Brandi was so concerned about interfering with a "Holy Process" told me how sincere, careful, and thoughtful she would always be as a healing medium for the dying and for the deceased.

— Brandi Zorzy
www.brandizorzy.com

Assisting the Dying and Their Loved Ones

Notice that the stories in this chapter are very different from each other, and yet, very similar. Remember, each person you assist is still an individual, with individual life experiences, and individual levels of awareness. For some, the focus could be their fear of dying. Others could be extremely confused, unaware, and some are completely and consciously aware. And others are holding back in hopes of resolving unfinished issues, unsaid concerns, and sometimes secrets.

Each of these stories are meaningful examples of how to guide the dying into a healing. But just as valuable and just as important, healings take place for the living as well. These very different pathways bring relief and a release for everyone involved. Say all the unsaid things to the dying. It will bring healing and will release the heavy burdens for everyone, alive or deceased.

Key Steps to Communicate with a Person in Their Death Process

Notice that the true life-and-death stories above involve one of more of the following steps:

1. First, become an excellent listener. Speak, then pause to listen and receive. If they are awake, you can discuss things out loud.
2. If they are unconscious, speak to them telepathically.
3. If you are not a friend or family, then verbally or intuitively inform the dying who you are. Then ask the dying person for permission to assist them. Receive the "pop" of yes or no. Honor the "no," if that's what you get from them, but try again later that day or the following days. Sometimes a "no" is only for that moment but not forever.
4. If you receive permission, then ask one question at a time (verbally or telepathically), then pause to receive the pop of words, thoughts, or images.
5. Slowly ask questions or make statements such as:
    - What are your thoughts today?
    - What is your body signaling to you?
    - Are you feeling worried?
    - What are you worried about?
    - Tell me what things you are wondering about.
    - Are you waiting for someone?
    - What kind of help do you want now?
    - Are you seeing your loved ones?
    - Do you see Angels or Guides who are here to help you?
    - What are these guides telling you?

6. When you hear that it is the right time, telepathically or aloud, direct the dying person to connect with the guide or loved ones who have come for them.
    - Look around and find the brightest loving helper that is here just for you now.
    - Talk things over with this loving helper.
    - Ask questions to your spirit helper now.
    - Ask your deceased loved ones if it's time for you to go.
    - Ask your guide if it is time for you to go with them.
7. Be an accurate bridge of communication between the living and the dying person. Communicate to the living exactly what the dying person said or has shown you. Say exactly what you receive verbally, telepathically, or in images, even if it makes no sense to you. Never interpret what you receive, just inform everyone.
8. At the same time, you are also communicating with your own personal Divine and Sacred specialty guides, so you are not working alone in this process. Ask many questions to constantly receive guidance as you assist the living and the dying. Do not do this level of work alone. Work together.
9. Ask all the family members to say everything to the dying that they want or need to express. Tell them, "Do not hold anything back." Saying important issues or unfinished concerns out loud deeply and forever helps the living and the dying.

VITAL POINT

Allow yourself to become the healer, the listener, the knowledgeable one and the trusted one.

Two Tips to Protect Yourself as You Guide Others

The nonphysical realms are much more complicated than the physical realm. It is profoundly important that the healing medium constantly remains vigilant of their own safety. A person who is new to mediumship frequently leaves themselves vulnerable to the complications of the nonphysical world.

Here are two valuable tips to take care of yourself with nonphysical beings.

Tip 1: Never Take a Deceased Person to the "Gates of Heaven."

Do not even imagine doing this! One of my students was so happy to tell me that he finally perceived a deceased person. He also realized that the dead person had not crossed over. So, he thought he was truly helping when he reached out and took her hand, then lifted upward, took her to the gates of heaven, and handed her over to a guide.

After he told me his story, he then desperately declared, "I became so weak and exhausted that I was in bed for days! I don't understand why I was so drained!"

I replied, "You were not just imagining this. When you took her hand and rose upward to the "gates of heaven," you were literally only one step away from death yourself! This is why you could not get out of bed for so many days."

Tip 2: Constantly Communicate with Your Guides

Constant communication with your specialty guides ensures you are assisting each individual in the most perfect way. It is the specialty guides that escort the deceased into the nonphysical realms, not you!

Most people report that they are terrified of their own death, and either block it from their thoughts or become preoccupied with it. The dying process is actually a birthing process. If only people could perceive this in its truest nature. We are giving birth to a less dense form of ourselves, a celestial form of a higher, more refined nature. We are releasing the heavy burden of a physical body and the thick burden of emotions and negative thoughts.

VITAL POINT

> You are already one with the nonphysical realms. Remember, sense, feel, and know that you are a nonphysical being more than a human body. Knowing this opens a massive doorway to understanding, connecting, and interacting with the nonphysical world.

Astral Project When You Cannot Get There in Time

Astral projection and remote-viewing are the more technical terms of how we can instantly travel across great distances to be with family, or a friend who is about to pass.

Over the years, so many people have told me how they suffer because they did not get to their loved one in time to talk to them. They go on to tell me their loved one was already in a coma. Please hear me now! You are not too late. It has been shown over and over again that someone in a coma, or so close to leaving their body that they can no longer open their eyes or speak out loud, still hear everything! So, say everything that you wish you had said a long time ago.

People who are near death are floating back and forth from outside of their body, and then floating back into their physical body. In this very fluid state of being, we are able to see and communicate with them as we project ourselves to them. It will be as if you are physically there with them. To the dying, it's as if you are physically there with them.

VITAL POINT

> Anyone and everyone can astral project to be with their loved one when you cannot get there in time! You do not need to be a medium. It will *always* feel as if you are imagining it. Do it anyway if the need arises.

I was in deep silence as I followed a path along a small river. Suddenly, Cathy's name leaped into my mind. I met Cathy in the nursing home where my sister lived. We quickly became good friends. Cathy had a severe stroke that left her immobile and in a wheelchair for many years of her life. While the stroke left her body frozen in contorted shapes that created an extremely crippled body, it did not interfere with her brain or her thought processes. She always said the funniest things and threw in a few curse words until I could not stop laughing.

I knew she was very ill and was in intensive care. She had called me five days ago to tell me she was now transferred to intensive care. When her name leaped into my mind, I noticed the feelings of her struggling.

Telepathically, Cathy said, "I have had it."

Even though I received those words quite clearly, it felt to me like she was not sure what to do about it at that moment. I stopped walking and looked out across the flowing water of the river. It was around 3:30 p.m. I communicated with my Divine and Sacred Guides in this way:

TZ: Tell me or show me now, is Cathy struggling to leave her body?

Guides: "Yes."

TZ: "Is it the right time now for her to release her physical body?"

Guides: "Yes."

TZ: "Would it be helpful if I inform Cathy on how to leave her physical body?"

Guides: "Yes."

I focused on Cathy to astral project to her. I projected my focus to her and extended my energy field toward her. I was instantly standing at her bedside. I was truly there with her. First, I told her this is Tina Zion, and that I was going to help her release her body. I said I must know if that feels right to you or not. I quickly received a clear undeniable, "Yes!" Since I received her permission, I continued.

I directed her in this way. "First, notice how light your body feels. Let yourself feel lighter and lighter. As you feel lighter, I want you to notice how light you are becoming . . . Notice now that you feel like you're lifting upward. As you release your body, I want you to look in all directions around you. Find the brightest light of all the lights around you. When it feels right to you, continue to lift upward and go to the brightest light of all."

I opened my eyes and looked at the river, and then I looked at the time. It was Thursday at 3:30 p.m. The next day, I was told that she had died the previous day. When I asked, "About what time yesterday did she pass?" After a moment of thought, her family said, "It was around 3:30."

The next night, I was just about to fall asleep when the name Cathy jumped into my mind. I opened my eyes, and there she stood next to my bed. She exclaimed quite loudly, "Look at me! I'm standing up!"

I responded, "Cathy, you look great!"

She confidently responded, "I know I do!"

I laughed and laughed. Cathy always made me laugh.

At the funeral, I sat with some other friends in the church. About fifteen minutes into the service, I realized I hadn't even thought about seeing Cathy like I always see the deceased during their funeral service. As discreetly as possible, I looked over at Julie's family and did not see her. So, I quickly looked all around the room and could not detect her anywhere.

So, telepathically, I yelled out, “Cathy! Are you here?”

“Yes, of course I’m here!”

I followed the sound of her voice and looked upward. There she was, hovering like a helium balloon would hover. Her very transparent form bobbing up and down like a helium balloon at the top of the church’s tall cathedral ceiling.

I said, “Oh, there you are. I thought you would be here.”

Cathy replied, “Of course I am here!”

Now, here is the strangest part of Cathy’s story. Just as I finished writing the last word in the description of Cathy’s funeral for this book, I heard a choir singing from my kitchen. Even I was freaked out as I jumped out of my chair and ran to my kitchen. My cell phone was sitting on the kitchen counter. Out of my phone, which was turned off, a choir sang the song, “Hallelujah.” You just can’t make this stuff up!

VITAL POINT

> Always ask the person, whether they are alive or dying, for permission before astral projecting to them. If you receive a “No,” you must honor it, but you can also ask again later. If you receive a “Yes,” then immediately astral project to them.

My dear, dear friend Elaine just asked me to add this to my book. Right now, as I’m writing this book, I am sitting outside. The idea of including a moment that Elaine and I had together just popped into my mind. Elaine’s spirit just asked me to share the sacred moment we had together. As I began to write, I heard two hawks calling to each other. I looked up to see them floating together in the breeze . . .

I woke up in the night to see Elaine standing next to my bed. She had astral projected to me. She clearly said, "I am very close to leaving my body now. I wanted you to know." The second she told me that, it seemed like she was sucked backward and instantly vanished. I then deliberately astral projected to her. I found her at home in a hospital bed. As soon as I arrived, she physically turned her head, and with a tiny smile she said, "I knew you would come . . . I knew you would come."

From now on, you can be at the side of your family, friends, or client—no matter how far away you are from them—by astral projecting yourself to them. You can also teach others how to astral project to their loved one when they cannot get there in time. Astral projection is simply controlled thought energy, focused in a certain direction. Our thoughts are energy, and energy also follows our thoughts. We humans can be completely in charge of our own thought energy. Thoughts focused in a certain direction, or to a certain person, causes your energy to stretch outward in that direction.

The healing medium astral projects with a laser-beam focus of thought energy. Remote-viewing is the natural ability to receive accurate intuitive information for the person you are assisting. You are able to astral project and remote-view across a small room or to the other side of the world—instantly.

Remember to Use These Steps to Astral Project

1. Ask the person verbally or intuitively for permission to astral project to them.
2. Stop all thoughts about yourself.
3. Focus on being in charge, and focus all attention and thoughts on the person you are checking in on.

4. Request the Divine and Sacred specialty guide to direct your focus to the person's energy field and body in order to receive accurate, detailed information about this person's illness or life struggles.
5. Think and feel that you are stretching outward to the person's name, voice, and body. Allow the guides to direct you. You are *not* to work at this. Allow the guides to take you to the person's physical body.
6. Think and feel that you have hypersensitive sensors at the end of your extended beam of energy. These sensors are alive, alert, active, noticing, and receiving everything.
7. Project your thoughts to the dying person in the same way you would talk to a person in front of you. Do not hold back on anything. Pause and receive all instant pops of information into your mind. It will come in images, tiny movies, and words.
8. When you sense you are complete, pull all your energy back into your own body.
9. Know in your heart that this is deeply real.

Chapter 9

Identifying the Level of Awareness of Each Deceased Person

The primary causes of death seem to be illness, injury, drug overdose, suicide, murder, starvation, and old age. No matter the cause of death, we humans do not become angels at the time of death. Many people think the deceased immediately go to heaven and become angels. I know this because I frequently hear that idea from individuals all around the world. We deceased humans tend to continue on as human souls and not angels. I have even noticed that ascended masters are aware and extremely advanced beings in human forms. Even ascended masters continue to be recognized as glowing human forms rather than angels.

I have said earlier that we have many choices at the time of death. But what causes the deceased to be troubled, and to remain troubled in spirit? This topic is extremely complicated and mired in intricate, multilayered emotions of distraught, unfinished events—things that should not have been said, or that *should* have been said.

Whether we remain on Earth as a troubled deceased is always based on the thoughts and emotions each person had at the moment of death. Who knew that every single one of us has a choice to make at the time of leaving our physical body? I have never heard anyone describe having choices, but this is exactly what I keep hearing from deceased people. The dead never call it a choice, but many describe making choices.

There is one primary reason trauma stays within the soul and comes forward into our current life. Traumatic events create traumatic emotions. Thoughts and emotions for humans are literally distinct frequencies of energy. Negative thoughts and emotions are dense, thick, heavy, slow, and sticky, and they are more likely to move forward from past lives into our current life. The energy of happiness, pleasant thoughts and emotions are fine, light, and flow very fast. Those happier times in our past lives do not tend to weigh heavy on our souls, so we rarely notice those pleasant past lives during a regression. It is the life of extreme emotions that always come to mind due to the burdens of heavy experiences causing heavy, lingering emotions such as regret, self-cursing, vows, drugs and alcohol, unexpected death, or tidal waves of raw emotions.

We have an uncountable number of choices as we leave the physical body. Leaving the physical body does not mean the person leaves the physical Earth. Many, many times, the deceased are in such a state of raw emotion that they frequently remain in that moment even after leaving their body. Human thought energy sometimes creates an energetic loop. In this case, a loop is created when the deceased continues to remember and continues to go over and over one exact moment of great negative emotion. Some have told me they are looking for hell because they decided they do not deserve heaven, so they remain on the Earth plane.

Here are some examples:

- They ruminate about a negative event they caused.
- They ruminate about a death they caused—or believe they caused.
- They remain in a bar where all their friends hang out.
- Some are focused on a certain alive victim who they abused, and who they continue to abuse in spirit.

- They refuse to go to the light because they made a vow to their spouse or friend that they will not cross over until they can do it together.
- They relive, over and over again, the moment they died or were murdered, which causes them to remain in that physical location.

It's this repeating loop of traumatic emotions, that creates "ghosts" and haunted locations. Living people witness a deceased person caught up in this loop of remembering something and feeling tremendous negative emotions. This continuous repetition over time thickens the already dense energy. The more the person in spirit repeats the memory, the more the density builds, and as a result, the more they become visible to the living. Dramatic, negative thoughts and emotions literally create a heaviness within the living human body but also within the eternal human soul.

The prominent negative emotions are: Panic, shame, jealousy, fear, terror, regret, guilt, obsession, hate, judgment, undeserving, anguish, disgust, anxiety, disappointment, agony, aggression, physical pain, confusion caused by dementia, drugs, heartache, loss, self-punishment, and extreme physical pain.

Our thoughts and our emotions at the instant we exit the physical body, is crucial in what happens as we transition into the nonphysical. We want to prevent the dying from experiencing these traumatic emotions so that they do not become lost, unaware of their death, or stuck in a never-ending loop of repetition for decades, or even centuries. Your primary goal is to attempt to bring them to a place of resolution, and possibly even peace, just before transitioning into the nonphysical.

There is a second, even more mystical cause of old thoughts, emotions, and memories of our past traumas, that travels forward with us into our current lives. Each life cycle is yet another chance to learn something. For many years, my private practice consisted of mental health counseling, hypnosis, and past-life regressions. Again and again, I have witnessed clients in deep hypnotic states who describe that their current life is their next opportunity to learn and improve from their past events, or their negative decisions or unhappiness.

They often go on to describe how their current life conflicts are identical, or nearly identical, to their most stressful past life. They often state that this current life is another chance to heal themselves and the other souls who were involved in past-life hatred or cruelty. At the same time, I frequently hear from regressed clients that the people involved in their past lives continue to look the same or similar to their appearance in this current life! They often admit they, and the others in this life, are still struggling as a group, in the same ways they have for multiple past lives.

Advancing our level of understanding, kindness, wisdom, and love, without any conditions, elevates our eternal soul, which then elevates the entire macrocosm. As we humans learn our lessons, our Earth life becomes more enjoyable, and we are much more aware of what is important and what is not important.

VITAL POINT

> Understanding, kindness, wisdom, and love elevates and advances our eternal soul.

Emotional Situations for Spirits

There do seem to be situations where people do not make conscious choices in their death process. If death comes instantly, it seems the individual has no time to process or even understand what just happened. Deceased people often suddenly appear in my car with me. They never realize they're dead. For example, they tell me they're always standing at that intersection of those streets, or at that railroad crossing, etc. If I ask them why they are in my car, they have no idea. Then they disappear to go back to the place where they died. Then the next day, they arrive in my car, not knowing why they do what they keep doing.

Another example of unexpected deaths are those caused by drugs. A person could have overdosed on street drugs, or they could have died while heavily medicated due to severe pain or disease, and so on. I have also assisted an elderly deceased male in my living room, who I determined—with the help of my Divine and Sacred Guides—that he used to live in my neighborhood and had died of severe dementia. He acted as if he still had dementia, because he unknowingly continued to hold that dense energy vibration associated with that illness.

I was contacted by a local man who had recently purchased a completely dilapidated factory. He quickly installed security cameras all over the place. He was quite upset because alarms kept going off late at night. Every time he checked the camera, he could see a dark, shadowy ghost floating across the floor.

He asked that I come to the building. I told him that as a medium I do not need to physically be at the location. He insisted, so I went. I asked the owner not to tell me where the camera alarm was being triggered, and I asked for permission to roam around the deserted building alone.

"Creepy" does not even come close to describing what was left of this ancient brick factory. I roamed around everywhere and didn't notice anything. I found my way to the lower level. I immediately saw arms flinging around, stirring up the air in the room. I saw the energy of two men fighting. One man was trying to kill the other man. The attacker finally hit the victim over the head with an object. I watched this man drag the body out of that room, and around a wall, and back into a completely dark room that had no windows. He pulled the body into the back corner of the room. I watched him bury the body in the only area of that entire lower floor that was not covered in concrete. No one had ever found his body.

I walked upstairs to the owner's desk. I told him what I observed and the location where it had happened. Together we walked through the building and down into the lower level where I saw the murder. I pointed toward the pitch-black room and told him the body was buried back in the far corner. We did not enter that area because neither of us could see anything. That's when this man told me that I was pointing into the only area in the entire building that had dirt floors.

I said to him, "If you hire someone to dig there, you will find him."

I never heard another word from the owner.

Here are other conversations you might have with troubled or confused deceased:

- Many struggling deceased simply have no idea that they've died. In fact, they seem quite surprised and sometimes shocked. Some simply do not believe you.
- Many tell me they were so bad in their life that they do not deserve to go to heaven. One man told me that he keeps his back to the light because he does not deserve to go to heaven.
- Self-punishment is a common theme. If they feel they were not punished enough in life, they will punish themselves.
- Many people, even after death, continue an emotional focus on a living person to the point of obsession.
- Some living people were so focused on their house, a building such as a barn, or their land, that they remain locked into that location after death.
- Yearning or craving alcohol or street drugs will hold them to the Earth and to certain locations where they hung out the most, such as a certain bar or pub. This is why I have rescued so many deceased people from bars, under bridges, or in alleys, etc.

- Occasionally, a deceased human remains in a certain location, repeating an action to continue a lifestyle they loved. For example, the deceased might have been the janitor in an old abandoned opera house, or a train engineer in an ancient train station.
- Many deceased people seem to continue on for centuries, reliving physical agony in a past life, such as being tortured or participating in bloody battles.
- Occasionally, a spirit person might remain in a church or a building used for religious practices. They might remain in that location due to their history of learning extreme religious beliefs or religious shaming in front of others.
- Severe levels of mental illness often create an attachment to a deserted building of a mental institution. The mentally ill behavior repeats into the nonphysical realm.

This last example leads me to describe a situation with a mentoring client on Zoom. This was my first session with this female client. She was quite nice and eager to learn. She sat at a long table, asking me appropriate questions. I could barely take in what she was saying because a wild-looking spirit woman with her hair standing straight up was screaming and running back and forth behind this very calm and attentive client. At the same time, the screaming, thrashing woman was showing me an old-fashioned building that decades ago would have been called an insane asylum.

The longer the session went on, the wilder and louder the deceased woman became. I finally stopped the client to inform her about the woman behind her. As soon as I asked the living client to stop talking so I could describe this to her, the deceased woman threw herself on the floor, screaming and pounding the floor. I described in detail what I was seeing and what the woman looked like.

The living client listened to me and then quietly said, "You just described my mother exactly. She was schizophrenic and spent most of her life in a psychiatric hospital."

VITAL POINT

Leaving the physical body in death does not mean the person leaves the physical Earth.

A student took immediate action after one of my courses! She describes this in her own words.

A Practitioner Shares a Story

An amazing experience! Exactly one month after finishing Tina's course, my husband and I went to look at a property with a house and land that we were looking to buy. I sent a fellow medium friend a picture of the house for her to give me a quick reading of it. She said there were dense energies there, like the land maybe used to be a war zone. With that in mind, on my way to look at the property, I powered up my toroidal field.

We looked at the house and didn't feel like it was for us, but we still went to drive around the land on a four-seated ATV with our realtor. The realtor and my husband sat on the front, and I rode behind my husband. As soon as we started driving, I started hearing, "Help! Help! Help!" That is when I realized the reason why I was there! I started remembering Tina's steps and called the guides of these souls to help them transition to the light. There were so many angels falling from the sky to assist them, it was so amazing to see (with my mind's eye, that is).

As I experienced this, my friend the medium texted me to see how things were going, and I started to tell her what was going on. She then asked, "Have you not seen the house?" I told her, "Yes, but that's not our house."

As soon as I texted her those words, the guides took me to the house. I could see how the Guides were instructing a whole bunch of other souls to leave the house. It was almost as if they were kidnapped and the Guides were showing them the exit. It looked like a movie scene! My friend also asked me if the land was a war zone? The guides said, "Not necessarily." They say that there are generations and generations of owners, employees, and slaves who lived here and did not know how to leave.

Then Archangel Michael sat next to me on the ATV and said, "I will accompany you for the rest of the trip." I love him! Archangel Michael put out a wave of blue energy like the sea, everywhere we went. Then I saw the guides selecting the souls, "You go here. You go there . . ." How incredible!

If I had to guess, I would say there were between fifty to sixty souls there. This process lasted more than half an hour. At the end, when we got back to the house where our cars were, I asked my guides to prepare a cleansing filter for all three of us.

— Claudia Gonzales
www.icanhealmyself.com

As time goes on, the more the spirit person repeats their movements and their dense emotions, the more there are opportunities for living people to notice them. The locations, like the one Claudia described, then becomes known as haunted. But, in fact, the common locations of haunted places are examples of looping. It can be due to dying at a trauma, or confusion, or unfinished business with one or more people in the living.

Remember, we have an uncountable number of choices as we leave the physical body. Leaving the physical body in death does not mean the person leaves the physical Earth. That continuous repetition of a certain moment creates "ghosts," and the "ghosts" then create haunted areas. The more the person in spirit repeats the memory, the more visible they become to the living. This could go on for decades, or even centuries.

Ten Possible Outcomes Immediately after Death

1. The individual completely releases the physical body and the physical world to join the nonphysical realm of the soul.
2. The dead remain at the location of their death to repeat that moment over and over again.
3. Some deceased tend to roam back and forth among living loved ones or remain with one living person. They often do this in an attempt to help the living person.
4. Many remain lost or confused and are often drawn to mediums but do not understand why they approach the medium. I often hear from the dead that mediums look different, or their light is different from the general population.
5. A troubled deceased human attaches to a newly deceased person only because they were near the person at the time of their death.
6. Occasionally, some deceased are attracted to another deceased person whose energy or struggles are similar to themselves. This often occurs with alcoholics or street-drug users.
7. Many are attracted to a negative location, where they spent a lot of time while alive, such as a bar or an abandoned house where homeless people are living.

8. A negative non-human entity is attracted to a newly deceased negative human. This will dramatically increase the deceased human's confusion and vulnerability.
9. Occasionally, an extremely negative deceased human is taken by specialty guides to a nonphysical location to literally be dismantled, to prevent them from causing more extreme harm on Earth.
10. In a rare situation, another deceased person who has not crossed over quickly leaps into the body of someone who just died, making it appear as if the original person did not die. This is known as a "walk-in."

VITAL POINT

Teach others that ghosts are human beings. They are humans who want or need something, and what they usually need is help.

The word "ghosts" is a very negative and scary word to most people. The word itself seems to take away a spirit person's humanity. I purposefully do not want to call the deceased by the negative title of "ghosts." They are no longer considered human beings in a nonphysical existence. A false message begins to develop . . . Ghosts are terrifying and will make you sick, or harm you, or kill you. It sends a powerful, gloomy message to the living: Be very afraid because ghosts will get you. It's important to learn and to teach others that these beings are very troubled humans who need help from a well-trained healing medium.

The Difference Between the Positive and Negative Deceased

I'm sure you have already noticed that some alive humans on Earth are sweet, kind, and giving people. They would dig into their purses or pockets to give you money for a bus to get home. These kind people might let you go in front of them in the grocery because you said you're running late. But just like here on Earth, not everyone is positive, kind, and giving. Negative people are takers—mean and hateful. Negative people continue to build a dark, thick density within their energy field and their body.

Immediately Notice General Characteristics of Spirit People

1. Is your immediate sense of the spirit positive or negative?
2. Do they feel as if they have already crossed over into the light?
3. Do they feel heavy, as if they have not crossed over?
4. Do they say they just want to speak to someone?
5. What is your first instinct of what they want or need?
6. Who or what do they keep focusing on?
7. Are they emotional or neutral?
8. Do they come up to your face or appear somewhere around you?

Identifying Negative Deceased People

At the time of their death, negative spirit people have the tendency to be so heavy with contentious, cold, and noxious emotions and actions that they tend to remain on the Earth plane as hateful, dead people continuing to cause problems for the living. Their personalities on Earth will continue after death. Some of those emotions that continue in death are anger, hostility, obsessions, possessiveness, control, viciousness, and hatefulness.

Here Are Some Characteristics of Negative Spirit People:

- They will appear with a more defined human form.
- That form is often a smoky dark-gray color.
- They will appear as if they are literally standing on the floor.
- They will move quickly, making shadowy flashes, trying not to be seen.
- There will not be any light or brightness to them.
- They will not be as transparent, so you may not be able to see through them.
- They do not readily cross over into the light and tend to remain on Earth.
- They might feel a bit scary because of their troubled energy.
- They might appear very close to you to make you think they are more powerful.

Identifying Positive Deceased People

At the time of their death, people who lived a more positive life will have a tendency to release this Earth plane to cross over into the light. They still might carry some emotions from all the things that happened in their life, but there is a large difference: They are not weighed down in such dramatic ways. They have some understanding about the human experience. They have achieved some level of forgiveness, caring, and in general, they have been givers and not takers of others.

Here are some characteristics of positive deceased people:

- They will appear in degrees of transparency.
- They will not appear as a distinct human form.
- You will be able to see through them.

- They will have some level of light, and occasionally, might seem to sparkle.
- They are usually floating inches to many feet above the floor.
- You might be surprised, but you will not feel afraid.
- They are more ready to release the Earth to cross over into the light.
- They will not appear very close to you.

A long-term mentoring student shares her experience with a distraught woman whose husband died. This is her experience as she goes deeper into being the communicating bridge for this loving couple.

A Practitioner Shares a Story

As a medical intuitive and a medium, there are times when deceased people appear to me with messages for their loved ones in the physical world. I am delighted to be able to communicate with them as they make themselves known in unique ways. Most of the time, my experience with this communication has been rather brief—a quick message from a deceased loved one for a client who is scheduled to come for a session; a confused person in spirit who appears somewhere in my home or in a public place; and the occasional spirit passenger in my car as I travel to my office. Sometimes the encounters are more ongoing, as is the one in this case.

I was quite surprised about a year ago to see my good friend's recently deceased husband appear in front of me one morning as I finished my meditation. My friend was extremely distraught over the loss of her beloved husband. Now here he was, literally down on one knee, frantically begging me to connect with his wife to deliver several messages. I felt an urgency and a bit of desperation in his pleading.

My friend had recently begun a new job, and the first thing he said was, "Tell her not to quit her job." He indicated that he was quite proud of the accomplishments she had made in her career and now had an opportunity to watch her excel in her new role. He also gave me information about the location of important papers needed to make final arrangements, along with details about attending to maintenance of their home. But most urgently, he wanted her to know that she needed to remain strong and present for their sons.

My friend, deep in her grief, at first was unable to recognize her husband's presence at all. He continued to come to me often. A retired ophthalmologist, he almost always began by telling me to clean my glasses. (My glasses are almost always covered with fingerprints!) He enjoyed getting my attention by turning lights on in the middle of the night, playing with electrical appliances, and frequently appearing across the room as I sat in meditation.

As I shared these messages with my friend, she began to sense moments of her husband's presence herself in her own home. Lights would flicker as she talked to him while alone in her house. She began to sense him as she did her own daily spiritual practices. My friend had never lived alone and was extremely concerned about her ability to handle the details of everyday life—taxes, home repairs, and maintenance of their properties. She began to notice that the repairmen she reached out to just happened to have an immediate opening or could help her with little extras that were unrelated to the job they had come to do. Things just seemed to fall into place much more easily than she had expected.

Her husband had mentioned to her before his passing that he must get the home ready for possible freezing temperatures by disconnecting the hose from the outdoor faucet, but he passed away before he could do this. When she attempted to remove the hose, the connection on the faucet was so tight that she was unable to loosen it by herself. Frustrated, she went inside to enlist the help of her son. When the two of them went back outside to disconnect the hose from the faucet, it was so loose that it practically fell off the house!

The best part of all this is that in communicating these messages to my friend, she has begun to see that her husband *is* around, that he *does* communicate with her, and that there *is* still a connection. She can now recognize that communication even as it comes in subtle ways. She recently shared that she heard him say her name loudly, as she was almost asleep and felt him touch her face.

I sometimes wake up to my under-cabinet lighting shining brightly in the middle of the night. It's always a sign from Spirit for me. The lights were bright in the middle of the night around Valentine's Day, as my friend's son delivered his ashes to the river Ganges as he had wished.

But the beauty in it all is that she now understands the continuity of the spirit. As intuitives and mediums, the opportunity to assist our clients and friends in realizing the eternity of our souls is the ultimate honor and privilege. I am so blessed to be able to do this work and be able to recognize the beautiful signs and messages that come from the spirit world! When we assist our clients in realizing that love is what remains even when our deceased loved ones are no longer physically present, we are doing the most important work of all.

— Betty Ann Dean, R.N., B.S.N.
bettyandretti@hotmail.com
vibrantbodyworks.com

Being a medium is not always tearful, solemn, or scary. Sometimes the dead are lighthearted, appearing just for fun and are delighted to be part of your session with their loved one. For example, one person in spirit, with a giant smile on his face, came to my client's session with an uncountable number of spirit dogs with him. He was laughing, I was laughing, and so was my living client!

Always remember: The dead are just as alive as you are.

Chapter 10

Working with the Confused or Needy Deceased

I have been in private practice for a long time. I was drawn more and more into professional mediumship because living people were frequently hindered by deceased people. Again and again, I discovered that a dead person was the direct cause of a physical illness or a terrible, confusing life situation for the living client.

Here we are taking the next massive step as energy healers: To become the healer for the dead and negative non-human beings. Historically, mediums have been recognized as only interpreters for the deceased, and it is up to the medium to request evidence from the dead. The historically trained medium is supposed to provide details to prove to the living client:

1. The deceased is real.
2. The deceased is truly who they say they are.
3. The deceased describes information that makes sense to the living.

Traditionally, the medium's goal has been to communicate and create a bridge between the deceased to the living client. We are now skyrocketing from merely communicating on behalf of the deceased, to phenomenal healing of the troubled, earthbound human spirits. Healing can always be successfully accomplished for a deceased human. It does not matter how long the individual has been dead.

Some have been dead for centuries. It is never too late to help and to heal.

Many deceased people deeply need your help. Please consider all nonphysical beings and all living humans as your clients. I offer guidelines to keep you safe and to keep you physically healthy as well. Many mediums are ill or die at an early age because they have no safety guidelines. You're not to be a victim or a servant to the deceased or to non-human beings. You are to be the commander, the boss, and the director of nonphysical beings.

The troubled nonphysical beings simply do not have the level of awareness that you have. Most struggling beings have no idea they are hindering the living. They should never be allowed to step into your energy field or your body. You do not want their struggles, their negative emotions, or their energy field to become yours. There is an uncountable number of needy living humans and needy nonphysical beings. There is only one of you.

Channeling with Safety

I am determined and committed to never allow:

1. Guides of any level, not even the Divine and Sacred, to enter my body.
2. Any deceased humans to enter my body.
3. Any non-human beings to enter my body.

There is absolutely no reason to allow this, nor is there a benefit. You are in charge allowing or forbidding any level of nonphysical beings into your body. They cannot enter you unless you consciously or unconsciously allow this to happen.

You then might ask me, "Don't you know that other professionals channel entities, and they speak through them and in their own voice?"

Yes, I do. It makes a more dramatic experience for an audience, but it is not necessary for communication with the dead.

I know many mediums who allow all types of beings to enter their body and speak through them. But hear this: At the time of writing this, I'm outliving most of them, and most of them were younger than I. My point here is that every time you allow beings into your physical body, they bring their energy with them. That energy could be vibrating with the disease they died with. That energy could be full of negative emotion or hostile, threatening ideas. Even the Divine and Sacred, who vibrate at a gloriously enraptured state, don't ask or even attempt to enter into a living human being. We would probably explode into pieces!

VITAL POINT

> It is not necessary to allow a spirit being to step into your body to be an excellent speaker for that being. Your physical body is often negatively affected by the energetic state of the deceased.

Later in this chapter, you will read about the "Transformation of an Advanced Spirit Person." This is an example of channeling. As I channeled for a deceased man who I will call J.H. He never tried, and never asked, to enter my physical body in order to speak to the group of people. He respectfully stood on my right side. He spoke aloud to me, and I simply listened to every word he said. He also showed me clear images and brief movie-type images in my mind. I then repeated out loud the exact words he said and described the images he showed me. I was literally his interpreter. Placing himself into my physical body was not necessary in any way, and it would not have improved the experience for him, for me, or for the audience.

Highly Aware Spirit People

Many spirits are just living their life in the nonphysical realm without thoughts of harming or interfering with the living. I awoke one night and found a male spirit, who looked like the well-known actor Nathan Lane, quietly sitting at the foot of my bed. He paid no attention to me. He sat looking out as if deep in thought. I calmly asked him why he was sitting on my bed. He answered that he wasn't sure why he was there. I asked him to think about it and look back to what brought him here. After a brief pause, he responded, "I followed that girl from [the hotel] where I was staying. I followed her to this house."

My granddaughter had just arrived at my home that evening. He named the same hotel where my granddaughter had just come from with her sports team. I told him it was not appropriate for him to be sitting on the bed of a woman whom he does not know. He instantly disappeared before I could help him transition into Source.

Another spirit person, who was just living his spirit life, kept sitting in a wicker chair in the corner of my bedroom. Every night, after going to bed, I heard the wicker chair make a sound that only wicker can make when someone sits on it. After a few nights of hearing a creaking chair, I telepathically called out, saying, "Who are you?"

I came out from under my blanket to see a very distinguished spirit man. I asked for his name. His first and last name leaped into my mind. I said, "Have you been sitting in my chair for the last few nights?" He clearly said, "Yes." So I said, "Why are you here in my house every night?" He answered, "I was attracted to this house because of all the spirit activity here." I responded, "Do you realize it is not appropriate for you to be in a woman's bedroom?" He instantly shot upward through the ceiling, and I never saw him again.

A Story to Learn From: Ann's Persistence Even After Death

Ann's body was in the casket at the altar of her church. I got there early and sat down quietly at the far end of the church pew, waiting for the service to begin. Ann suddenly rushed past me, heading to the front of the church. Deep within my mind, I yelled out her name. She stopped and quickly floated back to me. She was radiant, literally glowing with white sparkles and with a huge smile on her face.

"Ann, is there anything that you want me to tell them?" I asked. By "them," I meant her husband, her two very young children, her parents, or her friends.

She lifted her hands upward, and her glow shot upward as she declared, "Tell them it is ALL LOVE! It is just ALL LOVE!"

She did not wait for my reply. Ann quickly floated forward to the front of the church. As the service began, Ann crouched down in front of her husband and her two small children. I could not hear her words, but I could tell they were not aware of her. She then floated to her girlfriend who stood up front at the microphone, speaking to the large group of family and friends. Ann tried to assist her friend in telling a funny story about herself. She seemed to be having a grand time rushing around as if she was at the greatest party of all. Ann, the deceased young woman, is still the happiest person I have ever seen immediately after their death.

About two months went by. Suddenly, Ann stood at my bedside, telling me she didn't understand why no one was paying attention to her except for me. She said that she had been trying to communicate with her husband and children, but she realized she kept failing. Ann said that she finally remembered that I'd seen and talked to her at the church. She asked me to tell her husband that she is well. I said that I would.

But every day, Ann returned to my home, asking me to contact her husband, and every day, I forgot or decided it was too late to call, or something else came up that had distracted me. I had to face the fact that I was afraid to call him. He considered himself a strong Christian, very active with his church, and I was afraid he would not understand, or that my call might increase his pain rather than help him through his grieving.

As the days turned into a couple of weeks, Ann became more insistent. She began to follow me around the house. She stood next to my bed as I tried to sleep at night and stood there as I awoke in the morning. Each day, she seemed more agitated until I had no choice but to contact him.

Michael listened to my story of Ann's persistence without speaking, but I could hear the breathing and his tears on the other end of the phone. When she clearly stated, "I have been messing with the electricity in the house!" Her husband loudly gasped. "The ceiling fan in the living room keeps coming on when I'm in the house by myself! I knew that I wasn't turning it on and couldn't figure it out."

I responded, "Michael, we are electrical beings. Our physical bodies are electrical in nature. Our brains work with electrical impulses. When we get an EEG in the doctor's office, they are measuring the electrical impulses in our brain. Now there is an EMG that measures the flow of electricity moving through our muscles. An EKG measures the electrical flow in the muscle of our heart. Have you seen medics on TV giving an electrical shock to a victim whose heart has stopped? Well, that's because every single beat of our heart begins with an electrical spark, just like a spark plug does for our car!"

I continued, "The alive part of us is the electrical charge. We cannot stay alive in the physical without that electricity. So, when we die, the electrical charge that has actually connected us to the physical body releases from the body. The electricity or the alive current that was surging inside of our body never dies but continues in the nonphysical. This is why spirit people usually find it so easy to manipulate electrical appliances such as clocks, stereos, lights, and now ceiling fans."

He had stopped crying and said that made sense to him. He knew that Ann was with him because of their ceiling fan.

Not Every Deceased Human Needs Your Help

I was sitting in my car at the gas station, waiting for my friend to return from paying for the gas. I felt a powerful pull to look toward my left. I immediately saw a woman finish pumping gas into her car, and then sit down in the driver's seat and close the door to her car. For a split second, I wondered why I was entranced by this woman. But the next second, I knew why.

A man in the passenger seat turned his head and looked directly at me. He was only slightly transparent, so I knew he was a spirit person, and it felt like he hadn't been dead for very long.

Telepathically, loud and forceful he said, "I'm afraid she's going to get into a car wreck!"

I responded back telepathically to him, "Together, let's call in an angel to keep her safe from any type of wreck."

He loved my idea. Together, we called in a specific angel to watch over this young woman. An angel-type being rushed into the car, and the spirit man blinked out of sight. You just can't make this stuff up!

VITAL POINT

> Not every deceased person needs to be wrapped up and taken to the best place for their transformation.

Be ready to encounter a deceased spouse or parent who is clearly aware they are in the nonphysical realms. Their conscious decision is to help someone in their daily life. Many loving deceased will often tell you they are deliberately waiting here on Earth to help their loved one at the time of their death. Take note: This type of spirit person is completely different from someone in spirit who is obsessed and controlling a person in the living. If the man at the gas station had been controlling, he would be demanding, leaping out of the car and rushing up to me, demanding for me to help the young woman. Notice the difference between caring and controlling. It feels, and looks, very different coming from the deceased.

Transformation of an Advanced Spirit Person

I was privileged to be the channeling medium for a man whose dearest friend had just passed on. Doug and J.H. had known each other for thirty years. Their long discussions always revolved around a deeper understanding of the Universe, how it all works, quantum physics, life and death.

They made a pact, if at all possible, that the one who died first would consciously describe each step along the way during the process and then attempt to come back to describe their personal experiences of life in spirit. After discussing these things for thirty years, J.H. was diagnosed with cancer and died two weeks later.

Doug sat with his dear friend and listened to J.H. as he joked and laughed, but he also consciously shared what he'd experienced in the last two days of his life. He said, "I see and feel a thin membrane . . ." He then stopped talking, stopped responding, and made his transition on Doug's birthday. Doug said he felt it was J.H.'s way of honoring their lifelong friendship and their partnership to understand life and the Universe.

Just two weeks after J.H.'s passing, Doug asked me if I could intuitively connect with his friend. I checked in with my spirit mind and could not pick up on anything about him. I informed Doug about this, and told him that maybe it was too soon after his friend's passing.

A few weeks later, Doug asked me again. I faintly heard J.H. say from far away, "I'm just not ready yet."

Three months went by, and suddenly, I felt a rush of energy come up to me and heard J.H. declare, "Okay, I'm ready!"

I informed Doug, and he asked that his spiritual group be present when he and J.H. communicated through me. Keep in mind that I'd never met J.H. when he was in the physical, and yet, after the channeling, Doug told me that I sounded like his friend, used the same phrases, and gave evidential information throughout the entire session. His presence was stronger than any other spirit person I've ever connected with.

J.H. answered the group's questions with clear, thoughtful, and humorous information. His spirit body stood next to me while he responded to many in-depth questions from the group. He was dynamically alive! He was just as alive in his nonphysical form, as we physical humans were, sitting in the circle together.

While channeling this highly aware soul, he showed me images of his death process. As he verbalized his experience, he projected images to me. I saw him lying on a hospital bed. I then saw a transparent, milky-white shape rise up from his physical body. His transparent shape rose upward from head to toe at the same time, remaining parallel to the body. His transparent, milky-white shape remained in the same form as his physical body. As it rose ever so slowly, I could see thousands of threads between his spirit form and his physical body. Each thread connected the milky etheric form to the physical body from head to toe.

As his soul energy rose upward, the shimmery threads lengthened. His soul hovered about three or four feet above his body. As the threads lengthened, they also became thinner until they seemed to disintegrate. As thousands of the threads disintegrated, I noticed his transparent soul energy also disappeared. His eternal, alive, nonphysical presence seemed to evaporate like fog when the sun shone upon it.

Listen, Discover, and Allow the Tears

I sat in stillness as my client sobbed. Her husband had passed on two months ago. I gently asked that she allow herself to cry, so she continued to cry. When she felt calmer, she asked if I could attempt to contact her husband. I said, "I already see him standing in front of the stove in your kitchen."

She burst out in loud sobs that physically rocked her body. When she was able to calm herself again, she said, "He loved to cook!"

Inform your client whatever, or whoever, you perceive without judgment. In this example, I nearly made a judgment that this spirit man should not be focusing on a stove, especially as his wife was near hysteria over losing him. This, however, was a powerful signal between them. She knew immediately that he was present for her. He meant no harm. In fact, he came with love in his heart for his distraught wife.

You are not only a translator for the living and the dead. In a situation like this, you are also a communicator, a friend, and a gentle witness for a precious moment between two people that is intense but also extraordinary. Slow down and give your physical client time to imprint this moment in their memory. You do not need to talk every minute. In situations like this, silence is precious. Be comfortable with gentle periods of silence as part of your healing environment.

Here is a teaching story about telepathically talking, listening, and discovering. Notice my responses to my client. This session is full of teaching steps to assist deceased humans.

Client: I still have stuff come at me and stick with me. There are two times that something has stuck with me. There was a face of a man who stuck with me, but I don't know who he is. He was so clear that I thought, "What is going on here?" He has dark hair and a beard, and his hair is brushed over to the left side. He seemed to be mid-thirties to maybe forty years old. I thought, "What the heck are you doing here?" I did not feel anything negative about him. But I said, "You've got to go away because I've got to go to sleep now." But I kept thinking, "Why was this being so clear to me?"

TZ: Remember, never chase them away. You can tell them not to bother you right at that moment. But then tell them something like, "I will meet you tomorrow at a certain time and place." They are real people, so you must follow through with what you say to them. About when did this happen?

Client: Oh, okay. Well, it was about a month or two ago. But I still keep seeing him in my mind.

TZ: That's because he is still there with you.

Client: Oh! Is that right?

TZ: Yes! That's why he's still in your thoughts and images in your mind's eye. Now, if you would, but only if you want to do this, you can call him to you right now. The time that has gone past does not matter to the deceased. Tell him now to come to you and stand next to you in this room. Make sure you give him very clear directives.

Client: Now he is standing over by my left shoulder. But I don't know what to do next.

TZ: Okay. First of all, what you do next is based on what you are wondering about. First of all, it seems like you're assuming that he's someone you know or should know. That is not necessarily so.

Client: Oh! You're right. Okay.

TZ: So, first of all, check this out. Ask if you know him.

Client: (Eyes closed and quiet, then she spoke.) He says, "No, I was just drawn to you because of your heart. I need some love and compassion."

TZ: Ask him, how is he trying to get love and compassion from you?

Client: (Long pause, then client chuckles.) He says he wants me to hear his story . . . Tina, is this when you tell me that I'm crazy now, or what?

TZ: No, not at all. You are expanding your intuitive abilities now into mediumship! So, now ask him something else that you're wondering about.

Client: Can you tell me what . . .?

TZ: No, please do not use the words, "Can you . . .?" That is only asking them if they are capable of doing something. Ask him very directly: "Tell me now, what your story is."

Client: Oh! (A long silence.) He says he was murdered. What's interesting is that lately I've been obsessed with detective stories on TV around solving murders for quite a while. I just find them fascinating.

TZ: Well, then ask him what does he know about his own death?

Client: He says he was hanging around the wrong people. He was talking to somebody in a crowd, and somebody came up behind him and grabbed his neck with something. He still doesn't know why someone did that.

TZ: Ask him to check to see if he was robbed.

Client: No, he had some money but had drugs that he was carrying for someone. The drugs were taken from him. They didn't want him to be able to identify them.

TZ: Sounds like he knows he has died and left his body. Ask him why he's still here on the Earth plane.

Client: He wishes he could say goodbye to his sister! His parents had given up on him, but his sister was still there for him, and he appreciated that.

(Pause.)

Client: I am starting to feel very uncertain about myself, and what I'm getting, and what's coming out of my mouth.

TZ: No! I think you're clear as a bell. If I get to a place where I'm "wondering" if I'm receiving something correctly, I simply ask the deceased if I'm getting the information correctly, and believe me, they will tell you if you're right or wrong! So, just ask him right now if you're correct so far. Believe me, the deceased will tell you if you're wrong, and our Divine and Sacred Guides will tell you too! So, just ask him now.

Client: He says, "Yes, yes, yes! You are hearing me correctly."

TZ: Great. Even I did not know what to do to help him, or to help you either. I just asked my own Guides, and they told us to do the following . . .

Tell him to go to his sister right now and talk directly to her soul. Tell him he will be talking directly from his soul to her soul. It doesn't matter what she's doing now. But then tell him to come right back to you when he's done.

(Client mumbles to the deceased client.)

Client: "Yes, you can hug her soul to soul too." (Very long pause.) He feels like he really made a connection, and he was telling her how much her love meant to him, and he needed her to know how important she was to him. Then I had to laugh! (Suddenly, the deceased man began to discuss his dog with my client.) I'm wondering if I'm always an animal communicator too, because he's now telling her to keep his dog! I'm wondering if there will always be an animal in every story? Then he said the dog will always remind her of him. He knew that I couldn't take care of him. Wait! He just told me, "The dog is not a him. It is a her. She knew I could not take care of her." So, he just corrected me! Okay, he's back.

TZ: Let's help him to cross over now. Call in Divine and Sacred Guides who know exactly about him; wrap him in the comfort of a blanket of white light, and take him to the best place for his transformation into love and light now.

Client: Okay, I will do that. (Longer pause.) I'm told he was taken to a "soul-soothing place" to begin to love himself.

TZ: You really just did that. You're drawn to those murder mysteries because you are now to include mediumship, and you can use the TV documentary shows to actually help people who were murdered to cross over.

Client: Now that you've said that, I remember I have done some of this in the past, but I didn't know what to do with it before. In the past, I told them to go to the white light.

TZ: Please! Never tell a troubled deceased person to go to the light by themselves, because many of their own emotions might come up that prohibits them from crossing over. Do not give them so much credit that they will know what to do. You're working with the confused, unaware, or very troubled. Always call in Divine and Sacred Guides who specialize in crossing over this particular person and direct them to take the deceased to the best place for their learning and transformation into the light.

Client: Oh, okay! That makes total sense!

— Maribeth Decker
sacredgrove.com

What to Do When the Deceased Ask You to Contact People You Do Not Know

I have noticed that especially in public places, the deceased will approach you, demanding that you take their important message to their living loved ones. The problem is, you have no idea who, or where, their loved ones are!

Notice that this issue came up in the dialogue above. The dead person asked the medium to give a message to his sister. The medium had no idea who the dead person was, and did not know who his sister was or how to get in touch with her. What do you do then?

First, never say: "I cannot do that for you, because I do not know them." In this example, I asked her to direct this deceased man to do this for himself. The deceased will need clear directions from you. In this case, it was "Go to your sister now and talk directly to her soul. You will be talking directly from your soul to her soul. It does not matter what she's doing now. Go now. Come back to me. I will wait for you to give you the next step for your healing."

Terrified Teenager in My Basement

Most of the deceased who come to me are deeply confused and unaware. It is, indeed, as if they are in a state of "limbo." Again, deep negative emotions such as terror hold them to the earth. Here is the story of the terrified teenager in my basement.

The floorboards popped under the thick carpet near my bedroom door, then another pop over there, then a snap near the foot of my bed. The furnace vent crackled and made a continuous tinkling sound. I looked out from under my blankets to see the spirit person who was making all the noise, but no one was there.

The sounds continued and even escalated. I remember thinking that the past three nights had been so still and peaceful, but then my partner returned from a conference and all the noise began. I sat up in bed and astral projected outward to scan the house. I noticed nothing. I remained in bed as I scanned the downstairs and saw frantic flashes of low-level light, bouncing back and forth against the walls. I telepathically looked more closely to see a vague gray human form, flinging himself against the walls.

"It's okay. It's okay," I whispered to him. As I telepathically talked to him, I projected the feelings of calm and peace from my heart. "You are fine, but I want you to feel even better. I can help you feel better . . . First, notice that you're feeling better already."

I waited as his boomerang-type movements slowed and he came to a stop. When he calmed down and stood still, he projected horrible images to me. He was murdered in the bathroom of a gas station.

I continued to gently direct this young man. "Now notice all around you. Divine and Sacred Guides are here to help your transformation. Look around and find the best feelings and the brightest light of all . . . Only the brightest of all . . ."

His vague, gray, human form dissipated into tiny particles, spreading apart more and more until he disappeared. I pulled the blankets back up to my chin and listened . . . complete silence in the house again.

Seriously, I wouldn't have given this healing a second's thought, nor would I have entered it into this book. The truly interesting part came later in the next evening. As we sat down for dinner, I remembered to tell my partner about the teenage male spirit and what took place in the basement the night before. I first mentioned the banging and crashing sounds, but when I described the frantic flinging movements back and forth, her eyes widened, and she stopped me.

She told me that she had to stop for a bathroom break at a gas station during her four-hour drive home. As she got back into the car, she immediately felt as if someone was in the back seat, but no one was there, so she drove on.

As she continued, driving the last hour and a half, she kept noticing something in the rearview mirror. First, she saw a flash one way across the back seat, and then moments later, she would see the flash going back the other direction. This back-and-forth movement continued throughout the remainder of her trip home. Glad to be home, she immediately forgot to mention it and made no connection later that night of all the noise in the house.

Small Groups of Deceased Constantly Roaming

The energy of strong negative emotions tends to pull spirit people to each other. That tendency sometimes leads deceased individuals to group together due to their level of awareness. These spirits will sometimes be drawn to living people who are having the same or similar life problems and emotions.

For about a month, my family and I had major computer problems, and the family kept saying they saw shadows all over the place. As the month went on, the house was making more and more sounds of popping and boards cracking. I took one minute to check but did not pick up on anything.

One morning, my partner thought the roof had broken open under the weight of a huge snow that we'd received. I was asleep and did not hear it. Then our computer problems increased. The TV kept pixilating and going out.

At about noon, I went down to use the treadmill. I started walking and took the remote control in hand to turn on the TV. I began to scroll down the channels. I lost all control of the remote! It flew through all the channels, going up to channel 9,000. I pressed the Up button, and it flew up again and stopped on *Percy Jackson and the Sea Monsters*. I pushed the control again, and it raced all the way down to channel one. I pressed down again, and it bounced back to *Percy Jackson*, then stopped.

I said loudly into my basement, "Okay, you have my attention. Let's talk."

I got off the treadmill and sat down. I asked if they'd been causing all the problems for a month with the families' computers. I heard, "Yes." Then I saw a white mask over a hidden face. I asked, "Why are you showing me this mask?" I instantly saw an explosion in a college lab and a young male's face being burned away. I then saw other injured students. Then he showed me a vision of one person in a hospital bed. He then showed me that the injuries did kill this young man's spirit, as well as the other young males. The death of their spirit caused the death of their body. He and the others had physically died.

Out loud, I said to him, "I cannot imagine how horrible this was for all of you. I feel such a deep compassion for what you and the other students have been through."

He did not know why they were at my house. I telepathically explained that they came to my house because I can help them. I told the group I am a medium who also brings healing to troubled people. I can assist them to transform from this sorrow to love. I called in specific assistants to come and help these beings.

A circle of Divine and Sacred specialists quickly formed around the suffering group. I soon felt the sense of tragedy begin to lift oh so slowly. Then another being came in and wrapped a blanket of light around the spirit people but also wrapped the light blanket around the other Divine beings. Over time, they lifted up through the ceiling, then through my living room, and then out through the roof.

After everyone ascended through the roof, I checked the TV and the remote. All was working well. That night, the house was peaceful and very quiet... No pops or sounds of breaking boards. The computers and the TV did not fly up and down. (I have goose bumps as I write this.)

The Regretful

Regret carries a dense energy from a burden of heavy thoughts. Humans tend to carry a lot of regret. Some regrets happen when making a decision and later discovering it was not the best decision, or that decision created a negative outcome. A person holds a lot of regret when they do something that causes emotional or physical harm. It is impossible to name all the circumstances that lead to regret. Some deceased humans will simply not tell you what their actions were that causes them to avoid transforming into the light.

One spirit man told me that he knew there was a bright light. He said, "Yes, I know there's a bright light. I always keep my back to it."

I asked, "Why would you do that when that's exactly where you should go? It would be wonderful for you!"

He replied, "I did terrible things when I was alive, and I don't deserve to go to the light."

This is a rare example of a spirit person who knew they'd left the physical world but regretted his actions so deeply that he was choosing to continue his self-judgment and self-punishment.

A mentoring student and I were attempting to have a Zoom session. Her computer kept freezing on her end, but my computer was not freezing. It happened so many times that I finally said, "Let's stop for a moment. May I look around your home for a minute?" She gave me permission, so I telepathically looked around her office, and then went out and looked into her house.

I found a spirit man in the family room. He was actively interfering with the computer and electronics. I informed her of finding the man in her home, and how he was messing with the electronics. She said that her TV has come on twice on its own. I informed her that he caused the interference because he wanted her full attention. He said he does not want to go to the light because he didn't deserve to go; he deeply regretted many things he did in his life.

A Divine and Sacred specialist came. They talked it over for a long period of time until the spirit man realized he would not be punished. They both rose up together, went through the ceiling, and were gone. For the remainder of our session, the computer and Zoom were completely stable.

When the Cause of Death is Suicide

The deceased people who come to me the most all have one cause of their regret. They are people who have committed suicide. In this case, I experience multiple similarities among the dead. There seem to be consistent patterns with the deceased who have killed themselves. I do not find them emotional. They seem emotionless, or possibly as if they are numb in some ways. They are very factual and will give you details if you ask them questions.

I have noticed one detail lately . . . I don't think a deceased person who committed suicide has ever come to me on their own. They tend to follow a living person around and hang out with them as they continue to live their lives on Earth.

For example, a lovely young woman was seeing me for counseling. I noticed a young male spirit person following her to each session. When I knew her well enough and I thought she might be comfortable, I finally mentioned she had a deceased young man following her around and coming to her counseling sessions. At first, she didn't recognize anyone until I informed her that he'd committed suicide. Then she immediately knew him. He was pleased. She then realized she had a feeling as if someone was always watching her, but she never felt threatened.

He never caused her harm and was not a distraction in her life. He just wanted to be part of her life by following her around. So, as a medium, I was the translator for him. I shared with the young woman what he said when she asked him important questions about his death. Little did he know that he was about to receive assistance to transform from the Earth plane. And little did my counseling client know that she was about to receive a training in how to assist a deceased person to stop following the living, and to release the Earth to continue to learn in the nonphysical.

An older retired couple moved into a smaller home when they downsized. For their entire life, neither of them had ever witnessed a spirit person. In spite of never having any experience with spirit people, they finally decided to tell each other what they were experiencing in their new little house. Hesitantly and terribly afraid, each one shared with the other what they frequently saw. At individual times, this couple constantly saw a dead woman hanging from a rope in the ceiling of their living room. Each one was deeply afraid to tell their spouse. Finally, one of them shared the visualization with the other, and both were startled to find that not only were they seeing her hanging, but they were seeing her exactly in the same place, same clothing, and the same way she killed herself.

I could have attended to the woman for them, but for some reason, my guides directed me to give them simple "layperson" instructions to help heal this woman. This couple did their homework and never saw this troubled spirit person again.

I created my first simplified steps that I hoped they could follow on their own. I share these steps with you now in case someone you know needs help in the future. (This is not for the professional healing medium to use.)

Steps to Help a Layperson Go to the Light

1. Speak slowly. Send a prayer and invite in Divine and Sacred Guides who know exactly who this spirit person is and how this person is suffering. (You can also do this with groups of newly deceased people.)

2. In your mind or out loud, tell the spirit person what has just happened to them. Tell the deceased, "You died and are not alive anymore. Now, turn all your attention to the guide or guides who have come to help you."

3. In your mind, or out loud, tell the spirit person, "Now feel all the love coming to you from the guides."
4. Ask the guides to wrap the suffering spirit person in a blanket of warmth, security, and love.
5. Ask the guides to lift the spirit person out of this place and carry them directly to the brightest light of Source.
6. When a suffering spirit person is taken away to the light, you must then pray for healing angels to rush in and fill the entire area, the entire house or building, *and* the entire land with light, love, and healing.
7. Take a moment to feel the beautiful difference for yourself.

Healing Steps for the Confused and Needy

As a medium healer, it is vital that you assess each living client and each deceased client to discover if the deceased is, in any way, causing harm or illness for the living. The confused, needy, and unaware category of deceased humans is not malicious at all. If anything, they tend to be naive and complacent. They simply tend to hang around a building, an area, or a living human rather than releasing this world to go on with the expansion of their soul.

When looking for the cause of an illness or life struggle for yourself or your living client, you might overlook this type of spirit person because of their passive demeanor. How could they possibly be causing problems for the living? They can interfere with the living person's daily life in very subtle ways. They are so needy that they tend to drain energy from living people.

For example, a deceased person could have died of dementia, and their energy field now interferes with the living person they're following. That person does not get dementia, but they struggle to think creatively or clearly.

Another example is a spirit person who died from overdosing on a combination of alcohol and street drugs. He immediately followed his living family member every day, and stayed in his house during the night. He never meant any harm; however, the living family member suddenly began to have bad dreams and couldn't figure out why.

Here are the questions and the steps to take when you discover a confused or needy spirit person. No matter how innocent they may be, they could still be the direct cause of someone's illness, or the cause of someone negatively changing their life.

Questions to Ask Confused or Needy Deceased Humans

1. Do you know why you have come here?
2. Do you know why you have been staying around?
3. Tell me what is troubling you.
4. Do you know that you do not have a physical body any longer?
5. Do you know that you have died?
6. Let yourself remember how you died. Tell me what happened.
7. What have you been doing lately?
8. What places or people have you been focusing on?
9. Do you know you haven't yet crossed over into the light?
10. Tell me why you haven't let go of the Earth and gone to the light.

Steps to Remove, Transition, and Heal All Confused and Needy Spirit People

1. You have just discovered a spirit person in someone's energy field or their environment.
2. Never chase the intrusive spirit person away. They will go away for a short time but will always return.

3. Power up your toroidal field until your light is brilliant.
4. Telepathically ask the spirit person questions to specifically find out certain information. Ask each question, then pause and take what pops into your mind. That will be the deceased person responding to you. Your questions need to purposefully determine the reason that a spirit person is interfering with you or another person.
5. Ask these questions to determine why this spirit person is attracted to you (or the client). Ask each question, then pause to receive the pop:
   - How long have you been following me or the client?
   - Exactly where did you find me or the client?
   - What attracted you to me or the client?
   - What do you get from being with me or the client?
6. Ask these next questions to assist the spirit person with separating from the living person. Ask each question, then pause to receive the pop:
   - Do you know that you are dead and that you do not have your physical body anymore?
   - Do you know that you are causing harm or interference to the living?
   - I am calling in Divine and Sacred specialists to assist you. How many do you see?
7. Command: Divine and Sacred Guides who specialize in this particular spirit, completely and permanently remove the spirit from me (or client) on all levels and all dimensions. Remove all energy of the deceased and take them to the best place for their highest transformation into Light and Love now!

8. Watch in your mind's eye as the specialists remove and lift the spirit being upward and away. This transformation that you initiated is not only beautiful to witness but exhilarating to watch this positive change for everyone involved.
9. Remember—When any being is removed, we must always call in the Divine and Sacred healing guides and command: Fill every single space and place where that negativity used to be with cellular health, vitality, and (other power words that apply).

Chapter 11

Working with the Hostile, Hateful, Vicious Deceased

These are the individuals that living people call "evil" or "satanic." The truth about the spirit realms is that there are hostile, hateful, vicious dead people. This is a sensitive subject because of society's beliefs, philosophies, and religious or spiritual training. The good news is that they are more bewildered and unaware than the confused ones. These hate-filled spirit people do exist, even if your previous mediumship training told you that it does not exist. If you are a medium, intuitive, or medical intuitive, or if you are working to be, you must be open to learning about negative deceased people.

The deeply negative deceased can generate mild to severe physical illnesses, depression, personality changes, anxiety, and confusion for the living. Sometimes they have no clue that they cause any harm. Sometimes they deliberately cause harm, and even chaos. Why does a dead person interfere with the living? Why have they shown themselves to particular people? They have an uncountable number of reasons. It is uncountable because each one is an individual with an individual story.

As a healing medium, it's vital that you understand them as a troublesome, emotional mess that possibly affect your clients and will ultimately interfere with you if you do not prepare yourself. It will be extremely valuable for you to understand that the hostile and vicious spirit people are simply overwhelmed with dark experiences creating dark emotions, brought on from horrible life experiences in the physical world. If you're not prepared, you will be vulnerable. If you are prepared, because you are educated about them, then you are always more powerful than any nasty dead human can be. I want you to be more prepared than I ever was. I want you to be educated, aware, and alert for all possibilities in the nonphysical realms of life. I want you to be ready for this level of awareness and know you can handle that awareness with a commanding attitude.

This light is literally the spark-of-life energy and knowledge springing from Source. Both the dark realms and the light realms give us options and constant choices to make in developing our personal level of advancement and expansion.

Here is how one of my mentoring students describes this . . .

"I have had spirits try and scare me. Sometimes they send pictures to my mind of what they have done in their lifetime. When I'm assisting, I am the best version of myself. I feel so much love in my heart that I could never judge. I explain I know that is what you did, but it is not who you are. You have just forgotten. I often explain that life is a school, and they've done it tough here. I promise them that everything will make more sense when they cross over, as I know it to be true, that they are forgiven and loved. Hurt people, hurt people. I also have to say I don't take any funny business. I used to be a door person. So, I bring in my door bitch attitude sometimes, I am invincible, and I take no shit. I have dealt with some tough spirits, sex offenders, and hardened criminals. I remain empowered, strong, and compassionate."

You will not be surprised or caught off guard when you perceive the "negative spirit world." You will think to yourself, "Oh, there it is. I have learned about this from Tina's training, and I am prepared. I am capable of facilitating healing steps when the negative deceased is interfering. I am ready to be a healing medium for everyone no matter how ugly they are, or how ugly they are acting."

When fear surges though people, it is like a tidal wave of debilitating energy, leaving us diminished and terribly jeopardized. Emotions such as fear, guilt, shame, or remorse weaken areas in the human field.

The first time I taught mediumship, I was awake all night because I knew I had to teach about all levels of the most hateful, angry dead people and the details of how they interfere with the living.

I spoke this truth to a large number of students. When I finished, I looked out across the group. The energy shifted when I said, "Many of you in this workshop are energy workers or professional intuitives. I know some of you have had similar experiences with hostile deceased human spirits that I've described. I can see that awareness in some of your eyes. My hope is that some of you will now share what you have perceived. If you do share, you will help validate the details I'm teaching, and help the other students realize it isn't just me, Tina, who has these experiences."

Five students raised their hands to speak. They shared their own experiences with the strange, the weird, and the negative. The class then became eager to discuss this topic, and everyone began to breathe again.

Valuable Rules to Working with Negative Beings

Negative spirit human beings have no power, energy, or love of their own, so they attempt to take it from others. You, as the medium, are the one in charge and in a powerful position to assist everyone and everything involved.

Here are three rules for conducting a mediumship session with a client who is affected by a very negative deceased human:

Rule 1: You must now consider any level of an intrusive, interfering, hostile, dead human only as a client who needs you even more than your living client. This client might be a surprise, but they are still a client.

Rule 2: Never chase a negative deceased human away. Never try to get rid of them by using hostile attacks such as exorcisms. Do not try to get rid of them with kindness either. You must be more powerful than they are, and with this training, you will be.

Rule 3: You cannot kill a deceased human or a nonphysical being of any type. I know healers who tell me they stab them, or cut their heads off, and so on. The beings I'm speaking about are not physical. They are energy beings. Energy cannot be killed. It can only be transformed.

Many times, this "client" might be a surprise to you. This being is still a client who needs help and healing. This client, however, is also an obstructive interference for the living human client sitting in front of you. Both clients must be cared for. Both of your clients have come from Source. Everything from Source holds a spark of light. Even the negative and the dark beings come from the Creative Source of All. From the confused, unaware spirit person to the darkest of the dark deceased human, all beings have that same spark of light and goodness. They have lost track of, or forgotten, or do not feel they deserve it any longer. (See chapters 4 and 5 to "power up" daily.)

Understanding negative human entities as clients in need of relief will dramatically alter your beliefs in positive, life-changing ways. Negative humans have been forgotten, ignored, or have themselves become fearful of Source's light.

Signals of Negative Interference

When I look back over my earlier years of childhood and adolescence, I remember people who exhibited one or more of the following signals of negative interference. At that time, I was not aware of the spirit realm affecting people in negative ways. As a child, my experiences with the spirit world were sometimes eerie but also a natural part of my life. I had no idea that the spirit world included compassionate, selfless, loving beings, and at the same time, self-centered, hostile, egocentric beings with goals of power and destruction. Just like the physical world, the nonphysical world includes everything in between these extremes. Even the Bible states, "As above, so below."

As you describe negative interference to a living client, the information will not scare them if you point out that the negative being needs help and can be removed and healed. The information will never scare your client. It will always bring relief.

The following describes some of the primary verbal signals that a negative influence might be obstructing a human being. Be on the alert when you hear statements such as:

"I haven't felt right or well since I was at (a specific location)."

"I feel weird all the time."

"I don't feel like myself."

"I feel like someone is behind me, watching everything."

"I am having hideous dreams at night."

"I have gone to every specialist, and no one can find the reason for my illness."

My Grumpy Guy Experience

The key point here is to ask many questions to sort out what the hostile spirit being needed or wanted, and why he was causing me harm.

I became grumpier and more edgy, and one evening around 9:30 p.m., I became strange and distracted. I tuned in and called out to whoever was in the house. I saw (in my mind's eye) a middle-aged man, wrinkled, disheveled a bit. I asked him why he has been following me, and he said he wasn't following me. I asked him what he called it, and he said he was just hanging out with me.

"Okay," I said, "We'll go with that. Why have you been hanging out with me? You've caused me a lot of trouble."

He replied that it wasn't his fault, he didn't do anything. He never gave me a good answer why he was hanging around.

I asked him how he came to be "hanging out" with me. I instantly saw my office in my mind's eye. Then I clearly saw one of my colleagues, and I asked how he came to be with her. Then I saw my colleague's mother (who is in a nursing home), and then telepathically saw a tiny movie. Hostile dead man had come to the nursing home with someone else. I did not go back any further, as it didn't matter.

I asked him if he knew he was dead. He said yes. I asked how he'd died—in a bar fight, late in the evening (corresponding to about the 9:00 p.m. time I'd started fighting with my spouse). I asked him if he'd seen a bright light, and he replied he had, but he was ignoring it. He said he'd gotten into a lot of trouble in life, and he was pretty sure he wasn't going anywhere good. I told him it doesn't work that way in spirit.

He replied, "What would you know?"

I immediately directed the Divine and Sacred Guide who specialized in this man. I strongly stated to take this spirit man to the best place for his greatest good. I saw a male guide come in, with short brown hair. I'm serious, this guide had an air of resignation. The deceased man asked the guide how he knew him. The guide replied that he was one of his guides in the spirit world, and they have done this same thing many times before. In fact, this guide told the spirit man that he's been in this same situation many times. The guide then asked the hostile, agitated man to come with him. The spirit man agreed, and they rose upward and went into the light. All anger, agitation, and restlessness disappeared from me and from my house.

Yes, the enraged deceased are full of emotion and powerful concentrations of focused thought. Energy follows thought. If spirit people are trapped, it is only because they have trapped themselves within their own thought and emotional processes. Their focus may revolve around a certain person, an emotional event, an object, a building, or even a sensation such as drugs or alcohol.

Fear or guilt of facing God will bring a halt to a person's evolution as well. I do not see this as necessarily trapped, but they certainly do seem to be focused on the Earth plane because of the intensity of their emotions and thoughts. They are people who have also been functioning at a low level of conscious awareness. At death, we continue where we left off on Earth.

Never Frighten Your Living Client

Sometimes you hesitate to describe the details during your session with a client. That hesitancy is often caused by unusual details you witnessed during their session. You must never frighten your client, and yet, you must inform them of what happened. Sometimes I don't describe all that I've noticed or perceived. I always tell them they've released a great deal of negative energy, but if it's scary, I do not provide details. My guides tell me to always provide details of the client's healing process. I absolutely do not describe the look of a vicious dead person, or a strange non-human being that is about to be extracted from their body.

Instead, the details I provide include where the negativity is located, in or around their body. I will state that a large amount of negativity was causing harm to the client and making them physically ill. Or, for example, this negative burden kept them from owning their empowerment, almost like keeping them captive from living life fully.

I, myself, would be freaked out if someone told me that a terrible-looking being had just jumped out of me, and yet, I would want to know about the release of heavy negativity. There is a fine line here to draw. For example, I will not hesitate to tell someone that many thick black clouds have risen up and out of their body, or that their chest is full of rage and anguish. As a professional healing medium, ask yourself if the information would frighten or even terrify your client, or if it would bring relief to them? You must make that decision for yourself, keeping your client and their level of awareness in mind.

The Wrong Way to Confront the Hostile Deceased

Here are three examples of what happened during some of my first experiences with dealing with hostile deceased people. Remember, this is what *not* to do.

Example 1: The Mean Lady is Here

My daughter was working with a woman who recently moved into a new house. This woman shared with my daughter that their five-year-old son immediately had problems sleeping and woke up every night, crying hysterically.

Every night, he would tell them through his tears, "There is a mean lady in here!"

They could not console him and felt that the situation was even getting worse. My daughter went on to say that they did not really believe in ghosts or evil spirits, but now they were wondering if they had one in their home. They were also wondering if this might be the reason that Bible verses were painted all over the walls by the previous owners, attempting to disperse the evil spirits.

My daughter informed her that I do this type of thing for a living, and would she be interested in her mother doing a house clearing for them? The woman agreed out of desperation.

It was my call to action! I asked for the home's address, and then sat down to clear this place out. I immediately saw a very angry, haggard older woman with a hunchback who actually appeared exactly like a storybook witch. I was even more surprised to see that behind her stood the spirit of a professional-looking man in an old-fashioned black suit.

The woman glared and actually hissed at me, so I blasted her with white light. The battle was on! It was like Star Wars on the Earth plane! It was the first time I'd experienced a hostile human spirit with the energy to fight back. I was startled and afraid. She came at me multiple times, and I shot white energy back at her. She quickly disappeared. (I admit it now. That was the only thing I knew what to do back then!) The distinguished-looking man slowly faded away without taking any action. I was so full of myself and pleased. I thought I had just saved the day.

A couple of nights later, just as I was getting into bed, the haggard old woman came at me, screaming with rage. Again, I blasted her with white light until she vanished. I sat in bed, hyperventilating and afraid to turn off the light. The unexpectedness of the event convinced me that this was very real. This was a real and vicious spirit of a real woman who was enraged and very scary. This situation was way beyond what I'd ever experienced before, and I knew it was not over.

A week or so later, I sat with the monthly meditation group that I'd been facilitating for more than eight years. It was a large group of twenty-five women. I had just presented a brief talk about an aspect of meditating. We were sitting quietly in a large circle, settling down for our meditation. I felt so relaxed and had a smile on my face about the love that I'd been sharing, and the loving response I'd just received from the members.

And there she was again. Raging at me in her screeching voice with hatred in her eyes as she stood in the very center of the meditating women. I instantly looked around, worried about the other women, and what their reactions were to this invasion of our meditation. Each person continued to meditate so quietly with their eyes closed, individually drifting into their meditation.

At that exact moment, I knew I was in the wrong. This spirit person had her rights, and the right to feel all the anger she could hold. I suddenly felt compassion for her, that I now know came from all the love that this group of women surrounding me possessed. I was the teacher of a deep, heartfelt meditation, but it was the members who were living it at that moment . . . and I was not.

I sent flowing waves of love and compassion to her as she stood in the center of that circle. I telepathically asked each woman to send her all the love they had to give. I saw instant surprise on the witchy woman's face. She whirled around and ran through the closed door to the outside yard and disappeared. The door physically slammed so hard with a bang like a gun going off. We all jumped. Some opened their eyes, but everyone quickly resumed their meditating composure.

This time, I did not hyperventilate in fear. A peace settled within me. I knew deep in my soul that something profound had just happened.

Notice that blasting a spirit person, even a negative one, is never a healing. The negative spirit may leave, but they will just go to a different living person and continue to wreak havoc.

Example 2: Agitated Enough to Rip Somebody's Face Off

Remember: This is a story of what never to do!

My friend and I were sitting in the living room one evening when she asked if I would do an energy healing to her painful shoulder and neck. I agreed and placed my hands on her shoulders. Immediately, I felt a large male entity jump into me through the back of my neck, then though my body and my arms, and into my friend! His large, lumbering size felt like he was pushing my skin outward in all directions at once. This was not because of his large, wonderful vibration but because of the heavy density of his being. I was startled and tried to hide my concern from my friend so I wouldn't scare her. She didn't seem to notice, so even as an experienced energy worker, I decided I must have imagined it.

All through the night and into the morning, I kept thinking about that incident and what that deceased person had done. I knew he was real, and he was probably still within my friend's body! I went into a meditative state to intuitively ask my friend for permission to do a distance scanning and healing for her. I instantly received a yes. Because this was many years ago, my only tool then was to blast (and I do mean blast) everything with brilliant white light. So, I used the only technique I had at that time. I blasted that dead person that sat inside of my friend's body. My friend's aura instantly changed from dense mud to multiple clear, bright colors. Energetically, she instantly felt much calmer.

About an hour later, my friend called me again from her office. She immediately stated that she didn't know what was wrong with her all morning. She described herself as angry and agitated.

Her exact words were, "Earlier today, I wanted to rip somebody's face off because the world is so terrible." I panicked as she expressed these feelings, but I remained quiet as she talked. She then went on to say, "Suddenly, it was as if something had lifted from me, and everything was fine now. Isn't that weird?" She went on to say that she was having the strangest day and could not figure out why.

Whew . . . I felt relief as I described to her what had happened.

Notice that blasting a spirit person, even a negative one, is never a healing. The negative spirit will just go to a different living person and continue to wreak havoc. Remember, spirit people are real people too. They have the choice to feel pain and hatred, or love and compassion, just as we living humans do. Spirit people are also capable of resisting transitioning into the light.

VITAL POINT

Do not blast a negative spirit person with white light. Instead, provide a healing for them.

Example 3: A Brutal Deceased Husband

Remember: This is another example of what healing mediums should never do!

I met Susie virtually. She described how for the last four months, she had hit the back of her head severely six times by rising up from under things and banging her head on hard objects. She thought she must have a concussion. I asked if I could have permission to look inside her head. She responded with a yes.

I quickly heard the word, "worried." She strongly agreed that she worried that her brain was injured. I then asked guides for the cause of repeatedly hitting her head. I instantly saw a deceased man in the back of the room she was sitting in. In this situation, my guides informed me that she knew her attacker and I needed to tell her. I described the man in detail and said he had not crossed over, and he seemed hostile toward her.

She gasped and said, "I know exactly who he is!" He was her partner for many years. He was brutal many times, and she feared for her life.

I said, "He caused you to hit your head all six times. He is still trying to harm you." He told me that he was around her two months earlier, before he started causing her head injuries.

I asked him, "Why were you around her for two months before you began to hurt her?"

He said she'd begun to get so full of light that it pissed him off, so he began to hurt her. She had become brighter four months ago. It made him angry, so he began to push at her head.

I asked my client what she'd done four months ago that she became so bright.

She looked at her calendar and looked directly at me. "I began to study your teachings with two other women."

I was amazed, and her words deeply touched my heart to hear that her energy field had become so bright due to studying my books and taking my courses. I was covered with goose bumps, and I began to get teary. I was so touched by her words.

I reminded her that her brightness would always be more powerful than the man standing behind her. I directed her to feel her power. I had her call in Divine and Sacred guardians to specifically guard her from the hostile deceased, and together, we did the transformation steps.

She suddenly said, "Now he's fighting the Divine and Sacreds!" I directed her to keep repeating the commands until the guides lifted him up and away to the best place for his transformation into Light and Love.

She reached out to update me, stating:

"Thank you so much for the powerful session you did with me to clear out that negative deceased man from my energy field, who was causing me to knock my head multiple times and making it hard to recover from COVID. Since we did the session, I have felt bright and happy inside, with a clear energy flow that lifts me over the bumps of life. In my spiritual practices of meditation and Qigong, the energy is stronger and brighter and unimpeded. I feel happy and joyful, and looking forward to bringing this sense of aliveness to all my projects to help others. I can see the way opening to learning to do medical intuition and mediumship for others."

Never be intimidated or feel powerless with hostile deceased humans. Stand your ground no matter how horrible their actions are, or how ugly they look. Horrible, dangerous spirit people are still real people. They have choices to feel pain and hatred, or love and compassion, just as living humans do. They can resist Source, just as we living people can. You and your Divine and Sacred Guides are always more powerful than the struggling, hostile deceased or a non-human being. Remember, they all either need or want something.

When the Deceased Take Power from the Living

A colleague shares this dramatic story between two brothers, one alive and one deceased:

A Practitioner Shares a Story

A male client came in needing help with an energy that was in the basement. He described the energy as cold, dark, negative, angry and "something that you don't want to mess with, or be around."

The client shared that over the last few months, possibly up to a year, he, his wife, and his house were experiencing car troubles, electronic breakdowns, and plumbing issues. He started wondering if it was all due to this negative energy that was in his basement. He said the negative energy was getting worse. One night, while they and the dogs were all sleeping together in bed, the dogs stood up and started growling as they looked down the hallway toward the door that led to the basement. After a few moments, the dogs started barking in a protective way.

My client could tell that no one was physically standing there, and yet it felt like that same energy was beginning to move upstairs to the main living areas of his house. My client stated that he had tried to deal with the negative energy himself using sage, prayers, and asking it to leave, and it wasn't getting better. He found out about the medical intuitive work that I offer, and he scheduled a session.

After he shared the details of what had been happening, I began working with my client and with my Divine and Sacred Guides. Using Tina's mediumship steps, I zeroed in on the root cause, when the disruption started, when the negative energy began in his basement, and why the energy was getting stronger. Together, the client and I were able to use Tina's steps in identifying when the issue started, and gained clarity that the energy had entered his basement when his father passed away.

My client was able to identify that his living brother was angry and jealous of the relationships that my client had with his father and with his son. After his father died, his living brother's anger magnified and projected upon my client, his family, and his home. The brother's negative energy was so strong that it caused great disruption in my client's life, his wife's life, his home, their cars, electronics, and the plumbing in his home.

Using Tina's steps, I called in the Divine and Sacred angels, guardians, and protectors. I asked them to recognize that the negative energy around his living brother be recognized with compassion and love. The intention was to change and heal the jealous and angry emotions and behaviors toward my client, his family, and his home. In working with my Divine and Sacred Guides, they led me to write down steps for my client to take in order to regain his home, the relationship with his wife and son, and the rooms in his basement.

What's interesting was where this negative energy was presenting itself in the basement. It was the most important room to my client. It was his creative art studio. My client said when this started, he had no desire to be creative anymore, and he was hoping to get that back. There was also another room down in his basement that was dedicated to the train sets that he, his father, and his son enjoyed together. It was amazing to watch my client as the light bulbs were going on in his awareness. He understood why the energy was being focused in his home, and the intensity of where the energy was targeting. It was his creativity and the connection that he had with his father and his son. He described that his creative energy felt like it was being taken away or blocked since this negative energy was present.

By using Tina's steps to command and demand, my client left with a set of healing tools for himself and also working with energy with his living brother. My client felt so much relief and was also in awe that the energy was traced back to his living brother with jealousy and the anger. It all made sense to him by the time he left, and he felt like it was much more manageable in getting his home back and making it feel full of love, purpose, and meaning rather than coldness, jealousy, and emptiness. I'm so grateful for Tina's wisdom and medical intuitive steps that she teaches. She gives me the support to work with my guides and clients to come up with game plans that work to heal the living and deceased.

— Tammy Barton
www.illuminatingthesoul.com

I was in session, and I'd just informed my client that far, far back in her past, she completely lost her sense of self. It left her powerless and emotionally raw, even today, as if the situation had happened recently.

My guides suggested I ask her a specific question. So, I asked her, "What instantly jumps into your mind when I ask you this? When and how did you lose your sense of self?" She said that her husband had abandoned her forty years ago, leaving her with a toddler while she was pregnant with their second child. She added that her ex-husband had died two years ago. She and her two adult children were at his side as he passed. My client went on to tell me that she never told her children that she'd divorced him because he left her forty years ago.

Her emotions still felt openly raw to me, as if her husband's affair had happened last week and not forty years ago. I continued, "It also feels to me that one particular memory keeps coming up in your mind more than any other."

I asked her to go back to that memory and give him back his responsibility. I told her to literally take anything out of her body that was truly his. I went on to say, "You do not need to carry his junk or mess from his actions any longer. It is his to have and to learn from." There was a long period of quiet as she took this weighty energy out of her field. I then asked her to take back from him all that he'd taken from her. I then asked her to take back for herself all that she'd given away to him.

As she began to take her own empowerment back into herself, I clearly saw a man's shadowy form take a step forward as he walked right out of this woman's body. I had no perception prior to that moment that he'd been living within her body and her energy field. I questioned my guides why the ex-husband stepped out of this woman's body. The guides informed me that her ex-husband could no longer stay within her because she was instantly strengthening her own self-love and self-respect while doing this healing technique. He had to leave her because she no longer held the same subservient vibration that he needed and was draining from her. I noticed that he simply stood about three feet in front of her, as if he didn't know what else to do. I called in specialists for him to guide his transition into the light.

In this case, the man deliberately chose to remain in a situation that he'd helped create. In other words, rather than moving forward in his own development, he stayed within his ex-wife's field, where he felt comfort and familiarity. He was also constantly drawing energy from her and keeping her forever in a raw state of emotion. He had never left her. Literally and energetically, he just left her yesterday. This is an example of how real this level of work truly is. My client's weakened field allowed this man to continue his abuse of her. He continued the ultimate abandonment and betrayal until this healing practically ejected him from her body and energy field. She immediately looked younger and refreshed.

Healing Steps for the Hostile, Hateful, Vicious Deceased

You just intuitively perceived an enraged, vicious, and extremely negative spirit person. Here are the next steps to take:

1. Immediately direct your Divine and Sacred Guardian Warriors to surround you and completely protect you, now!
2. Immediately power up your toroidal field to its brightest and fullest.
3. Get in charge and in control. Feel fiercely powerful.
4. Direct this spirit person, "You back off now and see my Warriors!"
5. Ask the hostile deceased at least two important questions:
   - What drew you to me or this person, this house, or this land?
   - Do you know that you have come to me so I can help you?
6. Call in Divine and Sacred Transformational Guides who know this human.
7. Demand the spirit person: "Now you count the guides that have come for you and feel the love from the specialty guides. How many have come to help you?"
8. Tell the spirit person, "The specialty guides do not care how terrible you think you are. The guides can only feel love for you, no matter what you have done."
9. Direct the guides: "Completely and permanently extract all this spirit person's energy and cords from everything and everyone he has been negatively interfering with! Take him to the best place for his transformation into the light, now!"
10. The Healing: Call in Divine and Sacred Healing Specialists

to completely and permanently cleanse every single space and place where negativity used to be.

11. Then direct the healing specialist to fill every space and place where that negativity used to be with pure love and light, now!

Chapter 12

Be Prepared for the Complexities of the Nonphysical Realms

A student told me that multiple mediums described a deceased family member coming in. But those mediums also added that a second deceased human would show up that looked exactly like that deceased family member. In other words, two spirits kept appearing together, but they both looked like the same person. The student questioned me, asking how could two of the same deceased persons arrive together? I had no idea! So, I asked my Sacred Divines that same question because my human brain told me a couple of different options. They described exactly what was going on. They explained that the second duplicate figure, who always arrived a moment later, was a separate negative being interfering with the first deceased human.

When your living client is affected by one or more negative deceased beings or non-human beings with different levels of interference, you become the catalyst for change. And yes, there can be more than one entity involved with your client, and sometimes there may be many entities functioning at different levels, which results in a traumatized physical client.

In this example, you have the living physical client in your office, but you might have attached to them:

- A positive deceased loved one.
- One, or many more, negative spirit humans.

- One or more negative non-human entities. (See chapter 13.)

Just like people in the living, some nonphysical beings are shy and quiet, or in hiding, while others are aggressive and loud, and some are even lethal. All negative beings interfering with your physical client are simply in need of help just as much as the physical client in your office. Accept this concept, and you are on your way as an advanced healing medium.

A Practitioner Shares a Story: Spirits May Be Attached to Other Spirits

I had a session with a grieving mother, who was still trying to process the unexpected death of her nineteen-year-old daughter. She'd just left for college, was not making the smartest choices, and died in her sleep from side effects of party drugs and alcohol. The mom was still extremely sad but also admitted that she was actually very mad and angry at her. She tried not to be an overly protective mother and thought she had raised her child to make better choices.

We decided to invite the spirit of her daughter into our healing session and were planning on having a conversation with her to find more clarity. After we called out her name, the spirit that came into our awareness seemed very immature and didn't add much to our conversation. The girl had a very rebellious nature and showed herself wearing a black goofy outfit. She was sitting in a chair and gave us some arrogant attitude while chewing on gum with her mouth open.

"Chill, Mom," is all she had to say to us. "Don't take it so seriously."

Our efforts to have a conversation with her did not really succeed. I did not get the wisdom that could have contributed to a healing process. I was a bit disappointed. Tina then reminded me that spirits, which show themselves with a clear physical outline, might not be aware that they're dead and most likely haven't crossed over into the light yet. Transformed spirits appear less solid and are perceived as a very subtle form of energy.

After asking a few more questions to my guides, it was suddenly very clear that we were talking to a spirit attached to a spirit. This female spirit had taken over my client's daughter's body and was not aware that she in the meantime had passed too.

All of a sudden, I had three clients: The mom, the daughter, and the negative spirit who was in charge of all the bad decisions that had led to the girl's death.

I called in Divine and Sacred spirit guides who helped that spirit to cross over. Only then was I able to have a conversation with my client's daughter. She was very shy and felt extremely embarrassed. She could barely look her mom in the eye. She was so sorry she'd caused so much sadness and disappointment. She was just having a good time and had no idea that negative spirits could cause so much harm. She apologized to her mom and asked not to judge her for what had happened. Then I called in Divine and Sacred Guides to help her cross over as well. She told me she was excited and curious to meet that light now and become the stardust that fills the hearts of people with love and compassion.

I wrote this to the mother and will let you know if I hear back from her:

I was not happy with our last session and kept thinking about the energy work we did. I can't forget your statement that you had tried not to be an overprotective mother and that you thought you'd raised your child to make better choices.

I had a session with my mentor, Tina, and we analyzed the session together. When we invited your daughter into our healing session, I could not really bring together what I perceived and what you've told me about her. I was planning on having a productive conversation with her in order to find more clarity and to help you heal.

The spirit that came into our awareness, though, seemed very immature and had not much to add to our conversation. Our efforts to have a conversation with her did not really succeed. We did not get that wisdom that could have contributed to a healing process.

At first, I was a bit disappointed. Then Tina reminded me that spirits who show themselves with a clear physical outline are not aware that they are dead, and most likely have not crossed over into the light yet. Transformed spirits appear less solid and get perceived as a subtle form of energy. So, we did ask a few more questions to my guides, and it was suddenly very clear that we were talking to a spirit who had taken over your daughter's body. This spirit was not aware that she had passed, and even less aware that your daughter had passed too. That negative female spirit had made all the bad decisions that caused your daughter's death.

We called in Divine and Sacred spirit guides who helped that girl to cross over. Only then I was able to get through to your daughter to have a conversation with her. She was very shy and felt extremely embarrassed. She barely could look you in the eyes. She was so sorry she had caused so much sadness and disappointment. She was just having a good time and had no idea that negative spirits could cause so much harm. She wanted to apologize to you and asked to not judge her for what had happened.

Then we called in Divine and Sacred Guides to help her cross over too. I just wanted to share this with you, and I hope this helps you heal. Lots of love to you.

— Barbara Liniger
info@barbaraliniger.com

The Non-human Realm is Complicated and Multilayered

This happened in one of my mentoring sessions with a long-term student . . .

CLIENT: Last week, I was with a group of friends doing remote healing work together with a client with lung cancer. These other energy workers said their work has made him so much better. They said things like, "He is so grounded now, and he is so much better."

I did not say anything, because I was not getting that at all. I saw that he was drifting away, leaving his body more and more. The grounding they were doing was not enough. Then someone else said, "Yes, I see entities, but I'm not so good with entities, so maybe it's just an energy blockage."

I finally told the group that my guides just informed me that this man did not feel he deserved to be healed. Then the group literally started guessing and saying, "Maybe it's this, or maybe it's that. Maybe it's just an energy block."

TZ: You need to understand that most people do not have this level of training that I've done with you, and they do not have this level of awareness that you now have. They don't know what you know.

CLIENT: This man is not healing, and he needs much more than simply grounding. This man is dying!

TZ: Every time I find cancer, or my friend Dan finds cancer, we both find negative entities. Healing cannot happen unless they are removed first. This removal must happen first for positive changes to happen with cancer. Your friends couldn't deal with it when you mentioned that he does have negative beings interfering with him.

This is important to realize . . . When negative beings deeply interfere with people, the human spirits often avoid or reject treatment, and they cannot give you permission to remove entities. There is only one time that we healing mediums take action without requesting permission, and that is when a living human is so deeply interfered with by negative beings that they are unable to give permission.

CLIENT: Okay.

TZ: Now if you want, I ask you to really power up your field and direct your guides to do the powering up with you now. Do not even try to ask him for permission. You power up first! And if you want, we can practice with him now, if that feels right to you.

I want you to call in your most powerful guardians and warriors and Archangel Michael's legions, and direct them to power you up and also shield you.

CLIENT: Okay, let me do that first. (Long pause.) Okay, I did that. But now I see the entities eating away at his body and like feasting on him and eating his energy away. Now I see different types of entities.

TZ: This is common to find different types of negative beings all at the same time. For your practice, ask your guides how many types of beings are interfering with this man.

CLIENT: I got the number twelve.

TZ: For your practice, I want you to ask your guides for more information *first*, before the guides begin to extract them. Ask: When was the exact moment that these entities attached to this man?

CLIENT: The guides say it began twenty years ago.

TZ: Ask this: "What was happening in that moment that he became so vulnerable to the point that the entities began interfering with him?"

CLIENT: He is a super nice person. Back then, he was so vulnerable he just gave himself to everybody. He could not differentiate between good and bad. Everyone took advantage of him. He became more and more vulnerable. Now he looks like a dead cadaver on the floor, and all these beings are eating his organs. It's not a nice picture.

TZ: I know . . . Now, what does this leave you wondering about whether you could ask your guides for more information? Make this about your learning too.

CLIENT: I'm wondering, is he still healable, or is he just going to fade away? What is the best way to help him at this stage of his life? I get to remove all entities, and even if he does not make it and dies, he can die in peace without those entities.

TZ: What I want to point out to you is that many people think when the living person dies, all negative entities let go of that person at the time of death, but that is not correct. Sometimes those entities are attached to that person's soul for many lifetimes. Whether he lives now or not, you releasing those entities will give him relief for his next lifetime. This is how dramatically important this is for him, and also for you!

CLIENT: I am calling in spirit guides who specialize in each of these twelve different entities.

TZ: I would also call in specialty guides called the Carrion, who specialize in the most negative, dark beings of all. Call in all twelve of them and the Carrion. And stay back from this. Do not involve yourself in any way.

CLIENT: I see dark fumes rising. The guides are saying, "The party is over." Capture them and restrain them, because they are acting like they are going crazy.

TZ: Yes, sometimes you will see a great battle.

CLIENT: The dark steam is getting sucked up and out into the Universe.

TZ: Make sure you tell the specialist to remove all roots, tendrils, and particles.

CLIENT: The energy is getting quiet and still. Lots of noise as the guides carry away all these entities.

TZ: Make sure you keep directing the specialists to get every root, tendril, and particle out of him now!

CLIENT: Now I feel like he needs energetical CPR, because he's not moving at all.

TZ: Ask more questions first to see what is going on, such as: Has every one of them been removed, etc. Always ask more questions!

CLIENT: I scanned the back side of him. I asked that his heart be checked, and his systems. I get I need to ask that exhaustion, fear, and hopelessness be removed. A gentle guide is sweeping it from his blood and his fluids.

TZ: I would add that all cancerous tumors are removed now.

CLIENT: I am also adding a directive to reorganize his organs, because it looks like they are twisted and a mess to take it back to his original blueprint to their original state with all the fascia around them in place. I asked the guides to close the body back up so I do not see inside.

TZ: They keep showing me his feet, so please check that out too.

CLIENT: His feet look like metal and are not connected to the earth. The guides tell me it's like a robot. He cannot make his own decision about which way to go.

TZ: This is like an implant for control. Direct your specialists that all control mechanisms be removed now.

CLIENT: I see the metal disappearing and regular tissue grows over everything. He now wants to jump up and down in the grass.

TZ: Tell the guides to do that now with him.

CLIENT: Oh, this is helping him start his heart back up, like doing jumping jacks and skipping, with the guides holding him to assist him.

TZ: Ask the guides if there is anything else to do to assist with this man's health.

CLIENT: Fresh air, because he's also had pneumonia. The guides will continue to be with him now, so he does not get stagnant. He looks better now. He is inhaling better. Earlier, he looked like roadkill with all those entities on him. I know you told me in the past that all cancer has negative entities involved in some way.

TZ: Let me tell you something very important. When something is this severe, you must always keep yourself pulled back, and you do not ever need to watch the process either. What I did for you that I must tell you is when we began and noticed the severity of this man's situation, I directed the guides to place the Merkabah around you. This is a sacred geometric form, and I place it around me too. There are photos of it on the Internet. Notice the feeling of the Merkabah the second you see it. Notice the details and the power of it.

Important to Note: We healing mediums can alter and heal across time, space, and events. One of the most important details for the practitioner to discover is the exact moment when the victimized human became so vulnerable to the negative spirit world. It is key to discovering the moment causing the client's issues.

A powerful, permanent healing must always happen in this order:

1. Always remove ALL negative beings FIRST before other healings can happen.
2. After negative beings are completely extracted, other healings can more easily take place. (See my book *Advanced Medical Intuition*).

I had a session with a new mentoring client. He had only taken one of my courses and practiced with only a few clients. He mentioned that he couldn't sleep last night because something did not feel right in his house. He said it felt like a male spirit person was in his house, and he didn't feel like a good person. I directed him through the steps to invite in a new Divine and Sacred specialist who knew exactly about this male spirit. He did the invitation, then proceeded to the one-question interview: Are you truly at the Divine and Sacred level? He was successful with those basic steps. He then said he sees a dark form standing near a deceased person.

I directed him to ask his guide if the dark form was human or non-human.

"Non-human."

I explained to him that he now has a multilayered situation. There is a troubled deceased human who has a negative non-human attachment. The non-human struggled a little but calmed down when Divine and Sacred wrapped it in a white brilliant blanket of light. The non-human was now contained. Then I told him to direct the guides to extract the non-human from the deceased human and take it to the best place for its transformation into Light and Love. Then direct the guides to wrap the deceased human in a comforting white blanket of light and take that human to the best place for their transformation.

Steps to Direct Your Divine and Sacred Guides in Complicated Situations with Hostile Non-Humans

Complicated situations often entail multiple types of beings interfering with your client. For example, the living client might have one or more non-humans interfering, and at the same time, there could also be one or more negative deceased humans.

1. Always direct the guides to first contain the non-human.
2. Next, remove the non-human and take it to the best place for its transformation into Light and Love.
3. Then repeat the same steps for the negative deceased human.
4. Then fill all the empty space with light, love, and health.
5. Then fill the house or building and land with Light and Love.

Here is a good example of a multistep process to remove a group of drugged deceased males interfering with one deceased male.

The parents of a young, deceased man named Tim came to me for help with their unrelenting grief regarding their son dying of a drug overdose. Immediately, I called in the spirit helpers for the four deceased men, whom I immediately saw hanging around Tim. One left instantly with the angels. The other three took longer. I had to talk to them and explain about the angels and how they were there to help the three of them transition into the light. Those three slowly rose upward and left with the angels.

Then I was surprised. Suddenly, a fifth deeply negative and drugged deceased man came out of Tim. He had been hiding. He was vicious and cruel, and strongly attached to Tim. So, I repeated the process for him to leave and called in more spirit helpers, who assisted that one too.

When there is more than one spirit person interfering, the more negative and hostile beings will hide while the others come forward to receive your help. Make it a point to ask your guides if there are any negative beings hiding, and if so, direct the guides to extract it out of the living client.

VITAL POINT

> Always remember, the most negative and hostile beings will often hide while other nonphysical beings readily come forward for help.

Finally, I began to communicate with Tim. I called Divine and Sacred Transformational Guides for him too. I asked him to look around to see who arrived for him. He replied that angels were there. I asked him to count the angels who were around him, and he said he saw four angels. I explained to him that they were specialists who had come to help him in his transformation into the light. He did not question me at all. I asked him to turn it all over to his specialists.

What I witnessed next was simply beautiful. The angels had their arms stretched out toward him, and Tim just laid across their arms. The angels then wrapped him in something that looked like a blanket of brilliant lightbulbs. All the threads in the blanket were threads of white light. The angels then lifted upward with Tim in their arms. He was so calm and peaceful. He did not say anything to me or look my way. He gently transitioned into the light.

I kept Tim's parents informed every step of the way. I told them that Tim was able to do this now because of our meeting. He wanted to make sure that both of you were with me when he left. He was watching out for both of you.

Tim also said, "It really helped me when you got all of those dead druggies off me." I could tell that he meant it.

I went on to inform his parents, "I want you both to know that Tim's spirit was near both of you for quite a while. In my experience, most people who make their transition seem to be gone for about three months. I do not know why they're completely gone around three months, but that is the usual. When he returns, each of you will probably sense it right away."

It's Never Too Late to Heal Your Own Unresolved Issues with the Deceased

A healing medium guides a client through a soul retrieval:

A Practitioner Shares a Story

I recall a client who confided in me, stating that her dad had passed, and she thought she was going crazy. This client had all the feelings of being molested, especially at night. I don't allow any preconceived ideas so that I don't create any interference, which allows me to receive the clearest information when I tune in. When I tuned in, I saw a big deceased Greek man in her energy field.

He told me he loved his daughter. She was his favorite of all his many children. He was intimidating and possessive. My client confirmed this to be true, and her face took a shade of pride, and then shame. I explained to her that it's okay to love a man who was mentally ill; we are built for our survival to love our parents. He was unwell, and she deserved to be loved and kept safe. I told her that I was sorry he couldn't give her that.

I asked her to pull everything out of her that she'd taken on from the experiences with her father. Pull out all the shame, confusion, fear, and beliefs about the world, other people, men, or any dark or dense energy.

Then I asked what she wanted to do with it: Hand it back or take it away? She wanted to remove it from herself and hand it back to her dad. I directed her to watch as it came out of her body, watch as it left.

"Now hand it back to your father," I said, and then asked, "Did he accept it?"

She said, "No, he says he did nothing wrong."

I said, "It is not yours to carry. You are innocent, so give it back and place it all at his feet and watch his face."

She did. He turned away.

I asked that our most Sacred Guides now assist her dad with transmuting this energy and heal all that can be healed. I asked her to disconnect completely from him and to say anything she needed to say.

Next, I asked her to call back her energy through a specialty filter provided by our Sacred Guides. Call back everything you disowned or gave away because of these experiences with your dad. Call back all your power, all your light, purified and cleansed, back to you. See where it goes. Allow it to fill every cell, every atom, and every space between the atoms of your being. Notice what color it is.

I then asked my guides what to do next. They said to call in her grandfather. The grandfather had been physically abusive to her dad. Yet, the spirit said to call him forward. The grandfather's hand came through the light with a shot glass. The client's father took the shot and hugged his father, and then both disappeared into the light.

Boy, we humans have complex relationships. It reminded me to always let the client guide the session. She loved her dad. As abusive as he was, she'd said she was grieving him. If I had been judgmental to her or her father, she would have needed to repress her grief, but instead, she cried. Trauma enmeshed with love is complicated. Leave assumptions out of your sessions and have positive kind regards for all involved. My client said she felt immediately lighter, and the night terrors didn't return.

— Jade Osera
jadeosera@outlook.com

Soul Retrieval Steps to Heal the Deceased

It's never too late to heal a negative deceased human, and it's never too late to release and heal your living client as well. Life and death and relationships can always be altered into the positive. Here are the steps to accomplish a soul retrieval for a deceased person

1. A painful memory in the deceased person's life has come to the forefront.
2. Tell the deceased person that you want them to let their imagination unfold like a movie in their minds.
3. Ask them to imagine going back and standing with their younger self in the exact moment of the painful trauma.
4. Ask how they know their younger self is aware of them being together.
5. Direct both the young self and the current self to pull everything out of both their bodies that is not theirs. Completely pull out the traumatic event, the pain, the memories, all the ugliness, and give it back to their wrongdoer.
6. Tell the deceased person to take their time and make sure they get absolutely all of it out of them and give it all back. You will be still until they speak, so you do not interrupt their process.
7. Watch the deceased person's energy field as they respond to your request. If there is any residual darkness, tell them to get it all out

of both their current self and their younger self. Remind your client to do every step in partnership with their younger self.

8. Now direct both the deceased person and their younger self to call out for healing guides to create a perfect cleansing filter. Wait until the deceased person informs you that the filter is present.
9. Next, firmly tell the deceased and their younger self to take back absolutely everything that has been taken from them. Bring it through the cleansing filter and place it back inside both of them. To encourage the deceased person, use the same emotional words that they used to describe the traumatic event. Some examples to say aloud might be:
    - Both you and the younger you, take back everything that was taken from you.
    - Take back your confidence.
    - Take back your ability to love.
    - Take back all of your energy.
    - Take back all of your body.
    - Take back all of your POWER now.
10. Let the deceased person know you will be still until they speak, and to take their time making sure they get it all.
11. Tell both of them (the deceased's younger self and their current self) to look the wrongdoer directly in their eyes until they change in some way.
12. Ask them—the deceased's current self and their younger self—to talk it over with each other and see if there's anything else that needs to be done for a complete and permanent healing. Pause and allow both to check that out. Follow through with anything that seems incomplete for them.
13. Direct the current self to ask the younger self if they are ready

to leave that moment forever. If yes, tell both to release that event and to move forward, merging together before coming back into the deceased's present moment. Inform the deceased of the positive energetic changes. Direct the deceased to look around and see the brightest guide, and to go with that guide into a healing transformation.

The following is an excerpt from Heather McCutcheon's Book *Connecting the Dots: From Ad Exec. to Energy Practitioner.* Heather shared her unexpected awareness of a deceased person related to her Reiki client. Sharing her experience brought a phenomenal healing to her living client but also to the client's grandfather.

Mary, the woman with the broken tibia, came to see me after her grandfather passed. She was understandably grieving. He lived in one of the Southern states and Mary had intended to fly down to spend time with him before he left this world, but by the time she could get away from work and arrange a flight, she was informed by her family that there wasn't time. Instead, she had to settle for a phone call in his last hours, which left her feeling both short-changed and guilty.

In the weeks that followed his passing, she came in for a combination of massage and Reiki for relief on all fronts. As we were finishing up, and I had her head cradled in my hands, I felt a tangible pressure around my middle and up my back, as if I was being hugged from behind. I usually shared my intuitive impressions with Mary, as she was very open to exploring metaphysical phenomena, but at the same moment I felt this sensation, she began to cry. She was having her own experience, and I decided to keep my mouth shut.

Afterward, she told me she felt her grandfather's presence when I was holding her head and that's what had brought on her strong wave of emotion. I debated whether or not to tell her what I felt. The information I receive is not always verifiable, and I never want to come off as opportunistic or trying to manipulate someone's grief. I decided she knew me well enough to know I wouldn't do that, so I told her what I'd felt in the same moment she was having her experience of him. Her eyes got wide and filled with tears again.

"The last thing I said to him on the phone was that I was so sorry I wasn't there for him," she said, "and that I just wished I could give him a hug!" And then I got weepy, too. We sat there in silence for a moment, astonished at the experience we'd just shared—all three of us."[2]

— Heather McCutcheon, Reiki Brigade
www.reikibrigade.org

Healing can be successfully accomplished for people who want to heal. Healing can happen . . .

1. During a person's precious death process.
2. For someone who is already deceased.
3. For the living client.
4. For ourselves.

It does not matter how long the individual has been dead. It does not matter how far away they are as they're dying. It doesn't matter if they have been dead for centuries. It is never too late to help and to heal. Time and distance is never an issue.

Everything is energy. Energy is instant. Energy is forever.

2 Heather McCutcheon, *Connecting the Dots: From Ad Exec to Energy Practitioner* (Minneapolis: Hillcrest Publishing Group, 2015), 130-131.

PART 4

Non-human Beings are Everywhere

Chapter 13

Are Non-Human Beings Real?

Yes, they are real. This might be difficult to believe or even to imagine. If you haven't noticed them already, then it's time to notice so you're prepared for anything and everything!

No matter what, all beings—alive, dead, or non-human—must be considered as clients! When a non-human appears, they instantly become a client. This client happens to be some other type of being and not human. When non-human beings appear, you are now the healing medium to help them.

Always remember this: We are not victims of "bad" human spirits, and we are not victims of nasty non-human beings either.

I discussed earlier that all deceased humans are still just as alive as we are, and I ask that we mediums interact with the deceased as if they are alive beings, because they are alive! Now, I ask that you also consider all types of beings as alive. Even non-human entities are alive, and like humans, they also have many different levels of awareness and many personalities. Non-humans, just like humans, also have different levels of awareness, from kindness to high levels of aggression.

Complicated Interdimensional Realms of the Non-humans

Nonphysical, non-human beings are quite real. They are one potential cause of physical, mental, and emotional illness and life struggles for living humans. They are often the cause of deceased humans and the deterioration of living humans. Deceased and alive humans are so completely and deeply interfered with that they are not aware of non-human beings interfering and causing their constant traumas in life.

You will quickly learn that you are so much more powerful than any level of negative beings will ever be. You will confidently become the healer for all types of negative beings who are wreaking havoc with the living. One of my goals is to teach you now, so you will never be surprised or alarmed when you perceive strange beings. You will be trained and ready for anything and everything. You will come across a non-human or a nasty dead person and you will say to yourself:

"I know exactly about this type of being. It is a client in need of my help. I am completely safe and more powerful than it will ever be, because I am invincible with brilliant light, and I am the director of my Divine and Sacred team."

VITAL POINT

> With your Divine and Sacred team of specialists, you are always more powerful than any negative non-human entity will ever be.

Humans living on Earth are unpredictable. Dead humans are unpredictable. Non-human entities will always be unpredictable. So, be ready for non-human surprises! You are the interpreter, interventionalist, the psychopomp, the healer, and now the teacher. You are learning steps to work with resistance from the living, the deceased, and now with beings that are not human.

There is so much more happening across the unmeasurable space around the Earth. We mere humans, even healing mediums, know very little about all the non-human beings that exist. What you must know now is our Divine and Sacred team of specialists will always be more powerful than deceased humans or non-humans.

This might be a stretch for many readers, but other types of entities inhabit the Universe—more than we humans can even imagine. I will try to describe the beings that I have personally witnessed as well as beings that other mediums have shared with me. When creation happened, it was extremely creative! Once again, way beyond what even we can imagine. Just when I think I have perceived it all, I come across another entity that I have never seen before.

There is much more going on in life than humans.

Positive Non-Human Beings

Non-human beings exist, but not all are threatening or harmful. Some non-human entities are ornery and mischievous but do not intend direct harm. Some beings are part of the natural world of the earth, while others are a natural part of other dimensions, other planets, and other universes. We have never been alone.

If you have been hesitant to perceive the dead, then you might be even more cautious to consider working with and healing non-human beings. The nonphysical realms are real, and they truly exist. Nonphysical beings are also just as alive as you are. Even my own intuitive family never mentioned beings that are not human. I did not grow up with that level of awareness in childhood. I grew up far out in the country, so mainly I watched spirits of deceased farmers in the fields behind our barn.

The most common non-human does not seem to be recognized as non-human beings. The most known and valued non-human beings are angels and archangels. People accept angels as real perhaps because they are recognized by traditional churches. They are still not really identified as non-human beings among us. I have witnessed angels of all shapes and sizes and specialties. My life has expanded, brightened, and is full of love since I now work only with archangels and other beings at the Divine and Sacred level.

My first encounter with non-humans was delightful and surprising.

In my early twenties, I finally went downtown in the big city with a friend. We walked all around a small park in the center of downtown. We both stood and watched a gorgeous fountain that floated straight upward and fell in lovely ripples. The sun created little rainbows as the water flowed. I stood there in the city center, looking way up at the fountain of bubbling water just before it fell back into the pond.

I looked to my right at my friend to see if she was noticing anything, and asked her, "Do you see what I see at the top of the water just before it falls downward into the fountain?"

She squinted, trying to see something other than moving water and said, "No."

I was clearly seeing four female fairies who looked just like Tinker Bell in the Peter Pan story. I watched them, and they watched me. They bounced and played on top of the bubbling fountain but did not seem to be wet. When they noticed that I noticed them, they played, bounced, and laughed even more. That was the first moment that I became aware of the positive, playful, and beautiful non-humans that are with us.

I continue to experience many different groups or categories of non-human beings. Just like humans, some are sweet and truly kind, some seem anxious or irritated, some are grumpy, and others are vicious and cause harm whenever possible.

For example, I have experienced a friendly giant. He was so massive that his feet were the length of the five-acre field behind my house. His head was up in the clouds. When I asked for his name and why he was standing behind my house, he responded, "I am the Traveler. I am here to protect you."

He watched over me for three days and then vanished.

One more positive example is a golden dragon. My house was creaking, popping, and exploding with sounds. I had a large group of negative non-human beings trying to scare me. Instead of being frightened, I called out for Divine and Sacred Guides who specialize in this group of negative beings.

Bam! The explosive sounds stopped.

I telepathically scanned all around the house and did not perceive anyone or anything that stopped the wave of negative beings. My attention was pulled up and out to the roof. There stood a golden dragon across the length of my house, with flames coming out of its mouth. I nearly fell to my knees in gratitude and surprise.

I could go on and on about positive non-human entities, but we must move on and focus on the negative non-human entities since they're the ones causing problems and needing our help.

Negative Non-Human Beings

I will begin with a list of vicious entities that cause havoc and harm. I have witnessed these beings, but together with my dynamic Divine and Sacred team, we have come face-to-face with and brought healing and transformation with individuals of these categories. I have witnessed and dealt with the following:

Screaming banshees, some negative dragons, golem, trolls, mermaids, centaurs (half horse, half man) fauns/satyrs (half goat, half man) cyclops, goblins, a snake with a man's head, monsters of all kinds and sizes with grotesque faces with drooling fangs, extraterrestrials, shape-shifters, praying mantis, reptiles, clusters of slithering snakes, huge black spiders, bats, swarms of ant-like insects, trolls, and gargoyles.

Some will show flaming-red eyes without any visible body; or crooked, knotted hands with long claws reaching out for you. Any of these forms may leap at you unexpectedly. If you have done your preparation that I've described throughout this book, you will already be prepared and protected, and they cannot reach you. Your light from Sacred Source is too brilliantly bright and more powerful than they can ever be. They cannot stand the brightness, and it feels as if it's burning them.

Individuals of these groupings may appear in absolutely any location and are often attached to deceased humans or living humans. Some entities will frequently show themselves as monsters. Monsters tend to come in all varieties, shapes, and forms. You might see them with their mouths wide open, fangs dripping with strings of drool. They will all have flaming-red eyes that are creepy. Do not look into those red eyes, and do not cower in fear. It's just part of their elaborate show to weaken you.

I want you to be a prepared medium healer. I want you to be ready for anything, at any time, and in any form. Some of these alarming non-human forms, I later see in TV ads for horror movies and on book covers. My guess is that the creators of these horror movies and books have also experienced or seen these fearsome creatures from other realms.

My primary goal is to share this vital information with you so you're ready and won't go into fear. They are simply extremely hostile representatives of the negative part of life on Earth. If you already know about these beings, then you will be ready. Both human spirits and non-human beings, in nonphysical forms, cause illness and harm to the living and the deceased. Many energy workers, intuitives, and yes, even mediums are often not aware of this level of entity and not prepared. You must be prepared, and you must be in charge of yourself and your energy!

Every word within a thought attracts or repels nonphysical energy and nonphysical beings. We humans must understand the power of our thoughts. Negative thoughts and emotions may have negative consequences with entities of the nonphysical realm. People are always inadvertently summoning nonphysical beings, especially when they "channel" entities. Intuitives who channel are often allowing nonphysical beings to step into their physical body and speak using their vocal cords.

My first non-human experience occurred very early in my life. I had no understanding, training, or experience when I decided to send love to a disturbed friend of the family. I sat in meditation for a few moments, picturing this person in my mind. I filled myself with love and projected it outward toward the disturbed person. The second the love frequency reached that individual, their abdomen blew open, and an enraged gremlin-type entity flung itself at me and across the 1,500 miles between us. I'd heard about blasting negativity with white light. That was the only tool I had back then, so I blasted it with white light like a laser beam when it hurled itself at me. It shattered into tiny particles that lifted upward. I was hysterical with fear because I was not prepared. You will be prepared.

When I presented this segment in my workshop for the first time, it inspired the advanced day of my workshop. I could not sleep the night before my presentation.

That morning, trembling in front of a large class, I said, "We will begin today with the dark, but we will not end this day with the dark. We will end the day in love, light, and strength."

I then began to teach about the strange, the weird, and the negative. As I talked, the room became extraordinarily still. The students seemed immersed in my words. No one moved, or became angry, or ran out of the room as I expected. I continued on with my information in a neutral, matter-of-fact manner.

Negative non-human entities cannot be killed by stabbing them with knives or swords, or by asking your Sacred Divines to kill them. They are real beings, but they are also energy beings, and even physics says that energy cannot be killed. Deceased people and nonphysical entities exist in the nonphysical because they are all eternal and energetic, with either an advanced level of conscious awareness or no awareness.

I was once deeply involved in the healing portion of my client's session. I had only begun to send him Reiki energy when I intuitively witnessed metallic-looking clamps rising up from his spine. Each of the four clamps seemed to slowly release their grip, disconnecting one at a time from four different vertebrae along this man's spine. At that time, I had no idea what or why I was visualizing that release. As the clamps lifted away, I was startled when four faces of the aliens commonly called "the Greys" appeared right in front of my face. They were, indeed, gray with large black eyes devoid of any emotion. Once again, I had no training in how to deal with this type of intrusion. I blasted all four of them with the Reiki frequency of compassionate love and light. They backed off and faded from sight. The clamps lifted completely from that man's spine.

This man already knew that his life was compromised by invasive extraterrestrials. Once again, I was surprised that people usually have some degree of knowledge about their struggles with energetic beings. And once again, I was not prepared to experience these beings, let alone know how to handle a healing situation involving them. Do not go into fear, no matter what category of negative beings you are facing.

My friend Tom was struggling to breathe, and physicians could not find anything compromising his lungs. He asked me to look inside his body. I immediately saw a black dragon-type serpent tail wrapped all around his physical body. I intuitively scanned the entire length of the serpent and found its tail piercing his physical heart. It had stabbed him in the heart, then spiraled around his chest to hold onto him. I did not expect a dragon-type serpent piercing this man's heart and crushing his chest and lungs.

I did what I always do now: I called in my most powerful Divine and Sacred Guides who specialize in this being. I then directed them with all of my commanding might:

- "Completely and permanently extract every particle of this being out of (full name of client) now!"
- "Take it to the best place for its transformation into Light and Love now!"

- To the Divine and Sacred Healers: "Completely and permanently fill every space and place within (name of client) now with powerful cellular vitality; healthy, well-functioning lungs, and physical strength."

A Practitioner Shares a Story: When Entities Look You in the Eye

The healing medium must always be prepared for surprises and to take action accordingly. This practitioner is more powerful than any non-human being no matter how ugly if appears. Remember: Ugly does not mean it is powerful.

I was trained as a scientist in the early years of my life and am still surprised that the Universe decided to guide me toward spiritual energy work. It isn't in my nature to suspect entities and dead spirits right away, and I sometimes wonder if I overlook them. In this case, the entity stared me in the eye and hissed at me. The image was detailed and clear. There was no doubt—I had a famous "pop of information!"

I saw a vibrant, eighty-year-old woman for a healing session in person. She was struggling to walk since overlifting fifteen years ago and needed a battery-powered set of wheels to move around. She saw important doctors at famous hospitals and still had no conclusive diagnosis. Her symptoms did not make much sense from a medical point of view, and images did not give a solution. She either had no pain or immense pain in both her legs at night. She had to count her steps—if she only took one step more than her body allowed, her nervous system was on fire that night.

Her abdomen was so reactive that she did not allow any bodyworker to touch it or even send energy to it. She also had bronchiectasis and was just in the process of recovering from another pneumonia. She had a few good years when an osteopathic bodyworker was able to bring her some release. But that did not last, and a second attempt was not successful.

My first intuitive insight was that she was punished at night and was under constant control and supervision. She seemed to have surrendered to that constant threat and was surprisingly positive and okay with it. I stayed away from her abdomen but got permission to touch her sacrum. Instantly, a very scarry, scruffy-looking black entity tried to scare me away with a loud, furious roaring. It was a big creature that looked like a blend of a wolf, a mountain lion, and a hyena. Its eyes were bloodred, and I saw flames behind its pupils. The claws of its right front extremity were digging violently and deeply into my client's sacrum. I saw blood dripping from her bone, and its negative energy was circulating through her blood, taking possession of her whole being. That animal entity had no interest in giving up his prey without a fight.

There was no doubt that I needed backup. I called out for Divine and Sacred spirit guides. Twenty guides showed up and wrapped that entity with bandages of light. First the fire in its eyes started to diminish, then its eyes changed into a yellow, earthy tone, and soon the fur became silky and soft. A few moments later, the roaring creature became a tame black cat lying rolled up inside those blankets of light. Its nose was covered with its tail, and it was gently purring while the guides carried it out of my client's energy field.

In the meantime, ten Divine healers showed up, five on each side. They were touching my client's body with their hands along her sides. I was told that they were healing all the battle scars and filling her up with vitality, determination, confidence, and unconditional love.

"I love you, but you have to go now," said my client during

the release. It seemed that she was aware of that entity. My guides brought to my awareness that she had a second gain from it. It gave her passion and extra energy, made her feel alive. We called in a sacred guide to support her in those qualities—we made sure he was Divine and Sacred. He settled into her spinal cord, and he will from now on call back her energies at night, comfort and nurture her nervous system, and fill her up with vitality and strength.

The day after our session, I reached out to her and asked how she was feeling. I wanted to be sure that I did not upset her abdomen or nervous system. She just said she felt absolutely great, had a good night, and was planning on adding a step more today.

— Barbara Liniger
www.info@barbaraliniger.com

A Surprise Visit by a Satyr

I am a connoisseur of orbs. I love taking photos, then searching for orbs in the photos. I have also photographed faeries—yes, real faeries. I had already taught my grandchildren about guardian angels and faeries, topics they excelled with. So, I decided one evening, about 9:00 p.m., to take them out into the field behind my house to show them how to take photos of orbs. They were about eight and ten years old at the time.

I handed them cheap cameras (cheaper cameras seem to capture orbs better than expensive ones) and explained to the girls to call outward into the air: "Come here, orbs and faeries, and show yourself to me!" Then out we went into the dark night with our cameras, calling out to faeries and orbs. Faeries and orbs seem to love children. I still have the photos of all the orbs and faeries they'd found in those photos.

The next morning, while preparing breakfast, I noticed a slice of cooked bacon in the foyer near the top of the stairway leading to the downstairs. No one had been near the stove because I was still cooking breakfast, and the grandchildren were still in their bedroom. To my surprise, I suddenly noticed that my ceiling light, hanging by a chain with eight lightbulbs, was tilted at a severe angle.

I quickly thought, "Well, that is odd. How did it get so crooked?" So, I pushed it back into place only to find it crooked again minutes later. Then I noticed a slice of cooked bacon was again on the foyer floor, which was a room away from the kitchen stove!

The grandkids went home that evening. My partner and I were unwinding in front of the TV when, around 10:30 that night, we both heard a loud scraping under the floor of the living room. We put the TV on mute and listened but did not hear anything else.

A little while later, we prepared for bed and discovered that my cat did not join us as usual. I found her under the couch in the sunroom, looking all wide-eyed and terrified, as if she was hiding from something. It still didn't click in my brain that something was not quite right in the house.

The next day, I was alone and the house was quiet. I went downstairs to begin washing clothes and was startled to find a panel in the ceiling pushed back, leaving a gaping open hole in the ceiling. Still, I did not put all these weird events together. Then the light bulb in my head went off. That loud scraping sound was the basement ceiling panel being moved.

I scanned the house by astral projecting and remote-viewing. I saw nothing upstairs. I then sent my laser beam of energy to scan downstairs. I thoroughly scanned all the bedrooms. Then I went up into the gaping hole in the ceiling, going all through the space between ceiling and floor of the upper level—nothing. I then pulled my telepathic scanner back to my body, where I was physically standing at the bottom of the stairway.

I saw an arm and a young man's head coming out from under the steps. Pitchforks flew at me. I deflected them from my energy field as fast as I could, and I yelled out in my mind, "Stop that!"

The forks kept coming at me. I called out again, "Stop that! Let's talk. I think we can work this out!"

The pitchforks instantly stopped. I telepathically asked him again if we could talk about the problem we were having. (Okay, I always say to my students and clients that you cannot get too far-out for me, but I will admit, this was wild and crazy even for me.)

Hesitantly, a young man came out from under the space beneath the stairs and, shockingly, I saw that he had the upper body of a human male and the lower body of an animal. Please consider this . . . I was expecting a faerie of some sort. What appeared was the upper torso of a young man and the lower torso like a horse or goat with hooves.

I said, "We have been noticing many things being moved around the house, so I know you want us to know you're here. Let's work it out."

I did not receive any words but only the sense of mischievousness and a sense of readiness for a fight. Telepathically, I continued to try to communicate with him, but I didn't seem to be getting anywhere. So, I resorted to sending him love and white light. (When all else fails, I always use love and light in any circumstance.)

He seemed to fade away but with the feeling of irritation. That night, I went to the Internet to research this being, and I discovered fauns, which seem to be related to the general family of satyrs. A sensation of rightness washed over me.

While I'd seen him dwindle away the day before, I felt that he hadn't left the house yet. So, I began the telepathic dialogue again. I sent him the thought that I didn't know how he would be happy to remain in my dark basement under a stairway. I told him that I'd read he was from deep forests and mountains. That he was all about fun and wine and women. I pointed out to him that I was a grandmother and did not fit his interests either. (I had to giggle at that comment.) I talked to him about being happy again.

VITAL POINT

> Denying the existence of negative beings makes you vulnerable and not powerful.

He projected an image of a lush green wood, and a stream of water moving though a low area. It was as if I were standing in this place. I lifted my head up, looking through the top of the trees to see a very distinct mountain range; or sharp, pointed rocks; and the woods at its base. A sense of love rushed into me, and I knew that this being was communicating to me through images without words. I then saw a globe of the Earth in my mind and was pulled to northern Italy.

I then projected these thoughts back to him. "My goodness, you must go back to where you're the happiest. Follow your happiness, and it will lead you to the right place."

I repeated this sentiment over and over again, and I continued to see in my mind's eye that beautiful image of the mountain peak and the stream in the woods. I was washed with a sense of deep respect, and when I felt that respect for this entity, he lifted straight up through the floor, through the roof of my house, out a window, and into the sky.

I always say: "You just can't make this stuff up!"

Ann, my thirty-five-year-old counseling client, began the session discussing the sexual abuse she'd endured. She said it felt as if she would never be able to have children because her body and uterus feel heavy and ill. I asked her to sit and close her eyes and let her imagination give her an image of her uterus.

She quickly did what I suggested and instantly said, "It is hollow and black." I asked her to see what size it is. "It is the size of a basketball. The inside is a thick, dark maroon with red gelatinous stuff inside of it. I need to get rid of it."

I said, "Well, first ask it what it needs in order to get rid of the heavy gelatinous stuff, then wait and see what happens."

She described a scraping away of the gelatinous substance. This took quite a while as we both sat in silence. Ann then began to see a little pink tissue showing through and was pleased to see it. She dumped all the thickness into buckets, and filled many. She continued until the lining was all pink but then said, "It's still cold, but now light and heat are coming in and warming it up."

I watched her energy field make this transition from muddy blacks to bright pinkish orange. I was just about to ask her if this experience was feeling complete, but I stopped myself when I saw a dark, shadowy, human-type figure about three feet tall, walk out of Ann's body. It began floating toward me.

I instantly directed my Divine and Sacred Guides, "Ann and I need help with this entity, now!" I went on to ask for its highest good, and the highest good for Ann and for me. When it reached my right side, a powerful white angel placed her arms around the three-foot-tall figure and embraced it so lovingly. Holding it like a child, she turned away from us, and both of them floated through the wall behind me.

When Ann opened her eyes, I told her what I'd just witnessed. She exclaimed, "I've always thought that I had a gremlin inside of me! I have always seen it about three feet tall, exactly the same size that you just showed me!"

I reminded her that this being left her when bright light and warmth came into her lower abdomen. I said to this special woman, "This experience is very real. The dark cannot remain where the light is."

You Must Be the Boss, the Director, and the Commander

In every session, it is imperative that you are not only in charge of your living client but also the non-human entities you come across. In order to be the boss, the director, and the commander in a healing session for your human clients and your non-human clients, you must be the one who knows what you're doing. Here are five ways to make sure you remain the one in charge:

1. **Be Powerfully Fearless:** The energetic vibration of fear is heavy and thick, and it significantly weakens the human field.
2. **Be Powerfully Fierce:** This does not mean you need to be angry. The feeling of fierce is to feel intense, forceful, aggressive, and the one who is in power.
3. **Be a Powerful Director:** You are the official head commander of the session who knows your own abilities. No one else ever bosses you around.
4. **Be Ready for Surprises:** Mediums must always be ready for surprises during sessions with your human clients and your non-human clients. There will always be a surprise or two.
5. **Be Logical:** You must use common sense with nonphysical beings and common sense with your living humans. You must be able to convince your clients using logic.

A Practitioner Shares a Story

After your class, you (Tina) noticed that Susie, one of the students, had a non-human entity attached to her that appeared like a large praying-mantis-type being. After dinner, she asked me to get rid of the praying mantis in her being. I didn't feel ready, but I figured if she was ready, I'd better get ready! I sensed that we were going for the sixth-level dark forces, and I read your directive. We think you might like to know what happened . . .

When I laser-beamed into Susie, it was like a jet rocket to her lower back. Wow! As I continued the healing, Susie could perceive the following visions in her mind's eye:

- She saw the praying mantis as blueprints.
- Sixth-level entities, no leader. They work as a collective.
- Eight Divine and Sacred specialists arrived.
- The entities came in when she was four years old. She flew off a slide and broke her coccyx. This created a "leak," which allowed them to get in.
- Why did they pick her? Because they could easily hide in her sensitivity and creativity.
- She also saw clawlike, crablike attachments, blue flippers, gills and little legs.
- She recognized one of the specialists as Big Bird, her name for her big, giant, yellow, Divine and Sacred Guide. The specialists scrubbed her so much with soapy suds! Every piece was extracted.
- As she was healing, she began to shine with a beautiful red, orange, yellow glow!

I did not "see" any of this, but I was able to know it. Thankfully, Susie saw it all and described it. Neither of us could have imagined we were capable of reading people as medical intuitives before the weekend. The thought of removing the entities was also rather mind-blowing. We do understand that everything is in Divine Order, and that things play out exactly as they are meant to in the Universe. Thank you for building our confidence and giving us the tools to make this happen. We can't believe it was all in just three days!

— Judy Kerr
www.fcquantumhealing.com

A Practitioner Shares a Story: A Non-Human Being Took on the Character from a Movie to Possess a Teenager

I must immediately note that this anecdote involves a minor. Thus, written permission was obtained from the authorized guardian, who was the mother in this example.

Ideally, practitioners want to work with the client directly; however, in this case, the minor was so under the influence of heavy medications to control violent behavior, that she was not mentally able to participate directly.

Although I had permission from the daughter's mother, I also obtained permission from the daughter's higher self to continue due to the highly irregular situation. Another facet that is of paramount importance is that I informed the mother immediately that while I could do the energy work, I needed to do additional work in parallel by a licensed and credentialed mental health professional due to the dire circumstances.

While it's important for the mother to understand that the energy work needed to be done to optimize other traditional health care plans, it was critical for the mother to understand that additional work by a licensed mental health care professional was needed as well to address mental health at the physical layer.

In this situation, I had been contacted by a mother whose teenage daughter, with high functioning autism, had historically done well in school both academically and in extracurricular activities, in which she competed in championship events. However, during the summer before the next year of middle school, the daughter's behavior changed dramatically for an unknown reason.

The daughter had lost interest in academics and in the extracurricular activities she'd enjoyed and excelled at, and even worse, the daughter began talking about receiving threatening instructions from a voice or being inside her. These threatening instructions advised the daughter to rebel against long-standing family values and beliefs, and to reject her parents and sibling to the point of physically and violently harming them. Within a few weeks, the daughter went from excelling in school to being unable to read. She became a danger to both herself and to her family.

Understandably, her parents had taken her to be treated in several facilities over a few years, but the root cause had not been determined. By the time I was contacted, the daughter had been institutionalized for years and was on a pharmaceutical regimen to prevent her from harming herself or others. The look in her eyes was like those of a shark with a distant, glassy, dark, eerie look with no emotion or depth.

When I read the daughter's energy, I encountered a very dark, non-human energy who'd taken on the false persona of a most unexpected fictitious, but very recognizable, movie character. This movie character represented a position of great, controlling authority, and through this persona, a very dark, non-human energy was indeed controlling this girl and stripping her of her identity and everything she had known to be true. Even worse, this dark, non-human energy had convinced the daughter to take violent action against her parents and siblings.

Upon initially encountering this dark energy, I electrified my field with bright, blinding light and with emotions of love and compassion. I commanded: "I revoke, reject, repel all dark, negative beings and energies that want to do harm! *Keep me out of this!*" I immediately withdrew my own energy from the daughter's field through a filter that a Divine and Sacred Guide had created just for me. I called upon different Divine and Sacred specialists to take over every element of this work.

For example, one set of Divine and Sacred specialists identified where the connections from the dark entity were to the daughter at the chakras/organs and escorted this dark entity completely out of the daughter's field, while a second set of Divine and Sacred specialists did the filling and sealing so there would be no spare spaces within the daughter's field after the dark entity had been removed.

I commanded the Divine and Sacred specialists to encapsulate this non-human entity with the most powerful white light across all waves and levels, including all generals and managers. I then asked this dark non-human being the following questions:

- How long have you been connected to this daughter?
- What drew you to this person?
- What goals do you have by staying connected?
- In what way is hanging around the living not positive for you?
- Have you forgotten that you are a separate being and not part of this human?

When I reviewed with the mother what I'd found and that this dark entity essentially had gained access and overtaken her daughter by appealing to her idolization of the fictitious movie character, the mother gasped, as her daughter had, indeed, been idolizing this formidable movie character for several years to the point of dressing up as this character on a regular basis.

It is so important to set expectations and reiterate in such situations that energy work needs to be done in parallel with traditional mental health care, as many holistic practitioners are not licensed, trained, or credentialed in the many areas needed to allow diagnoses, care plans, and further progress.

— Maryann Kelly
IntuitiveServicesInsight.com

A Practitioner Shares a Story

I saw (intuitively) that Mary was surrounded by very dark negative entities ripping her apart and she was screaming and terrified. I could not tell how many, as it was a hot situation with multiples of dark entities attacking her.

I called in Divine and Sacred Guides. Four archangels appeared and surrounded her and the entities. They put a faraday cage around her that 'froze' the entities. A second light shield was immediately put around her which separated her from the frozen entities. The entities were totally encased in a donut shaped field in a frozen stasis. The negative non-humans were whisked away by the Divine and Sacred Guides and taken to the light. Mary then collapsed on the ground from fatigue, fear, exhaustion, and almost broken. But I sensed she was a warrior of the light. I called in her Divine and Sacred Guides and four surrounded her.

I then asked to be shown the exact point of origin that these entities began to interfere with Mary. I received the following:

- She has been in battle for 35 generations.
- She was 'brought down' as a Light Warrior to unseat a dark power.
- I saw her on a throne confronting the 'head' dark one.
- She then defeated and neutralized the leader.
- But there were two others who were next in line for leadership. They were both behind her and were covered with a cloak to not be discovered.
- She has been in battle with these two cloaked beings for eons.

I then asked Mary to go back to that exact moment when this battle began. I asked the Divine and Sacred Guides to extract the cloaked ones as well as the 'head' being. All were given assisted passage to be transformed swiftly!

I then directed Mary to remove all negativity from herself and give it back to the moment. Light Warrior Mary came to stand beside the current Mary. Through a light filter they took back their power, life, health, beauty, confidence, love, safety, security, wholeness, courage, protection and their mission.

Light Warrior Mary and the current Mary then merged. Together they both came back to the present moment. I then saw Light Warrior Mary standing before me. Mary's mission was restored as a Warrior of the Light. She will suffer no more. I called in her Guides to continue to power her up and maintain her toroidal field for at least the next four weeks to further ensure that she is shielded from all negativity and dark forces completely and permanently in all dimensions, on all levels and in all timeframes. So be it!

— Vera - The Attunitive www.theattunitive.me

VITAL POINT

Just because non-human beings are ugly, it does not mean they are more powerful. It just means they are ugly. Ugly non-human beings are still clients who need you.

Please notice four details in the following story.

1. Notice how calm she remained when seeing the non-human being.
2. She took charge of the situation.
3. She created a healing for the entity.
4. She also received clear validation when her friend immediately perceived it as well.

A Practitioner Shares a Story

One day, driving to a family festival in my car full of kids, I passed a church and noticed an energy that appeared to me as a black scaly dragon on the point of the steeple. I had seen dragon-type energies in nature before, but this had a negative energy to it. I sensed it feel me engage with it. It swooped down and was behind me. We pulled up moments later to the busy festival. It was a long drive, so my kids were desperate to get out and meet up with our friends. I thought I'd deal with this thing by going to the bathroom and clearing it from there.

As I was walking to the toilet, a shaman friend of mine came to say hi. She said in my ear as she hugged me: "Jade, there is a massive entity with you!"

I laughed and said, "Yes, I am aware of this."

She asked if I wanted her to clear it. I said "No, it's okay; I'm about to do it now."

I cleared the massive entity by calling in sacred space, asking for an expert who works with this particular entity and was of the utmost sacred and compassionate frequency. I commanded that it be cleared now, and permanently, to a place of healing and compassion, where it can no longer influence or do harm. It was gone. I ran my energy and joined my kids. This was important to me because sometimes it is alienating to see things others do not see. I love being connected with others who see these realms, as it makes it less disconcerting.

— Jade Osera
jadeosera@outlook.com

The following is an example of taking rapid steps for resolving negative interferences. Energy is instant, which allows healings to be instant as well. It will only take as long as you think it will take. So, if you believe it will take hours, it will. If you believe it will take minutes, it will.

A Practitioner Shares a Story

My friend is a medical doctor. She called to tell me two days ago that she thought there was a ghost in her house and spoke about some paranormal activity. I immediately sensed that it was malevolent and related to her daughter, who has some issues. Today, she called back in a panic. She said she woke up not feeling well but went to the office and began seeing patients. When she called me, she was on a bed in an exam room, unable to get up, doubled over in pain, which she described as ten out of ten, similar to being in labor.

> Using your [Tina's] directive, I asked how long it was there (two days) and followed your procedure. There were ten entities with a leader. Within five minutes, her pain went to five out of ten, then to three. A few minutes after that, she was in shock that she could walk and was in no pain, off to see patients. I was stunned that it was so simple to send them off. I gave immediate gratitude that I was again shown that I can do this.
>
> — Judy Kerr
> fcquantumhealing.com

Be the Boss with Extraterrestrials

Not all extraterrestrials are harmful. The Greys seem to be the most common aliens known to humans because they create terror and often negative physical conditions. Like all interfering deceased humans or interfering non-humans, we mediums must take on a commanding presence in order to be the one in charge and not become another victim. Be the boss and commander of your team.

I was drawn to look into this client's back. I looked up and down his spine. Then I saw four metal clips one attached to each of the four vertebrae. The second I noticed the clips; four Greys approached me. I only saw their faces with those massive, empty black eyes. In my mind, I forcefully said, "You back off now!"

Of course, they floated back a few feet. Again, I forcefully said, "I am removing these clips, and you are never to bother him again."

Each clip released from his spine, lifted, and floated away, and so did the Greys.

A dedicated mentoring client emailed the following experience she had with non-human entities. Take note that frequently, the more negative, sinister beings often hide while the less negative might show themselves to you first, which signifies they are ready for your healings.

The following story was offered by a mentoring student. Notice, too, that you might be perceiving much more than you allow yourself to notice.

A Practitioner Shares a Story

I want to share a brief follow-up after completing my homework today. I reviewed the steps for removing non-human and dark entities *first.* I powered up differently today. I followed the new sequence of commands and included each color from the rainbow, and *I love it.* It felt much more protective, and I felt calmer and in control as a result.

When I commanded the Divine and Sacred to encapsulate the non-human beings interfering with my client, I found there were still three in hiding. None of them seemed to be interested in leaving. They were quite a cruel bunch. For the first time, I felt like I knew exactly what each of them looked like. The three in hiding had fang-looking teeth, and one had creepy-looking horns, but I knew I had to help everyone today.

I took my time with these beings. I asked them questions just like you guide us to do. I learned that the beings have been with this person for most of her life. Her mother had attracted them to my client. I was shown a person her mother interacts with (someone who calls themselves a medium), who had drawn them in initially. I believe this person may be well aware that these non-human entities are attaching to her clients.

These beings wanted to spread misery through my client. I explained to them that none of them can progress their own development in this way. As I explained, I could tell they understood because their ugliness started to fade away. I watched the horns sink and the energy become less. They were trying to hang on to the client with a death grip. I felt them start to let go.

I had them count the specialist guides who came to help, focused on the love, and reminded them that I'm an expert in helping beings just like them. It took a little while, but I patiently waited while they separated. Then I filled *all* that space, where the beings used to be, with divine love and healing for my client. I love powering up in this new way! When I truly tuned in, I realized I can see and observe much more than I think I admit to myself. I also noticed that I felt calm, confident, and in control of the Divine and Sacred Team. I did not get anxious during this work. I just stayed focused and collected.

The nonphysical realm is just as complicated as the physical realm, with just as many complicated relationships. Do not go into fear or worry that you will come across complicated, scary things with your clients. We tend to get clients that we can handle and are ready for.

A Woman with Cancer

I love sharing this story with anyone who is venturing into healing mediumship. It was the first time I met with this woman. -Remember—I don't want the client to tell me anything until I have informed them what I perceive first. This will take at least the first five to eight minutes at the beginning of the session.

I astral projected like a laser beam and landed into this woman's right lung. My team of guides took me to a darkened area in the lower lobe of her right lung. She said that I was correct. She was told the cancerous lesion was located there. I continued to go deeper into the darkness inside her lung, but I did not perceive cancer in my usual way. I did, however, see a human-type face, and when it realized that I'd found him, it opened its enormous mouth and showed long, fang-like teeth dripping with thick drool.

I was not surprised to see an entity, but I was surprised that it quickly turned away from me as if it were shy. The guides directed me to tell this woman that she had a non-human entity causing the cancer.

I softened my voice and said to my client, "You have a negative being in your lung, and it is causing this cancer."

Try to believe me when I tell you what the client said. She whispered, "I have been aware of it since childhood."

She went on to describe a female spirit who used to "bother" her. She described the spirit as very sad and depressed. My client said she also felt very unhappy when the female spirit was not around her. She hadn't seen the spirit person since she was a child, but she always knew it was with her. This woman no longer visualized it because the being no longer hovered around her. It had merged into her body and was the cause of cancer.

Now I must tell you this . . . So far, after all these years of doing this level of work for others, there has always been a negative non-human entity within a person with cancer. One hundred percent of cancer patients have severe interference by one or many more negative entities. Keep that in mind as you work with more and more clients. My colleague and dear friend is also finding this connection.

VITAL POINT

> No matter what is going on with your human clients, complete healing cannot take place if there is a negative interference. An extraction is required first before you continue with other healing steps.

A Practitioner Shares a Story: Profound and Complicated Levels of Interference and of Healing

We Are Never Given Anything We Cannot Handle!

A mother wrote an email to me wanting to bring her daughter, Suzy Q (Tina's commonly used fictitious name for confidentiality), to see me for her mental health issues. She explained that no one was able to help her daughter's life struggles. Upon receiving the information on how the Medical Intuitive sessions would be conducted, my prospective clients both gave their permission to proceed.

Hours before the rescheduled session, Suzy Q cancelled again, citing mental health issues and postponed indefinitely. I received information from my guides that there was interference and that I could proceed with the session, remotely. I wrote to both Suzy Q and her mother explaining that I could still carry out the session remotely and that Suzy Q was not required to attend. The mother responded positively and gave the go ahead and my guides confirmed it was a green light to proceed.

As I was preparing for the session, I saw and heard a single earring drop on my bedside table. My earrings are always together on a chest of drawers further away. I knew there was someone around me and asked who it was. I saw my two huge warrior guides standing closely either side of me and thought, 'oh ok here we go, buckle up!' I felt completely calm and knew I would be safe and protected; my warrior guides had my back!

I heard Tina saying in my head: "You have studied this. We have talked about this. You are ready now!" I arrived in my office and "POWERED UP", with my personal Toroidal Field. I began the session and commanded: "I invite in now only a

Divine and Sacred guide who specializes in creating the perfect sacred and safe place around me and my client Suzy Q for the most perfect work and healing that is about to happen.

In my mind's eye I looked to my right and sensed Suzy Q was there but could not see her. When I went in closer to look, she was completely covered in black shield and had three dark beings surrounding her, standing on the ground and facing her. They were of a vague human form and were a very dark smokey colour. I sensed very, very dark energy and immediately pulled my energy out. I intuitively commanded: "I repel and reject NOW all negative beings and all energy that does harm. Keep me out of this and keep me safe.

Once out and observing from a distance I invoked, "Sacred Specialists from Source Light to instantly and completely encapsulate NOW all the dark beings interfering with Suzy Q with Pure Sacred Protective Light."

I saw six Sacred and Divine specialists for this kind of situation appear, two for each of the three dark beings. I commanded: "Extract NOW all negative/dark force commanders, managers, and all beings within their network. Take every one of them to the best place for their complete and highest transformation into Love and Light." They were wrapped in pure healing white energy and were escorted towards and disappeared through the Light.

I turned my attention towards Suzy Q and still could not see her. She was still encased in black darkness. I asked my guides: "Tell me/show me now more about this black darkness surrounding my client Suzy Q". (Tina has often said in her trainings: "Be prepared for surprises!") The information that 'popped' in were the words: 'Hive' and 'Queen'. The three dark beings that had been removed were protecting this very dark of darkest entity Queen that was in possession of my client.

I commanded again: "I invoke Sacred Specialists from Source Light to NOW immediately encapsulate and contain this dark being with Pure Sacred Protective Light. Extract all negative/dark force commanders, managers, and all beings within their network. Take every one of them to the best place for their complete and highest transformation into Love and Light." I saw four huge, very tall and very bright Archangels appear, surrounding Suzy Q. They put a containment field of light around the entity encapsulating Suzy Q. I then noticed a surgical white laser beam cut through the darkness up through the front of Suzy Q, along the Conception Vessel I heard the word: "Impregnation". I asked later of my guides "Tell me now the exact point of origin of the cause of this dark entity around my client, Suzy Q." I received information that the origin of this situation was through a rape at 14 years old with drugs involved.

Once the laser cut had completed, the 'Queen' entity was peeled off Suzy Q and immediately encapsulated in Pure Sacred Protective Light. There was some resistance from the entity, and I repeated several times the command that the entity must go with the Archangels to the Light. After a while the entity successfully transitioned into the Light. My attention was taken back to Suzy Q. I called in the most Purest Loving Healing Specialist to completely and permanently fill every single space and place in all dimensions, in all time frames and on all levels where this negativity used to be, with health, vitality, and the loving light of source." Four specialist healing guides appeared to envelope Suzy Q with a beautiful blanket of healing light.

There was more healing to be done. Suzy Q was dimly lit in different areas of her body. I beamed in closer to get a better look, knowing it was safe to do so now that the very dark energy had been cleared. I started to scan her body from top to bottom. I saw that there was a large flat thick rectangular metal plate sitting above her head and a metal band around her forehead. There was a sense of dizziness from her.

I called in a Divine and Sacred Guide who specializes in clearing and removing interferences and negativity from Suzy Q's head NOW. A specialist guide appeared and was working very hard to remove the metal plate. The guides were removing gently dozens of fine metal probes that were piercing her brain. The guides then removed the metal band. I commanded: "I call in now the purest Healing Specialist to completely and permanently fill every single space and place where the negativity used to be with health, vitality, clarity and the loving light of source." Beautiful healing light was pouring into all the spaces and places by a healing specialist guide.

I then noticed a blockage around her throat, like being choked. I received the words, "I can't speak", "I don't know who I am". I saw more clearly there was an energetic cording around her neck that when followed back, originated from someone that was trying to have some control over her at some point in her past. I went through the soul retrieval process, where I asked my client telepathically to go with her younger self back to the person and give back all the negative feelings and thoughts to that person.

Once complete, I asked her to bring in her guides to create a perfect cleansing filter through which they could both take back from that person all their confidence, ability to love, personal empowerment, energy, health, strength, intelligence, body, beauty, hopes and dreams. Once completed I asked them to merge together and come back to the present moment completely and permanently whole and healed.

I went around to her back and noticed there were cords

attached to her adrenals causing fatigue. I commanded: "I call in the Purest Healing Specialist to completely and permanently clear and remove all negative cords, all tendrils and all roots of the cords from Suzy Q's adrenals NOW." Once this was cleared, I then commanded: "I call in the purest Healing Specialist to completely and permanently fill every single space and place where the negativity used to be in Suzy Q's adrenals with health, vitality, clarity and the loving light of source now."

I then commanded: "I call in NOW, Specialist Healing guides to remove all negativity and heal with bright healing light energy Suzy Q's throat, chest, stomach, bladder and hand." I waited patiently while two guides were working throughout her body removing all negativity and beaming in beautiful healing light in all the spaces and places where needed.

A bright beam of pure light came down from source to fill her entire body completely from head to toe. I sensed her soul was being reconnected to source and she became a brilliant beautiful white energy body. Her four guides still surrounded her with a gentle layer of translucent energy. They were helping her with a shield of brilliant pure light until she had the strength to "power up" herself.

We are never given anything we cannot handle as we are part of an amazing team of spirit guides!

— Vera - The Attunitive www.theattunitive.me

Specialized Healing Steps for All Non-Humans

It is vitally important to be the commanding leader with intrusive, negative non-humans. It is important to know that the invasive non-human entities do not care if they cause the human host to die. They do not care because the entity is draining the human's life force, which eventually causes death. This will surprise many readers, but at the time of the human's death, the hostile non-human entities continue to be attached even after death, because they are attached to the energy of the deceased human's soul. They frequently remain attached to the soul for many lifetimes.

You must take care of yourself first and foremost before you take care of your clients. It's like the airlines directing the passengers to place the face mask on yourself before helping others. It is the same for mediums and healers. If you are struggling in any way, then there is little you can do for others.

Notice that the following steps each have a different focus. The first set of steps focuses on *repelling* all negative beings from you and your daily life. The second set of steps focuses specifically on *extracting* negative non-human entities from you, or your living human clients, and sending them to the best place for their transformation.

Daily Steps to Repel All Negativity from Your Own Life

1. Every day, direct or command your Divine and Sacred Warriors and Protectors: "I revoke, reject, and repel all negative beings and all negative energy from my body and my life now!"
2. Electrify your energy field with brilliant, bright, sizzling light by doing all the steps of the toroidal field. Feel each step of the toroidal field as you do it.
3. You are fierce, powerful, and in charge.

Healing Steps to Extract Negative Non-Human Entities from the Client

1. You have realized that a negative entity is creating an illness, cancer, or life problems with this person.
2. Never frighten the client. Do all remaining steps within your mind (if your guides ask that you do not inform the client).

3. Stop, electrify your own energy field with sizzling brilliant light *and no fear.*
4. Direct your warrior protectors in a commanding way: "I revoke, reject, and repel all negative beings and all negative energy that is causing harm! Keep me out of this!"
5. Strongly invite in Divine and Sacred Guides who specialize in this particular entity.
6. Request the Specialists to immediately encapsulate *all entities* causing illness or within (full name of client) with powerful white light.
7. Strongly request that the Divine and Sacred Specialty guides *completely* and *permanently* remove and extract *all* levels of this entity from the client *now!*
8. Keep directing and strongly insisting that all negative cords and roots leave the client immediately.
9. Now request the Specialty Healing Guides: "Completely and Permanently fill every space and place where that negativity used to be with love, God's light, and cellular health and vitality now!" (Use any other words that describe what your living client needs.)

PART FIVE

Children, Animals, Buildings, and the Earth Need You Too

"Consciousness sleeps in mineral, dreams in plants, wakes up in animals and becomes self-aware in humans."

— Rumi

Chapter 14

Children and the Nonphysical Realms

Some mediums specialize in working with children. While I do not consider myself specialized in this area, I've had many spirit experiences with my grandchildren, and I've worked with some of my client's children as well. I have talked about the spirit realms with my grandchildren from the time they could understand simple verbal language. As we chat together, I include spiritual information in a very natural way. I include ideas about the nonphysical realms in our conversation that allows them to feel free to openly share what they already know, and what experiences they are having with spirits.

Some families treat it like it's a natural part of daily life and awareness. Dead family members come to you for a check-in. Like my family, some receive this contact during their dreams, and some receive it as a surprise when they walk into a room; some enjoy the contact and encourage it, and some are freaked out by it. Yet, no matter how we receive or react to it, my family talks about it and shares their stories when we get together for birthday parties or holidays. It's just part of our experience. This acceptance creates a safe and normal environment for intuition to flourish.

Teach, but Listen More to the Children

Listen to children when they are very young. They are naturally aware and intuitive, because adults haven't had enough time yet to interfere with their memories or their wisdom. It is this casual acceptance that allows spiritual expression to take place. It is this openness or critical constraint that is passed on to other generations.

Children are drawing the energy fields of people and animals around them. Many children really do have invisible playmates or scary dead people in their bedrooms, because they naturally perceive the deceased and the nonphysical world. They often interact with deceased children throughout the day because those children have not crossed over. Those deceased kids might have died in that house years ago, or they were drawn to the living children from a house next door.

One colleague describes a memory in her own childhood . . .

> My mother tells a story of when I was young, I talked to a little boy in my room on a rocking horse. He was dressed in old-fashioned clothing, knickers, and a puffy shirt. When asked, I described the boy to her. My mother, a somewhat superstitious woman, recalls being freaked out how I described what he wore, because it matched clothing from one hundred years ago.
>
> I was so young I couldn't have even seen clothes like this anywhere. My mother had told me to tell him to go away and ignore him. I can guess that this is when I closed my intuitive sight. It wasn't until I started energy healing in my twenties that it returned with a bang. The reason I tell this story is to let you know we all have access to these abilities within us. It is our natural way to be connected and receptive to information.

The demolition of our natural intuitive abilities begins in such subtle ways. Parents, teachers, grandparents, friends, and other children will be the first ones to tell a child, "The picture you just drew is not right. Your mother is not purple. You know she has brown hair!" "Your dog is not green. He is a white poodle!" Parents quickly declare, "No one is there! That is your imagination," or, "You just had a bad dream."

We adults are sometimes thoughtless or afraid ourselves. Teach your clients who are parents to normalize the nonphysical world for their children. Beliefs are only thoughts that we were taught in our earlier years as children. Beliefs are not necessarily truths. Teach the adults that many of our beliefs are false ideas or fears that the adults around us had, and we children soaked them up. Now it's time to learn some new ideas.

I share with you this scary story to take away your fear. Notice the many steps to bring healing for everyone and everything.

A mother contacted me to ask if I would see her three-year-old daughter. I explained that I don't need to meet in our office. I can check in with her daughter intuitively, and I will ask the child for permission to do so as well. The worried mother quickly informed me that the little girl tells her that her bed shakes at night, and she sees people in her room. The mother also informed me that her child is fine but then suddenly says things like, "I want to cut off your head and burn it."

I quickly asked her not to tell me anything else. (Do not allow clients to give you details of what is going on. Information from the client, or in this case, the mother, will interfere with information you receive from your guides.)

The three-year-old girl was hesitant to work with me, so I talked to her like the grandma that I am, while observing the little girl's energy field. Immediately, I saw a dark, cloudy energy surrounding the child so severely that I couldn't even see her own energy. I immediately powered up my toroidal field and called in my own Divine and Sacred guardian warriors. A large eye approached me with needles and arrows shooting out toward me. Then ugly faces came rushing at me. Then I perceived a young ten-year-old boy in spirit form rush out of the dark cloud. I saw the wheels of a car and sensed that he'd been hit in an accident.

Then I saw the little boy face down on an operating table, receiving surgery on the vertebrae in his neck. He did not live through the surgery. As he left his body, I watched him enter this little girl at the moment of her birth in the same hospital. (Now I have many clients . . . the mother, the alive little girl, angry little boy, and negative non-humans). I was shown that the boy continuously went in and out of the tiny girl, and when he was not possessing the girl, he was hiding inside of a furnace vent in the floor of these people's home.

I asked the deceased boy to notice that he still feels terrible even as he moves in and out of this little three-year-old girl. He agreed. I called in Divine and Sacred Guides to wrap him in a white energy blanket of comfort and love and take him to the best place for his transformation. Off he eagerly went.

I drifted toward the little girl's house again. My guides and, surprisingly, Archangel Michael appeared, although I hadn't asked him directly. This told me things were serious and dark. He waved his sword all around the girl, and the dark disintegrated around her. She looked lighter and felt happier. Her aura changed to a rich purple.

Next, I was pulled to the land where the child's house was located. It was completely void of any nature spirits and had no energy at all. I called in Divine and Sacred specifically for this particular piece of land. I requested that the aliveness rush back in and fill this space, and this land, and the home where this little one and her mother lived. I asked their guides to restore happiness and health to the people, their home, and the land right now, and to maintain happiness. I intuitively informed the little three-year-old, "All the negative beings are gone now."

A week later, the mother of the three-year-old informed me that her child was a little better the next day, and by the weekend, she was like a different child.

This is a dramatic but powerful example of how many children's fear starts in their bedroom. Teach children they are not victims of spirits. Teach children how to be in charge of their bedroom.

Tips for Parents to Prevent Night Terrors in Children

1. Talk at their level of understanding and their level of development.
2. Ask what do they hear or see.
3. Never have a surprised look on your face. Be calm and matter-of-fact.
4. Use the name that a child calls the spirits. (E.g., monster, mean man, etc.)
5. Tell the child that together you both are calling out into the air and asking for the biggest, strongest angel to come into the bedroom.
6. Help the child get to know the angel . . . tell the child to ask *all* the questions such as its name, looks, how it is dressed, etc. Ask the child to draw a picture of their angel to hang in their room.
7. Tell the child that the entity, monster, etc. must do what you and angel tell them to do.
8. Tell them the monster is afraid of you and the angel. It knows you and the angel are the boss of your bedroom.
9. Tell the angel to wrap Monster in a blanket and take it to heaven or the sky.

Living Children and the Nonphysical Realms

Children have just arrived from the nonphysical world. We adults need to listen more closely to what they say as soon as they become verbal. Listen closely to the details they say, then ask them to tell you more.

Sometimes asking questions makes children become quiet. Instead, make statements such as, "Hmm . . . Tell me more." It feels very different to little kids. Young children perceive nonphysical realms quite easily because they haven't had experiences yet to think they are separate from it.

When my son was nine years old, he suddenly looked up at me and said in a very confident voice, "We are not very important. It's like we're just a bugger in God's nose." Then he turned around and ran outside to play.

My grandson Jesse, around five years old, called out to his father, "Daddy, Tom is at the door and wants to come in." My son said, "Okay," and then walked over to the door and opened it so Tom could walk in. My son already knew that his dear friend Tom had just died two days ago, but my son opened the door to allow Tom's spirit in.

A Twelve-Year-Old Becomes a Healing Medium

We walked down the streets of Cardiff, Wales, in search of a restaurant for lunch. I had just finished teaching my course, Become a Medical Intuitive. My daughter and granddaughter were traveling with me. As we came out of the Cardiff restaurant and walked up a street, I noticed a spiritualist church, so we stopped to read their event board. We then got in the rental car and headed to the hotel.

My granddaughter immediately asked us if we heard whispering. We looked at each other, and neither of us could hear it in the car.

She kept asking if we heard the rapid whispering, and we tried to hear it, but nothing happened. She thought we were teasing her.

I said, "I think you've picked up a person in spirit. In your mind, tell the spirit person to slow down her speech so you can hear her more clearly. Ask if the person is male or female."

Lacey listened and heard female.

I said, "Ask her to tell you her name."

Lacey heard, Judie.

My daughter and I were very excited and began to think of many questions for the granddaughter to ask Judie. My granddaughter continued to clearly receive Judie's responses.

Judie was eager to talk to us, through my granddaughter, about her life and death. She was drawn to my granddaughter because her own daughter looks very similar. Judie said that her daughter had died at the age of fifteen from a disease. She was also aware that she, herself, had died in 1936. My granddaughter could see that she wore a gray skirt and jacket and shoes with short heels. She went on to say that she worked as a secretary.

I asked many more questions, and Lacey was able to hear Judie's detailed responses. When asked why she stayed here on the Earth plane and did not go on to the light, she stated that she must continue to look for her daughter. All three of us felt that her daughter had crossed into the light a long time ago.

By this time, we were back in our hotel room, where my granddaughter and I could assist Judie more easily in a quiet environment. I think we needed the quiet much more than Judie did! I walked my granddaughter though the basic steps to assist a spirit person who is somewhat unaware (She had searched for one hundred years for her daughter and had no idea that her daughter had immediately transitioned to the light right after her death.) She remained in a "lost realm" trapped by her thoughts and emotions of finding her child. She had forgotten to move into the light on her own. So, together in our hotel room, we assisted this lost, unaware soul to cross over into the brightest light. The three of us quietly witnessed bright, sparkling energy surrounding Judie as she released all of those lost years in old, old thoughts and old, old emotions.

Living Children are Comfortable with Deceased Children

I received a call from an exhausted mother of a three-year-old. She hoped I could help her and her son. I expected her to describe some terrible illness or disease, but instead, the young mother told me that her son is too happy. His happiness, as she put it, really was not the best for him. Every night, her three-year-old stayed up most of the night laughing and playing. She described his exhaustion but also added that her son is physically "sick all the time."

Before I begin to work with living children, I ask them for permission no matter their age. I also inform the parents that I must ask their child for permission before I proceed. I tell the parents that if their child says no, I have to honor their choice. Most parents will push you to ignore the child's refusal. If the child does refuse the help (which would be very unusual in my experience), quickly check for interfering negative forces that are much more aggressive than the child's quieter soul energy. In this case, I received a big "yes" from this enthusiastic and very happy three-year-old boy.

Young children tend to communicate through images rather than verbal information. When I sent my laser beam out to the three-year-old boy, I received a visual of a female child who appeared to be about the boy's age. Together, they showed me how they sit in the boy's bedroom and throw toys at each other. I heard them laughing and saw toys flying. I began chuckling too, until I noticed an energetic cord connecting them together. The child in spirit was very playful but, at the same time, she was drawing energy from my three-year-old client. This explained why the mother reported that lately he'd been sick all the time. While playing in the midnight hours was taxing, the cord was funneling his energy away. This little jovial spirit child was unintentionally pulling on her playmate's life essence.

I received all this information in just a few split seconds of my initial check-in. When I shared this first piece of intuitive information, the mother gasped for air. She said her son had a female twin who did not live. We were both covered with goose bumps.

VITAL POINT

> Listen closely to the children. They still remember the wisdom of the nonphysical realms where they just came from.

A Practitioner Shares a Story

This mentoring student had a beautiful experience with a four-year-old. Children of that age do not know how to fake stories. With that in mind, read this fascinating experience.

> A friend of mine called me to say she wanted my insight on an issue with her four-year-old daughter. She had taken her daughter to a physio, and he could not find anything wrong. However, her daughter was randomly dragging her leg or walking with it at an angle out to the side.
>
> As I tuned in and connected to her young daughter's energy over the phone, I immediately became aware of a small girl in spirit who was not from our current period. She was running around, but she wore weird crutch-like objects on her legs. I described what I was seeing to my friend and continued to focus on the girl in spirit.
>
> I curiously asked her a few questions: Where and when had she first connected with my friend's daughter? The spirit girl showed me that she had joined my friend's daughter at a local vintage shop. My friend corroborated this, saying that it had started after they were vintage shopping.
>
> This is not unusual, I explained, as sometimes old items (especially cherished items like dolls, etc.) have an energetic connection to a spirit who has not yet crossed over. The girl showed me that she was attracted to her daughter because they were around the same age, and she wanted to play. This

experience was before I had read Tina's books and participated in her workshop, so I did not have the steps back then to follow. So, instead, I created a sacred space and opened a portal to the spirit world using my hands and light, but more importantly, I did this quickly and did not watch the girl go into the vortex of light.

My friend remarked with surprise in her voice that her daughter was walking normally again. After I hung up the phone, I turned to look at my four-year-old daughter, and she was suddenly walking with a limp, exactly the way my friend had described to me. This was not expected. I closed my eyes and checked in again to find the same spirit girl laughing and running around my daughter now! Lesson 101 in crossing spirits over: Make sure they leave.

"Okay, cheeky girl," I said. "Do you have a mummy?" she nodded yes. As I asked, I looked for signs of fear or excitement. I got the expression of excitement in her face. "Okay, let's call mummy forward." I again created sacred space, opened the light and saw her mummy on the other side, holding out her arms. I watched the girl jumping through to her mum as I closed the portal. My daughter returned to walking around, completely unimpeded and normal once more.

As my mentor, Tina, would say, you cannot make this stuff up!

— Jade Osera
jadeosera@outlook.com

Children Remembering Their Past Lives

I was visiting family members who I rarely get to see. I was drawn toward the little boy who was sitting on the floor, entranced with many little toy soldiers. I watched at a distance so as not to disturb him. He was always unusually quiet. He could sit up and play with toys, but he consistently refused most toys. He insisted that he only play with tiny toy soldier figures. He sat for hours, moving the soldier figures into patterns, and then he would crash some of them together as if they were in many great battles. If his parents asked him to do something else, he would say, “No! I have to fight!” Take note that he did not say he was busy playing. He said in a very firm commanding voice, “No! I have to fight.” His parents were not open to past lives, but I am left wondering if he was deep within an old memory.

I beg every reader of this book to watch and listen to the children around them. Especially listen and watch children from the age they begin to talk to around six years old. During this time frame, children are still so close to the spirit realms that they talk about their past lives and their life in spirit just before they entered this current life. They talk about a past life, and they also seem to already know about angels too, even if the family has never talked about them.

Here is another example of past-life memories from my own family. My daughter and my little four-year-old granddaughter got into a little argument in my kitchen one day. The little four-year-old put her hands on her hips, then yelled, “Don’t you remember when I was the mommy and you were the baby?” My surprised daughter said, “No, I do not remember that.” My granddaughter angrily responded, “Well, I remember when I was your mother!”

A few days later, that same granddaughter and I took a nap together. I woke up with her shaking me as hard as she could. She was wide awake and so excited when she said, “An angel came in that door and kissed me here on my hand!” She asked full of excitement, “Did you see her?” My heart was about to burst in wonderment, but I gently said, “No. That angel was only for you.”

Deceased Children Struggle Too

Discovering a Surprising Complication

Mike stood up to leave the mentoring session we were having together and said he saw a short being about three feet tall behind me, and he felt that it seemed to be about me and not him. He didn't know what to do about that, so I guided him to ask the being some questions. The being said that it was here for me. I suggested that Mike ask it some questions. Was it human? Mike received the response, "part-human." He asked it, "What is its goal to be here in this session?" It responded, stating it needed to speak to me without Mike.

Later that evening, I sat quietly and found the being still standing in my office, slightly behind the chair I sat in. The being seemed to be an elemental connected to the woods behind my office. I asked her what she meant by being part-human? I then saw a child stuck to the left side of the elemental's head. The elemental confirmed by saying she had a human fragment attached to her, and she wanted the child to move on.

I immediately realized, for the first time in my twenty-five years, I was experiencing something new and something extremely unusual. I had an Earth woods elemental here in my office. That elemental was interfering with a human being. At the same time, the human was in turn interfering with the elemental. Not only that, but the human being was the fragmented soul of a human child. How could this be?

VITAL POINT

> Living children and deceased children will still be children and act like children.

I called in specialists for both of them. As I did, something suddenly shot toward me in anger. I was shocked because, up until then, the elemental seemed quite gentle and in need of assistance, so when something leaped out at me as if to attack, I was stunned but immediately protected myself. When I asked, I was shown that it was the child lashing out in anger. The little girl showed me that she experienced such a depth of love for the land and woods that she'd left behind part of her soul essence, and for some unknown reason, that portion of her soul had attached to the elemental.

I continued to call in assistance for both. A separation slowly happened, and the human child lifted and away, still not feeling especially happy about the change. The elemental scurried out the window, running back into the woods. My coworker later informed me that at the same time this was happening, she had been speaking the Invocation by Betsy Bergstrom, which directs and includes spirits of the land. We both felt this allowed the elemental to come forward and look for assistance.

Who knew that humans could attach onto an Earth elemental, a nonphysical being of the Earth plane, and cause some level of discomfort and a request for help from a living human? You just can't make this stuff up!

Helping Deceased Children Was a Surprise

One weekend, I noticed loud banging sounds in the house. Not the usual pops and cracks, but very loud sounds like a door closing, or something hitting the house or roof. I was tired and trying to lie down for a nap, so I reached out telepathically and said, "I hear you, but I need it quiet to sleep right now. I will talk with you later." The noises ceased immediately, and I took my nap.

Later that evening, I telepathically reached out again and said, "I said I could talk later, and I'm ready now." Immediately in my mind's eye, I saw a young girl, about ten or eleven years old, with big eyes and dressed in an old-fashioned girl's dress with some frills around an "apron" and puffy sleeves. She was quiet, shy, and didn't say anything. I was so surprised that she would be making so much noise.

I said "hello," and then a young man popped in right beside her. He was tall, gangly, and angular, looking about sixteen years old. He was dressed in overalls and a plain shirt, and they were clearly together.

Here is the noisemaker, I thought. I said "hello" again and asked them how they came to be here. The boy replied he didn't really know. The young girl said nothing.

I asked them if they knew they were no longer living. The boy replied they had "kind of suspected," because no one would talk to them or help them anymore. I asked what they needed help with, and he said they were trying to find their family and get back home. I explained to them that the people they were around would have helped, but they couldn't because they couldn't see them.

I asked him where he had first seen me. He intuitively showed me the hospital I'd recently visited. Ah—that made sense. This happens often if I go to a hospital. So, I asked him why they'd followed me. He said he could "see me a little better," so he hoped I would be able to help them.

Because they were both children, I didn't ask them how they'd died. I told them I would help them, and that I was going to call in special helpers for them. I asked the kids if they had seen any bright lights, but they didn't know what I was talking about. I told them to look for helpers to come now. I called out for Divine and Sacred Guides who specialized in these two kids to come and take them to the place for their highest good and transformation. I saw a young, dark-haired woman come and place her arm lovingly around the young girl, and a taller young man with dark hair come and put his hand on the young man's shoulder. They all turned away from me, and there was a bright, beautiful light. From the light came two older people, a man and woman. It seemed it was these kid's family members that they had been looking for, as they hugged them fiercely, and then they all went into the light.

A Practitioner Shares a Story

I have a memory from a past lifetime that allowed me to experience what it feels like to be a spirit that does not cross over. I was in the US in the early nineteenth century in a Southern area of America. I lived in a very well-to-do family, and there were people working in our fields. My sister and I were playing with the neighbor boy when he took us to a secret tunnel, we didn't know about. We went in, and he stayed at the entrance. From what it looked like, it was an alcohol-prohibition tunnel. The neighbor boy closed the big round door.

My sister and I began struggling for air. Then, to my shock, I popped up through the earth to the entrance of the tunnel. I stood next to the boy, laughing, thinking he was playfully scaring us by trapping us in the tunnel. The next scene I recall was when he opened the big round door and saw our lifeless bodies inside.

After that, my mother was holding my lifeless body, sobbing and repeating, "No! No! Please don't leave me." So, I did not leave her. I stayed. I was a spirit. I felt weak and vague. I remember realizing my parents had died, and now a new family lived in the house. I remember watching the kids of this new family playing. I knew that I didn't belong there anymore, but I was completely unsure of what to do. I was so spaced out and confused. I felt like I'd missed my opportunity, and now I was too weak to take any action.

Time passed, but I was unaware of time. It did not exist. The next scene I remember is a woman coming to the house . . . a woman of color. She sat on the bed and didn't look at me, but she spoke to me. I cannot remember what she said to me, but I looked up above me, and my parents were there, reaching for me with such loving faces. I went into the light with them. That is all I remember. I love this memory, as strange as it sounds, as it reminds me of what it feels like when the etheric body misses its call to go. It gets denser and denser, and is neither aware of the etheric realm nor the physical anymore.

— Jade Osera
jadeosera@outlook.com

(Did you, reader, notice that Jade mentioned a woman of color? I believe that the woman of color was a medium and knew that the spirit of the little girl needed help to cross over. She gave her that help, and off she went to her parents in spirit, after nearly a century of being lost and confused.)

Even I Was Stunned

I was teaching a mediumship course. We were near the end of my five-day course, so everyone knew all the important steps to take to assist troubled deceased people to cross over. It popped into my head to create a practice session that I had never used before. My guides directed me to give this specific assignment to the students: Ask your Divine and Sacred Guides, who specialize in the deceased, to bring only one gentle, kind, or confused deceased person to them who needed help to cross over. I emphasized that the deceased person *must* be gentle, kind, or confused.

Some of the students sat in their seats while others went outside. Up to that point, we had only been working with each student's deceased family members. I was so excited and curious to see what happened and how the students would do with this assignment.

When I asked that everyone return, volunteers shared their stories of the troubled deceased that were brought to them and, with the help of their guides, the steps they'd taken to assist the deceased. Many tears were cried as students described the stunning beauty of observing the guides wrap them in a blanket of comfort and lift them up and into the sky.

Then one student slowly raised his hand and said, "My guide brought me a small child around the age of five. I was informed that this child was murdered, and it happened somewhere close by here."

Then two more hands went up. These two students explained they also helped children who had shown them they had been killed nearby. After the stunned look on my face subsided, I checked with the students to make sure that these last two children were assisted into the light. We discussed how important and vital our mediumship abilities truly are. I stood in from of this group and said, "The healing of these distraught deceased children is only the beginning of your healing medium career."

Working with deceased children is always special and memorable. Working with their living relatives will always be emotional but will bring the most profound healing you will ever witness. Allow people to express their sorrows. All you need to say is, "I am here with you." Then stop talking and become very quiet. Simply be there with them until they can become quiet as well. That is another level of healing taking place.

Chapter 15

Animals and the Nonphysical Realms

It makes me smile when I write this. I teach all over the globe, and with every course I teach, no matter where I am, or what country I'm in, someone approaches me at break time to make what feels like a confession.

"I thought I'd better tell you that I'm an animal communicator, and I hope to include intuition, mediumship, and medical intuition in my work communicating with animals. But I really don't want to work on people at all."

And my response is: "Oh, that is absolutely fine. Lots of people tell me they have no interest in working with people. Everything I teach, even all the steps I teach, and also the steps to work with Divine and Sacred specialty guides are exactly the same for all animals!"

They are so relieved and happy when I tell them that . . . but it's very true!

Believe the Animals

Animals are not capable of imagining things or making things up. What they perceive is real. The day before I wrote this chapter, a friend told me how her dog began whining and looking upward. Then he moved his head as if he was following something all around the ceiling. Maybe animals are mediums too. Here is another example of animals perceiving nonphysical beings.

A Practitioner Shares a Story

I was contacted by a middle-aged woman who had been living with her calm, loyal dog for several years. It had been just the two of them in the home for these several years. Her usually calm dog began to catapult off the sofa in the living room and bolt into the kitchen in a frenzy, searching for something that was clearing getting his attention. However, every time the woman went to the kitchen, she saw no one there. This same distressing behavior continued, so the woman scheduled a session with me.

I began with reading the dog to find out what he was experiencing. When reading animals, I find it helpful if I ask the pet to show me with pictures what they're experiencing. Animals can create, in vivid detail, what's happening from their point of view. Since pets and animals don't have the ego and emotional factors that can get in the way with humans, they are very direct and actually welcome communicating with someone who is interested in what they're experiencing.

The dog showed me a repairman who had come into the kitchen about two weeks prior to repair the refrigerator. The repairman himself was fine and intended no harm and efficiently went about his work on the refrigerator. However, unbeknownst to the repairman, an earthbound spirit person tagged along on this service call. When the service call was over, the repairman left, but the spirit person stayed behind in the kitchen of this home. The dog was aware of this spirit, which was a foreign spirit to this dog. So, the dog considered this spirit person's energy as an intruder. When the dog repeatedly became aware of this spirit energy, he did, indeed, catapult off the sofa and bolt into the kitchen, seeking to find the intruder and protect his owner.

When I asked this spirit why he was lingering in the kitchen of this home, he said it was because he was afraid to ascend, and because the woman's home reminded him of his former home, where he'd had a loyal dog companion as well. I worked with my guides to help this spirit man happily ascend.

When I relayed this to my client, she asked me how could I have possibly known that she'd had a refrigerator repairman over about two weeks ago? I said her dog had shown me that event. I explained that her dog was, indeed, sensing this spirit and was doing his job to alert her that there was a strange presence in the kitchen. I explained that the spirit had since ascended. The woman later reported that her dog had stopped catapulting off the sofa into the kitchen and returned to his calm self.

— Maryann Kelly
www.IntuitiveServicesInsight.com

The following is a brief example of how even professional intuitives for people or for animals seem to question their own abilities. I hope I was able to teach this animal communicator just how accurate she really is.

My precious cat, Nicki, has been calm her entire life. Around the age of fifteen, she became a nervous wreck. Even as a professional medium and medical intuitive, I couldn't figure out what was causing this huge change in her personality. I decided I needed help and made an appointment with an animal communicator. I knew this woman personally but had never needed her services until now. I explained how my cat was now a nervous wreck when she has always been "calm, cool, and collected."

The animal communicator called me back a couple of days later to deeply apologize. She kept saying that she just could not get any information about Nicki. Then she apologized again and again.

Now I tried to calm her down. I ended up saying, "Well, okay . . . but just tell me any little thing you got."

She hesitated. "Well, this doesn't make any sense, but I kept seeing a large aquarium, so I know that can't be right."

"*What*!" I declared it a little too loudly. I then told this woman that she needed to stop questioning her amazing intuitive abilities with animals.

Now she was the one who said, "What?"

I informed her that one of my family members had just gotten a boa constrictor and placed it in a massive aquarium in the kitchen. At night, it tended to move around a lot, stretching itself upward to the top of the aquarium, and then down again.

I told her, "Nicki was showing you exactly what was causing her anxiety!"

VITAL POINT

> Always accept the most instant thing that pops into your awareness, even when it doesn't make any sense. This applies when working with both humans and animals.

A medical intuitive student told me about this story. A client's dog was falling over unexpectedly and more frequently. The veterinarian kept focusing on the dog's nervous system, which would be the usual cause of the animal falling over. The veterinarian could not find anything wrong. The medical intuitive, who trained with me regarding humans, telepathically investigated the animal. In her mind's eye, she saw the image of an EKG test strip. She told the dog's human that she was given that information and asked the person to request that the vet check the animal's heart. The veterinarian listened to the medical intuitive.

He found that the dog's heart was the issue. This dog's human had a pacemaker placed into her dog immediately.

Animals are Affected by Negative Human Spirits Too!

Animal communicators and intuitive healers always begin with at least two clients: one animal, and one or more humans. But sometimes there is a third individual involved . . . a negative deceased person interfering.

My Friend's Parrot was Suffering

My friend Denise has a huge African Gray parrot named Taco. They have been together for many years, and it seemed to be nothing but joy and laughter. But then, one day, Denise called me. She said suddenly Taco has pulled out most of the feathers on his chest and has never done that before. I was so surprised. She asked if I would intuitively check in with him to see if I can figure out what was going on.

Later that day, I astral projected outward to stand next to Taco. I asked him to show me what was troubling him so much that he was pulling out his own feathers. I waited and waited some more. He showed me inside the house at night, which I thought was a bit strange at first, so I waited. My attention was pulled to the dark outside. I began to see an older man in spirit walking down the street, heading toward Taco. The spirit man floated into the house and right up to Taco's cage. This nasty spirit began poking and poking a stick through the bars of the cage, trying to stab Taco. Then I saw the nasty dead man doing this same thing night after night.

I called in my Divine and Sacred Guide who excelled at dealing with the dead man. That guide followed my directives to rap him tightly in a blanket of peace and lift him up and away from Taco and this house, and take him to the best place for his transformation into love and light. Away he went, kicking and fighting against the tightening blanket. Within days, Taco's feathers began growing back!

A Practitioner Shares a Story: A Spirit Person Attached to Sonia's Basset Hound

Tina's medical intuitive training and step-by-step methods have expanded the level of information that I receive regarding individual animals. With Tina's training, I can now sense and see the history of the animal. The medical intuition training takes me to the cause of an animal's behavior or struggles, which has been very helpful.

For example, I now see and sense a rescued animal's history and what has happened to them in the past. My training has shown me that deceased people might also be the cause of an animal's behavior.

Sonia's young basset hound named Tammy started acting afraid of the front door. In addition, she reported that Tammy was frequently frightened. Her other two other dogs' behavior hadn't changed. Sonia's family had been in the house for a year, so this was new and unexpected behavior. When I connected with Tammy, I asked her and my Sacred Divine Master of Animal Communication to show me why she was now frightened of the front door and being in the house.

As I got quiet, I noticed an older woman in spirit attached to Tammy. The woman was not mean-spirited; it was not her intent to upset Tammy. She had stayed on Earth, looking for her own dog, whom she missed immensely and was worried about. When she saw Tammy, she thought Tammy was her dog. So, she came into the house through the front door, thinking it was her house—just like she would do when she was alive. She loved spending time with Tammy. But Tammy found her frightening.

As Tina says, I now had another client, one in spirit. I helped this woman understand that she was in spirit now. Then I invited her to really look at Tammy to see that Tammy wasn't her dog. And I asked her to see that the house was not hers either. When she realized these truths, I also explained that she was scaring Tammy, because I knew that wasn't her intent. Sonia also shared these truths her, talking out loud to her as if they were having a conversation. Because they were!

I invited Divine and Sacred beings, who were masters of helping people transition, to join us. They stood by the woman in spirit and offered their hands to her. We asked the woman to go with them now to a wonderful, safe place. Sonia declared that the woman couldn't visit again, as it wasn't her house, and it would frighten Tammy. The woman willingly left with the Divine and Sacred beings. We then worked with Tammy to extract and remove her fear and transform it into love and light. I invited Divine and Sacred masters of healing to join us. I then created the command to extract and remove the energy of fear, and shared those words with Sonia. Sonia spoke the command to the masters, and we watched them clear Tammy's energy. Then we asked them to replace the fear with the energy of "This is my house, and I'm safe in every part of the house" the immense love her family had for her.

Sonia continued to tell Tammy some version of "This is your house, and you're safe in every part of the house" daily. When I followed up with Sonia about how Tammy was doing, Sonia told me, "She's doing so good! Thank you!"

— Maribeth Decker
www.sacredgrove.com

A Practitioner Shares a Story: A Spirit Being asks Suki to Play

Our adopted rescue, Suki, had lived with us for nearly a year and had adjusted well, when suddenly she started waking me up at 3:00 a.m. to go out. She hadn't done this before, and she didn't go to anyone else on the nights I wasn't home. I talked to Suki, and got the sense that a spirit suggested that Suki wake me up to play. We sensed that it was the previous owner of the house. I was able to talk to the spirit to quit it, and then helped them move on from this Earth plane. I then talked to Suki about sleeping through the night. Sure enough, Suki now sleeps through the night and does not even wake up when my alarm goes off!

— Maribeth Decker
www.sacredgrove.com

Sometimes Animals Have the Choice When to Leave Their Body in Death

We both helplessly watched as our dog, Tabby, had a severe seizure. After the seizure, our dog became quiet and lay on her side, but she was still breathing. We both laid on the floor next to her. We noticed that Tabby's body became noticeably flattened as she grew closer to death. We also quickly noticed that each time we stroked her, Tabby's body instantly became fuller. It only took a few minutes for us to realize that each loving stroke of our hands across her body was signaling Tabby to come back into her body. We continued to lay on the floor but stopped touching her. Tabby quickly released her body and passed on.

Being an animal communicator is a specialty. Being an animal communicator and a healer is even more of a sacred specialty. Over the years, I have worked with practitioners who are accustomed to using the title of animal communicator. I point out to the animal communicators, and now I point out to you, the reader, that after taking my courses or reading my books, the methods and techniques are the same for people and animals. All steps can apply to animals.

As you apply these methods with animals, please deeply realize you are also an animal healer. Your human clients who come to you for their animals will notice the difference as you point out the healing that you accomplished. Place these key words on your website: Animal Healer and Communicator. You will stand out to your human clients.

Chapter 16

Buildings, the Earth, and Nonphysical Beings

Haunted places are always considered terrifying and often demonic. A haunted building or area generally means that living people have had many experiences there with nonphysical deceased humans or non-human entities. Living people usually have the same repetitive experiences, which should show that they're truly witnessing the same beings over and over again. To me, this is evidence of the reality of troubled beings in that area.

A friend approached me regarding a building they'd just purchased to expand their business. They asked me if I would check into the building. I immediately said two things to them, "Yes, of course, but do not tell me why you want me to check in with your building."

They then said, "When can you schedule a time to meet us there to scan the building?"

I responded, "I never need to go to a building to pick up intuitive information. All I need is the full address so that I can astral project to the correct building."

I put it aside for a day or so, but then I woke up about midnight. I was supposed to astral project and scan that building now.

I saw the form of a man sitting on a small couch looking out a large window. He was horribly depressed and told me he had lost everything, meaning his money. Someone cheated him in some way. He loved that his name was on the front of this building.

This spirit man's emotions in the 1950s was still negatively affecting that room and that building. The people who had worked for him suffered too, so their dense emotions were there as well. Because of this, he was still sitting there in that building, in deep remorse as well as anger over his employees losing their jobs. He also kept showing me that he'd killed himself there. I saw cars out on the street that now would be considered quite old. This was showing me that this event was a long time ago. I asked him if he was aware that he was dead. He said he knows because the cars sometimes look different to him over the years.

I asked him if it would be okay for me to help him cross over.

He said no. "Because I will be punished for killing myself."

I assured him that I would call in the most loving Divine and Sacred angel, and he will only feel profound love from the angel. So, he agreed. I called in the angel, who put her arms out to him.

Then I saw something I'd never seen before. The man put his arms out and hugged the angel as the angel held him. I told him to ask the angel to take him to the best place for his transformation into Light and Love.

The angel said, "I will take you there." They lifted away together.

Then I called in the Divine and Sacred cleansing specialists to remove all residual negative energy from that building. The cleaners said they were removing it from that building, but they were also removing it from the entire area around that office. I saw them go all over the place. They even went across the street from this building, then behind this building, and then around the block with something like a giant vacuum. They vacuumed the land under the building.

He was the original cause, and much more than just part of the grief. He was absolutely the cause of the grief in that building because he was still sitting there, creating it day after day, decade after decade. He had been there since the 1950s. Remember, the guides cleaned up the entire building and the buildings surrounding it. They went across the street, and then they went everywhere. It was kind of comical to watch. Then I asked my Guides, "Is this address done now, or does it need anything else to be positive for everyone?"

I am serious. I heard: "The inside walls could use a brighter color of paint for people to feel better."

When I told the owners I received a request for brighter-colored paint from my guides, they both said, "That's exactly what we thought too!"

You just cannot make this stuff up!

VITAL POINT

> Never just do a healing and cleansing for the building or home. Specifically healing the land must be included for a complete positive change to happen.

If someone asks you to check out a home, building, or other location, please realize there is no need for you to physically go to the actual location. You can astral project, and then remote-view to the exact address. You do not need a photo, but you can use one if that feels right for you. Last, always, always direct the guides to cleanse and heal the land beneath the house or building.

Always Direct Your Guides to Cleanse and Heal the Land Beneath Troubled Homes or Buildings

I finally lay down in bed in a New Mexico hotel that I'd been yearning to stay in for years. I went to sleep immediately. But I woke up many times. This happened three nights in a row. It was like I was constantly witnessing life-and-death battles every night. It was the same scenes over and over. When I checked, my traveling partner had the same strange dreams!

In our shared dreams, there was only one building, and that was a church with a tall bell tower. On the second morning, I walked out of the hotel, and there was the church I'd been seeing in my dreams. I checked the history of that area and found that it was the bloody battle ground between the Spaniards and the Native people.

Here is the point I want to make: The earth absorbs human energy. That is why you should never heal the home or building and believe the healing is complete. *Always* cleanse and heal the earth beneath it.

A Practitioner Shares a Story

> A friend gave my name to someone who said she needed to have her house blessed because "weird things were happening." When I arrived at the house, the owner wanted me to know that she bought it new about ten years ago. She began by telling me that she had placed several cherry tomatoes from her garden in a dish on the table. The next morning, the tomatoes were gone. There was no mess, no droppings from a mouse. The fan above her stove was on, and the large burner on the stove had been turned on and left on high. She was stumped but not yet alarmed. So, she put out more cherry tomatoes, and the same thing happened the next morning. Again, no tomatoes, and no evidence as to what could have happened to them.
>
> This time, she set up a video camera that would catch the whole scene on film. She set up the video and set out her tomatoes. The tomatoes once again were gone, and the fan and burner were running on high. There was nothing recorded on the video.
>
> That is when she was given my number. Because this took another day, she once again set up the video camera. When she

showed it to me, I couldn't stop laughing. This time, there, with its little front feet up on the dish, and its big eyes looking at the tomatoes, was the most cartoon-looking real mouse I have ever seen. The strange thing was that the tomatoes were gone, but the video just showed the mouse looking at them!

After a few minutes of banter about it all, I proceeded to bless the house. As I walked around her living room, doing what I do, I was overcome by a huge wave of undeniable sadness. It made my words choke in my throat. I didn't know what to do (I hadn't taken Tina's training yet), so I just started talking to the sadness. I asked the sadness if it had taken the tomatoes and left the fan and burner on. It admitted it had. I asked if it came into the house with someone who had been there visiting. It had not. I asked if it came in with other people's things she was storing in the garage. It had not.

I then asked the sadness what it was doing in this woman's house. It said that it was from the land (meaning the land the subdivision had been built on). Its ancestors had once lived on that land, and now the sadness just roamed around, occasionally going from house to house as it could. The sadness told me some other things about his history as well. He and his ancestors had been displaced. He knew he was no longer among the living and knew he was disturbing the person who lived in this house.

I told him that she was of the light, but not the Source of Light, and that he would feel much better if he just left out the door and went into the Source of Light. (Once again, I did not yet know about Tina's tip to ask the Divine and Sacred Guides to help the spirit person and me. I was "winging it.") I assumed he left, because the sadness lifted, and I resumed blessing the house. Big-time blessing!

I called the owner the next day. She said the tomatoes had

stayed in the bowl, and nothing had been turned on. The day after that, she called to tell me that she had gotten up the next morning to a dead mouse lying on the floor in front of the sliding doors I had just ushered Mr. Sadness through.

Now, fast-forward a couple of weeks. I have now read most of Tina's book, *Become a Medical Intuitive,* and I've asked for volunteers to practice on. One of the people who volunteered lives in one neighborhood over from the house I had blessed. She told me that she and her husband had recently attended a fascinating lecture on the history of their area. She said that a portion of the lecture was about "Night Marchers." They are believed to be spirits of people who lived in that area and were involved in a battle so bloody it turned the river red. These traumatized spirits still roamed that land!

Crazy, huh? As Tina has said, you could never make this stuff up! Not in a million years.

— Lewanna Godinez
mauilu1595@gmail.com

A small house down the road has had at least nine different individuals or families move in and then move out within six months up to a year later. I met the owner of the larger house next door. He told me that his mother used to live in the tiny house next to his, but she'd passed away many years earlier. He was finally ready to rent it out. But now I noticed the families were constantly coming and going.

After all those years, I finally thought that maybe I should check out the house, since it was having one of its lengthy empty times. I was met by a hostile senior citizen who was not happy that I was astral projecting into her home. She was furious and came at me. My shield went up immediately, and she bounced off it.

My first thought was, *I don't know how anyone who is unaware that deceased people are real and alive, could withstand one night in this woman's house.* I'm giggling as I write this, but I'm serious.

Needless to say, I talked to her, explained to her, and convinced this spirit woman that she was deceased, and it was possibly time to allow another family into that house. She was finally convinced when she looked around to truly see a gentle, glowing, beautiful guide telling her it was now her time to shine and to release this house.

Again, I did the steps to heal and release a troubled hostile deceased human, and then cleansed the acres of land that the house sat on. The current family has remodeled and lived there for over two years now.

Hmmm . . . maybe this stuff is real.

A Practitioner Shares a Story: Why Does This Home Feel Sad, Heavy, and Uneasy?

A daughter asked me to assess her childhood home where her parents still lived. Decades ago, ever since her parents could recall, this home just felt sad, heavy, and uneasy. Although the daughter had long since moved into her own home, she and her siblings still felt uneasy when returning to this home to visit their parents. When they asked me to do a property clearing on this property, including the home, I took the following approach:

It's imperative to include the entire property, including all the structures (home, barn, shed, wine cellars, etc.) and to include the uppermost point of each structure as well, such as the attic along with closets, basement(s), and crawl spaces under portions of the structures. What also must be included is the entire property's perimeter from the surface of the land all the way down to the core of the Earth, as the root cause could be many layers down under what the basement is now.

I directed my guides to immediately reveal to me all that

was hidden now for a permanent and complete clearing. My guides directed me to assess this property, beginning with the uppermost points on the roofs of the structures (home, barns, sheds, etc.). I went down foot by foot, from ceiling to floor of each room in the home, and each space in the barn and shed, paying attention to items that caught my attention, such as thresholds between rooms, thresholds between hallways, mirrors, windows, or any other items presenting dark, negative energy interference.

As I conducted the property clearing within the structures as described above, and by going across the uppermost surface of the land, including the entire area within the perimeter, the ominous feeling of heaviness increased and became a palpable, collective fear as I proceeded many feet under the basement. I encountered a group of forty unascended souls whose fear was truly palpable. While their bodies had passed, their fear kept their souls tethered to the earth to the extent where they were afraid to move or even make a sound. I asked them what they were waiting for, and they said very softly, in fear of being overheard, that they were waiting to be taken to the next stop. I asked them what next stop they were talking about? The spokesman for the group replied softly that they were waiting to be taken to the next stop on the Underground Railroad.

My heart sank, as no wonder there was palpable fear permeating throughout this property for generations. I explained that hundreds of years had actually passed, and that while I understood what they'd meant by the Underground Railroad, I had even better news for them. With the help of my guides, I assisted these souls to finally ascend and reunite with their loved ones. It was a moving reunification, and the ominous feeling of pervasive fear, heaviness, and sadness lifted from the bottom-most point under the basement all the way to the uppermost point of the structures and across the entire perimeter of the property.

The parents living in the home, and the adult children returning there, consistently remarked how much better the property felt without those feelings of sadness, heaviness, and uneasiness. Also, the daughter who had contacted me to do this property clearing later told me that she'd confirmed that the structure, on the land where her childhood home was, had indeed been a church that had been documented to be a stop along the Underground Railroad!

— Maryann Kelly
www.IntuitiveServicesInsight.com

Chapter 17

We are Never a Finished Product at the End of the Spiritual Assembly Line

Do not find yourself sitting under a tree waiting for life to happen, or for someone to save the day. Life is constantly happening within you and around you. It's time to be the boss, the director, and the commander of yourself and the nonphysical realms around you.

Based on all my lifelong experiences as an intuitive, medium, regressionist, and counselor, plus all the documented experiences that these mediums have shared with you in this book, I can clearly state that we humans have many choices throughout our life and our death. We can hold on to the stuff of life; we can contemplate our thoughts, deeds, and actions; and we can focus on our physical pain and emotional traumas of the physical world. We can stab at our own heart while in the physical and continue to do so in the nonphysical. We could rejoice at the sacred moment of moving from the physical to the nonphysical . . . entering into infinity.

I realize I've kept many secrets about the realities of the nonphysical realms. I realize I have kept quiet about my years of "high-def adventures" with the spirit world, but not anymore.

I have a four-foot-tall wooden statue of Kuan Yin, the Goddess of Compassion. For years, I thought that she was reminding me to be compassionate for all the living and deceased beings struggling here on Earth. But as I write this book, I now realize she is my reminder to be compassionate to myself and my soul.

> "Once we were particles of light . . . Now we are Beings of Light, Radiating Love."
>
> —Rumi

A Few Thoughts to Bring This Book to a Close

- Humanity simply needs to learn that we are all intuitive, and we are all mediums.
- Every living person is a physical and nonphysical being at the exact same time.
- We all live in physical and nonphysical realms at the exact same time, even if we don't realize it.
- Deceased people experience the physical and the nonphysical worlds at the same time as living people. Perceive all nonphysical beings first as a client in need.
- Understanding negative entities as clients in need will dramatically alter your beliefs in positive, life-changing ways.
- Light is literally the spark of energy of thought and knowledge springing from Source.
- Having both the Dark and the Light gives us options and constant choices to make in developing our personal level of advancement and expansion.
- Never chase deceased people or non-human entities away, or try to "get rid of them."
- You are now the healing medium, ready to help entities as you also help the living human clients before you.

The spirit world lives in conjunction with the physical world. It's the physical world that seems to have problems accepting the unseen. One world is not trying to take over the other. The nonphysical realm, and our deceased loved ones, are struggling and learning just as the living. People still living in the physical world can truly allow their deceased loved ones to continue to touch their lives in positive ways. But the troubled ones need our assistance. They are just as alive as we are, and they are able to learn as we learn.

These two worlds of the physical and the nonphysical are not separate or mutually exclusive. The nonphysical realm does not attempt to take over everyone's bodies or our lives in hostile, consuming ways. The unknown in our lives is not always the devil, although many people think it is. It is simply unexplored worlds and realms. We are not separate from nonphysical in any way. The air is rich and thick with wisdom. We do not rise upward into higher consciousness, and Spirit does not flow down to us. We are already surrounded and immersed in higher awareness. We are already breathing, walking, and living within the wisdom of the cosmos.

Many, many times I close my courses with this. It feels like a prayer to me.

I am supernatural and so are you.

I am intuitive and you are intuitive too.

I am a natural medium and you are a natural medium.

We are not separate from the spirit world.

We both have one foot in the physical and one foot in the nonphysical at the same time.

Kindness does not make the world go round. It allows the world to *continue* to go round.

A Message From the Divine and Sacred to You

"Become the medium who heals the living, the deceased, the nonhumans, the animals, and the Earth . . . healing all levels of the Soul."

Appendix

Steps to Astral Project and Do It Ethically

1. Always ask the person for permission to begin. This keeps you functioning ethically.
2. Stop all thoughts about yourself. Get "you" out of the way.
3. Direct your Divine and Sacred specialty guides to completely and permanently guard and protect you in all ways now. (This way, you are ready for anything you perceive.)
4. Focus all thoughts and all your attention on the client, home, building, land, animal, etc.
5. Think and feel that you are stretching outward to the place, object, or person. Allow the guides to direct you. You are *not* to work at this. Allow the guides to take you.
6. Think and feel that you have hypersensitive sensors at the end of your extended beam of energy. These sensors are alive, alert, active, and noticing everything.
7. Pause and receive all the instant pops of information in words, images, feelings.
8. At the end of receiving the information, direct your Divine and Sacred Guides to create a powerful cleansing filter around you. Pull your energy field back through the filter so that only the pure you comes back into you.

Astral Projecting to Receive Information on Deceased or Nonphysical Beings

Your personal well-being and safety will be enhanced by astral projecting outward and all around your body, home, or work.

1. You have just noticed a general sense that a spirit person has arrived near you.
2. Important: Do not search or try hard to find anything. Only passively notice.
3. Notice if words, phrases, thoughts, or images pop into your mind. It will feel as if those things come out of nowhere. Thoughts from a deceased person will not feel like your own thoughts. Things that are said by a deceased being will not be said in ways that you would say it.
4. If you do not hear sounds, words, phrases, or see images, do not be discouraged. Keep yourself in the position of noticing, and do not take any action.
5. When Spirit does speak words aloud, the words will either be soft whispers or a booming voice. Messages from friends and relatives who have passed may be brief, sound muddled, or they often repeat the same statement over and over.
6. First listen and receive their information. Then talk to them! Have a conversation. Ask one question or make one statement in

your mind. Then pause to receive the "pop" of their answer. Give the spirit person time to respond to you by speaking or showing you images.

7. If you struggle to understand their message, you simply give them some common-sense directions. For example, "Slow down," "Speak louder," "Tell me more details," or "Send me a picture of what you are telling me."
8. It's up to us to focus our complete attention on receiving. Do not try hard to do anything, and do not take action. Passively receive.
9. Inform your living client exactly what you perceived from the deceased, and exactly the way you received it, even when it does not make any sense to you. *Never* paraphrase the words of the deceased. Repeat every word or action exactly as you received it.

Questions to Get to Know Your Guides

- What name can I call you by?
- How do you qualify as a specialist in ?
- What do I need to do to work well with you?
- Do I need to actually see you as we work together?
- What should I notice when you contact me?
- How will I know you're there?
- How will you help me with intuition or mediumship or healing?
- What is the first step I should take to work excellently with you?
- What is the first step you will do to work excellently with me?
- How often can I ask you questions?
- Tell me one thing I need to do to work with you better.

- What should I notice when you contact me?
- How often can I ask you questions?
- What signals have I been missing from you?

Watch Your Thoughts and Commands, and STOP Using Ones That are Not Useful

- A meaning that is too general.
- A meaning that is too vague.
- A word used in a broad manner throughout society.
- A word that does not direct guides to take an action.
- A word that suggests you are only asking the guides if they can do something.
- A word that tells them to give you something negative that is also hindering your client.

Primary Words That SHOULD NOT be Used in Directives or Commands to Your Guides

- Wish
- Hope
- Want
- Help
- Can
- Ask
- Need
- Heal
- Trying

- Take care
- Would you
- Will you
- Could you
- Give Me

Examples of Unclear, Weak, or Vague Commands

- Give me the (name of the issue) this client is struggling with now.
- I wish for some guidance to increase my abilities.
- Can you show me the meaning of that symbol.
- I hope you will bring kindness to his heart.
- I ask that the negativity changes.
- I want you to help me.
- I need to know what is wrong with (client name).
- Help me please.
- Heal this client.
- Take care of this client's knee.
- I am trying to be intuitive.
- Would you give me intuition?
- Could you increase my abilities?
- Will you tell me the first steps to take?

Steps to Extract Negative Cords from Yourself

Direct your Divine and Sacred Guides using these commands:

1. Completely and permanently extract all negative cords sent to

me from needy or controlling people. Give all the cords back to the senders now to help them realize they have their own power.

2. Completely and permanently fill all places where the cords used to be with cellular vitality, glowing health, and amazing energy now.

Your Daily Scanning Steps

1. Your focused thoughts become like hypersensitive sensors. First send your ears, eyes, and fingertips all around your energy field, then inside your physical body. Notice your sensors scanning 360 degrees throughout and around you. Remember to scan your backside, under your feet, and above your head.
2. Notice the instant images or thoughts that pop into your awareness. Take note of the words or images that pop into your mind.
3. Notice where your field and physical body is rich with energy.
4. Look for areas that seem, feel, or look different from the rest of your field. Look for areas that are thin, weak, dim, open, torn, discolored, and any tunnels or leaks. (Leaks can appear anywhere from bubbles rising upward to gushes of energy leaving you like a fireman's hose, or even larger.)
5. Look for objects or impressions of objects in your field or body. Do not be alarmed if you discover objects such as dark cords, knives, arrows, spears, or other objects. Take it as important information of the cause of your struggles in a certain area.
6. If you become aware of objects, then notice the exact location of foreign objects, or other things within your physical body and your energy field.
7. Always notice the pop of images or thoughts that leap into your mind.

Steps to Direct Your Toroidal Field

- Think it, and the energy will follow in this order.
- Imagine inhaling upward through the soles of your feet and filling every cell. Imagine breathing in and upward, *each color, one at a time*, in this order: Red, Orange, Yellow, Green, Blue, Purple, White.
- Then breathe into the soles of your feet and fill every cell with fire-like energy of violet, burning off all negativity within and around you.
- Then breathe into the soles of your feet and place a brilliant white sparkle inside of every cell in your body.
- Then breathe into the soles of your feet and fill every cell with precious, electrified golden energy.
- Feel as if you are a brilliant light bulb.
- Open the crown of who you are and allow your brilliant light to shine up and into the cosmos.
- Ground yourself. The cosmos notices your new brilliance and sends energy wisdom downward into your field and your physical body, then back down into the Earth. Then repeat all the above steps, pulling energy back up into your body to ground yourself.
- You are training yourself to constantly be empowered.

Opening and Closing Each Session You Do for Others

1. At the beginning of each session, direct your specialty guide: Create the perfect, sacred, and safe space for the work that's about to happen. You may feel it, or you may be able to see it. Intuitively invite each client to join you in that space.
2. At the end of each session, or at the end of each day, direct your

specialty guide who excels in cleaning and clearing your energy field: "Create the ideal cleansing filter for me now."

3. Command: "I bring me, and only me, back to me, clean and clear through the most perfect filter provided for me."
4. Inhaling deeply, draw your energy back into your physical body through your thoughts. Sometimes you might see a thick substance clinging to the filter. You will be pleased to know you're not bringing that back to yourself or into your life.

Practice: I Give Back to My Heart Now

1. Place both hands over your heart.
2. Command: "I give love back into my own heart now, equal to all the love and care I have given to others."
3. Allow yourself to send and feel the energy of love going deep into the organ of your heart and its energy center.

Key Steps to Communicate with a Person in Their Death Process

Notice that the true life-and-death stories involve one of more of the following steps:

1. First, become an excellent listener. Speak, then pause to listen and receive. If they are awake, you can discuss things out loud.
2. If they are unconscious, speak to them telepathically.
3. If you are not a friend or family, then verbally or intuitively inform the dying who you are. Then ask the dying person for permission to assist them. Receive the "pop" of yes or no. Honor the "no," if that's what you get from them, but try again later that day or the following days. Sometimes a "no" is only for that moment but not forever.

4. If you receive permission, then ask one question at a time (verbally or telepathically), then pause to receive the pop of words, thoughts, or images.
5. Slowly ask questions or make statements such as:
    - What are your thoughts today?
    - What is your body signaling to you?
    - Are you feeling worried?
    - What are you worried about?
    - Tell me what things you are wondering about.
    - Are you waiting for someone?
    - What kind of help do you want now?
    - Are you seeing your loved ones?
    - Do you see Angels or Guides who are here to help you?
    - What are these guides telling you?
6. When you hear that it is the right time, telepathically or aloud, direct the dying person to connect with the guide or loved ones who have come for them.
    - Look around and find the brightest loving helper that is here just for you now.
    - Talk things over with this loving helper.
    - Ask questions to your spirit helper now.
    - Ask your deceased loved ones if it's time for you to go.
    - Ask your guide if it is time for you to go with them.
7. Be an accurate bridge of communication between the living and the dying person. Communicate to the living exactly what the dying person said or has shown you. Say exactly what you receive

verbally, telepathically, or in images, even if it makes no sense to you. Never interpret what you receive, just inform everyone.

8. At the same time, you are also communicating with your own personal Divine and Sacred specialty guides, so you are not working alone in this process. Ask many questions to constantly receive guidance as you assist the living and the dying. Do not do this level of work alone. Work together.
9. Ask all the family members to say everything to the dying that they want or need to express. Tell them, "Do not hold anything back." Saying important issues or unfinished concerns out loud deeply and forever helps the living and the dying.

Questions to Ask Confused or Needy Deceased Humans

1. Do you know why you have come here?
2. Do you know why you have been staying around?
3. Tell me what is troubling you.
4. Do you know that you do not have a physical body any longer?
5. Do you know that you have died?
6. Let yourself remember how you died. Tell me what happened.
7. What have you been doing lately?
8. What places or people have you been focusing on?
9. Do you know you haven't yet crossed over into the light?
10. Tell me why you haven't let go of the Earth and gone to the light.

Steps to Remove, Transition, and Heal All Confused and Needy Spirit People

1. You have just discovered a spirit person in someone's energy field or their environment.
2. Never chase the intrusive spirit person away. They will go away for a short time but will always return.
3. Power up your toroidal field until your light is brilliant.
4. Telepathically ask the spirit person questions to specifically find out certain information. Ask each question, then pause and take what pops into your mind. That will be the deceased person responding to you. Your questions need to purposefully determine the reason that a spirit person is interfering with you or another person.
5. Ask these questions to determine why this spirit person is attracted to you (or the client). Ask each question, then pause to receive the pop:
    - How long have you been following me or the client?
    - Exactly where did you find me or the client?
    - What attracted you to me or the client?
    - What do you get from being with me or the client?
6. Ask these next questions to assist the spirit person with separating from the living person. Ask each question, then pause to receive the pop:
    - Do you know that you are dead and that you do not have your physical body anymore?
    - Do you know that you are causing harm or interference to the living?

- I am calling in Divine and Sacred specialists to assist you. How many do you see?

7. Command: Divine and Sacred Guides who specialize in this particular spirit, completely and permanently remove the spirit from me (or client) on all levels and all dimensions. Remove all energy of the deceased and take them to the best place for their highest transformation into Light and Love now!
8. Watch in your mind's eye as the specialists remove and lift the spirit being upward and away. This transformation that you initiated is not only beautiful to witness but exhilarating to watch this positive change for everyone involved.
9. Remember—When any being is removed, we must always call in the Divine and Sacred healing guides and command: Fill every single space and place where that negativity used to be with cellular health, vitality, and (other power words that apply).

Healing Steps for the Hostile, Hateful, Vicious Deceased

You just intuitively perceived an enraged, vicious, and extremely negative spirit person. Here are the next steps to take:

1. Immediately direct your Divine and Sacred Guardian Warriors to surround you and completely protect you, now!
2. Immediately power up your toroidal field to its brightest and fullest.
3. Get in charge and in control. Feel fiercely powerful.
4. Direct this spirit person, "You back off now and see my Warriors!"
5. Ask the hostile deceased at least two important questions:
    - What drew you to me or this person, this house, or this land?

- Do you know that you have come to me so I can help you?

6. Call in Divine and Sacred Transformational Guides who know this human.
7. Demand the spirit person: "Now you count the guides that have come for you and feel the love from the specialty guides. How many have come to help you?"
8. Tell the spirit person, "The specialty guides do not care how terrible you think you are. The guides can only feel love for you, no matter what you have done."
9. Direct the guides: "Completely and permanently extract all this spirit person's energy and cords from everything and everyone he/she has been negatively interfering with! Take him/her to the best place for his transformation into the light, now!"
10. The Healing: Call in Divine and Sacred Healing Specialists to completely and permanently cleanse every single space and place where negativity used to be.
11. Then direct the healing specialist to fill every space and place where that negativity used to be with pure love and light, now!

Steps to Direct Your Divine and Sacred Guides in Complicated Situations with Hostile Non-Humans

Complicated situations often entail multiple types of beings interfering with your client. For example, the living client might have one or more non-humans interfering, and at the same time, there could also be one or more negative deceased humans.

1. Always direct the guides to first contain the non-human.
2. Next, remove the non-human and take it to the best place for its transformation into Light and Love.
3. Then repeat the same steps for the negative deceased human.

4. Then fill all the empty space with light, love, and health.
5. Then fill the house or building and land with Light and Love.

Soul Retrieval Steps to Heal the Deceased

It's never too late to heal a negative deceased human, and it's never too late to release and heal your living client as well. Life and death and relationships can always be altered into the positive. Here are the steps to accomplish a soul retrieval for a deceased person

1. A painful memory in the deceased person's life has come to the forefront.
2. Tell the deceased person that you want them to let their imagination unfold like a movie in their minds.
3. Ask them to imagine going back and standing with their younger self in the exact moment of the painful trauma.
4. Ask how they know their younger self is aware of them being together.
5. Direct both the young self and the current self to pull everything out of both their bodies that is not theirs. Completely pull out the traumatic event, the pain, the memories, all the ugliness, and give it back to their wrongdoer.
6. Tell the deceased person to take their time and make sure they get absolutely all of it out of them and give it all back. You will be still until they speak, so you do not interrupt their process.
7. Watch the deceased person's energy field as they respond to your request. If there is any residual darkness, tell them to get it all out of both their current self and their younger self. Remind your client to do every step in partnership with their younger self.
8. Now direct both the deceased person and their younger self to

call out for healing guides to create a perfect cleansing filter. Wait until the deceased person informs you that the filter is present.

9. Next, firmly tell the deceased and their younger self to take back absolutely everything that has been taken from them. Bring it through the cleansing filter and place it back inside both of them. To encourage the deceased person, use the same emotional words that they used to describe the traumatic event. Some examples to say aloud might be:
    - Both you and the younger you, take back everything that was taken from you.
    - Take back your confidence.
    - Take back your ability to love.
    - Take back all of your energy.
    - Take back all of your body.
    - Take back all of your POWER now.
10. Let the deceased person know you will be still until they speak, and to take their time making sure they get it all.
11. Tell both of them (the deceased's younger self and their current self) to look the wrongdoer directly in their eyes until they change in some way.
12. Ask them—the deceased's current self and their younger self—to talk it over with each other and see if there's anything else that needs to be done for a complete and permanent healing. Pause and allow both to check that out. Follow through with anything that seems incomplete for them.
13. Direct the current self to ask the younger self if they are ready to leave that moment forever. If yes, tell both to release that event and to move forward, merging together before coming back into the deceased's present moment. Inform the deceased

of the positive energetic changes. Direct the deceased to look around and see the brightest guide, and to go with that guide into a healing transformation.

Daily Steps to Repel All Negativity from Your Own Life

1. Every day, direct or command your Divine and Sacred Warriors and Protectors: "I revoke, reject, and repel all negative beings and all negative energy from my body and my life now!"
2. Electrify your energy field with brilliant, bright, sizzling light by doing all the steps of the toroidal field. Feel each step of the toroidal field as you do it.
3. You are fierce, powerful, and in charge.

Healing Steps to Extract Negative Non-Human Entities from the Client

1. You have realized that a negative entity is creating an illness, cancer, or life problems with this person.
2. Never frighten the client. Do all remaining steps within your mind (if your guides ask that you do not inform the client).
3. Stop, electrify your own energy field with sizzling brilliant light *and no fear.*
4. Direct your warrior protectors in a commanding way: "I revoke, reject, and repel all negative beings and all negative energy that is causing harm! Keep me out of this!"
5. Strongly invite in Divine and Sacred Guides who specialize in this particular entity.
6. Request the Specialists to immediately encapsulate *all entities* causing illness or within (full name of client) with powerful white light.

7. Strongly request that the Divine and Sacred Specialty guides *completely* and *permanently* remove and extract *all* levels of this entity from the client *now!*
8. Keep directing and strongly insisting that all negative cords and roots leave the client immediately.
9. Now request the Specialty Healing Guides: "Completely and Permanently fill every space and place where that negativity used to be with love, God's light, and cellular health and vitality now!" (Use any other words that describe what your living client needs.)

References

McCutcheon, Heather. *Connecting the Dots: From Ad Exec to Energy Practitioner.* Minneapolis: Hillcrest Publishing Group. 2015.

Newton, Michael. *Journey of Souls.* Woodbury, MN. Llewellyn Worldwide, 2002).

Stuart, Brooke. "On the Toroidal Field." December 7, 2022, https://www.drbrookestuart.com/on-the-toroidal-field.

About the Author

TINA ZION is a fourth-generation intuitive medium and internationally considered an expert in medical intuition and mediumship. She is a first-place gold award-winning author and instructor. Tina teaches courses: ***Medical Intuitive Practitioner, Advanced Medical Intuition. Be Your Own Medical Intuitive and Mediumship for the Troubled Deceased.*** She has taught in the United Kingdom, Europe, New Zealand, Australia, Canada, Mexico and throughout the US. She is also a faculty member for multiple spiritual centers in the US.

Tina's books are selling in over forty-five counties. She is the author of ***Become a Medical Intuitive, Advanced Medical Intuition, Be Your Own Medical Intuitive, The Reiki Teacher's Manual,*** *and* ***Reiki and Your Intuition.*** Tina is also a contributing author in Michael Newton's book, *Memories of the Afterlife.*

Tina worked as a psychiatric registered nurse with a national board specialty certification in mental health nursing. Tina is a Gestalt-trained mental health counselor. She holds a BA in communication and management, a certification in clinical hypnotherapy, and specialized in past-life regressions. She was also certified through the Michael Newton Institute for Life Between Life Regressions. She has taught Reiki for over ten years.

Tina now focuses on teaching people to be extraordinary practitioners of medical intuition and mediumship.

Tina's website: www.tinazion.com